Pragmatism, Postmodernism, and the Future of Philosophy

The **Routledge American Philosophy Series** presents original philosophical work advancing traditions of American thought so as to address new intellectual issues and global problems, as well as historical and theoretical studies of pragmatism, classical American philosophy, and related developments in American thought and culture.

Series editor
John J. Stuhr

Series advisors
Susan Bordo
Vincent M. Colapietro
John Lachs
Lucius Outlaw
Cheyney Ryan
Richard Shusterman

Books in the series
A Community of Individuals
John Lachs

Pragmatism, Postmodernism, and the Future of Philosophy
John J. Stuhr

Pragmatism, Postmodernism, and the Future of Philosophy

JOHN J. STUHR

Routledge
NEW YORK AND LONDON

Published in 2003 by
Routledge
29 West 35th Street
New York, NY 10001
www.routledge-ny.com

Published in Great Britain by
Routledge
11 New Fetter Lane
London EC4P 4EE
www.routledge.co.uk

Routledge is an imprint of the Taylor & Francis Group.
Printed in the United States of America on acid-free paper.
Typography: Jack Donner

10 9 8 7 6 5 4 3 2 1

Cataloging-in-Publication Data is available from the Library of Congress.
ISBN 0-415-93967-4—ISBN 0-415-93968-2 (pbk.)

Cover image: *Hercules* by Francesco da Sant'Agata. By kind permission of the Trustees
of the Wallace Collection.

For John Lachs and John J. McDermott
teachers, mentors, friends

Contents

Time held me green and dying,
Though I sang in my chains like the sea

—Dylan Thomas

Acknowledgments

Grateful acknowledgment is made to the following publishers and individuals for permission to reprint selections from the following copyrighted publications:

Ernest Hemingway, selection from "Big Two-Hearted River, Part II," *In Our Time* (New York: Charles Scribner's Sons, 1925), p. 212. Copyright 1925 by Charles Scribner's Sons. Copyright renewed 1953 by Ernest Hemingway. Reprinted by permission of Scribner, a division of Simon and Schuster, Inc., and by the Ernest Hemingway Foreign Rights Trust.

Wallace Stevens, selection from "Parts of a World," *The Collected Poems of Wallace Stevens* (New York: Alfred A. Knopf, 1954 [1942]), pp. 256–257. Copyright 1954 by Wallace Stevens and renewed 1982 by Holly Stevens. Used by permission of Alfred A. Knopf, a division of Random House, Inc., and by permission of Faber and Faber, Ltd.

I am indebted to many persons who have provided comments, suggestions, and criticisms of my concerns in this book: Vincent Colapietro, Charles Scott, Rick Lee, Shannon Sullivan, Nancy Tuana, and Jeff Nealon, colleagues at Penn State; John Lachs; Robert Innis; John J. McDermott; Noelle McAfee; Mike Sullivan; John Lysaker; Bruce Wilshire; Richard Shusterman and the members of our 2001 NEH Summer Seminar on pragmatism and American culture; Frank Ryan; Mark Johnson; Andrew Light; Laura Canis; Michael Hodges; Tom Burke; Micah Hester; Thomas Alexander; Bill Lewis; Tom Hilde; Nikita Pokrovsky; Margarita Zakarotonya; and, Sun Youzhong. I have tried to learn from and to take their insightful ideas at every turn.

Penn State University, its College of the Liberal Arts, and Dean Susan Welch supported a sabbatical leave that supplied that scarcest of resources, time. With the generous initiative and arrangements of Bertis Downs, Danielle and Francois Roux at La Colombe d'Or in St. Paul de Vence, France, supplied the place—indeed, the perfect place.

Eloise, Jennifer, and Robert Stuhr have provided support, inspiration, and delight on a daily basis beyond expression. For more than twenty-five years, John Lachs and John J. McDermott have shown me not only what it is to think philosophically but also what it is to live philosophically. I dedicate this book to them.

Introduction

Change happens slowly and rapidly, as expected and as surprise, happily and unhappily. But it always happens. Even if persons wanted or attempted to remain unchanged, still they would not be able to think and live in the future just as they or other persons now do in the present or as others have done in the past.

As a result, each person constantly faces a Herculean labor that is both personal and practical: to determine how to think differently and live differently in the future from how one does at present, and to act now so as to most fully move one's thought and life in this, rather than some other, direction.

American pragmatism, particularly the writings of William James and John Dewey, provides remarkably rich resources for addressing this issue: a radically experiential philosophy; openness, hope, and an insistence on embodiment, enactment, and putting theory into practice; a tolerant and pluralistic concern for individuals, their growth, and their differences; an urgent commitment to communities and democracy as a way of life; and a realization that philosophy is criticism and production and so is always concerned with values and creation.

These past resources, however, are only resources, and they only partially help. They are not permanent or ready-made or complete solutions for persons who must think and live in the future. As a result, anyone who would think or live as a pragmatist in the future, anyone who would extend but not try to repeat pragmatism, must strive to think differently and live differently from pragmatists of the past.

In this book and from this pragmatic tradition, I am trying to think and live differently.

In the context of pragmatism, the need to think and live differently is real not merely because change is real but also because, with respect to different futures, pragmatism presents real limitations as well as resources: an account of inquiry insufficiently attuned to issues of power, struggle, and multiplicity; a radically democratic ideal in need of response to threats from new technologies and the defects of liberal governments and societies; a pluralism in tension with pragmatism's understanding of its own values, methods, and future; and a view of philosophy as criticism that needs to become more critically self-reflective about its own history and effects, and about challenges to its very existence in possible postcritical societies. Here, in the context of James and Dewey, the writings of Deleuze, Adorno, and Foucault, for example, can be helpful tools for thinking more critically and living differently.

This use of pragmatism and postmodernism has nothing to do with fore-cast or foreknowledge. This book is not a horoscope, and I am not predicting or proscribing the future of philosophy in general or in anyone's specific case. Instead, my use of pragmatism and postmodernism has every-thing to do with action and hope. I am attempting to articulate, advocate, and establish—or, better, to suggest and evoke—hope for a different way of thinking and living. This is a different pragmatism and a different post-modernism (though traditionalists and "ism" police may find it so different as to wonder if it is pragmatic or postmodern at all). It is a genealogical and critically pluralistic way of thinking, and it is a way of living of great, ordinary love and sadness.

In this book, I am trying to think and live better this love and sadness.

In chapter 1, I take up Emerson's call that we must avoid thinking and living retrospectively, that we must do more than write the history and criticism of earlier generations, that we must enjoy an original relation to the universe. In its largest sense, this is an educational task, and pragmatism offers crucial, liberating tools for this task: the distinction between educa-tion and schooling; the use of growth, the goal of education, as a criterion for social criticism, and an understanding of education and democracy as intrinsically and reciprocally linked. Even in liberal democracies, these insights have been submerged by powerful cultural forces and organizations that shape meanings, characters, lives, and social relations on behalf of other agendas. In both theory and practice, these postliberal agendas stand in opposition even to ideals of education as growth and democracy as a way of life. Accordingly, after the twentieth century, any genuine pragmatism—pragmatism in practice as well as theory—must reconstruct these ideals and articulate new means for their realization.

This is an immense undertaking, one requiring Herculean strength. Is a liberal, pluralistic democracy up to the challenge? William Ernest Hocking, a now obscure American philosopher, thought that it was not. He developed criticism of liberalism that is far more penetrating than that of more recent and better known radical, communitarian, conservative, and religious opponents of liberalism. Stripped of its faulty idealistic metaphysics, Hocking's three-part argument is instructive for the future of democracy: liberalism, he argued, cannot maintain sufficient social unity; it promotes rights as privileges in a way that undermines the social goodwill presupposed by the exercise of rights, and, it produces self-indulgent persons who fail to enact the values of liberal democracy in their own lives. Hocking's own authoritarian and absolutist solution to these defects of liberalism is no solution, and I explain why this is so in chapter 2. Nonetheless, Hocking's critical question remains: Do liberalism and pluralism and democracy suffer from permanent defects, or do they contain the resources to address adequately these problems in the future?

In chapter 3, drawing on John Dewey's distinction between democracy as a form of government and democracy as a way of life, I develop an affirmative, or largely affirmative, reply to this question. The consequences of understanding democracy as a way of life are far reaching. First, it renders democracy an idea, but an ideal only in relation to action undertaken toward its realization. Second, it makes clear that the meaning of democracy is essentially moral—essentially a claim about what kinds of cultures should prevail and essentially a commitment to those social processes that produce commitment to this claim. Third, the role of faith, a democratic faith, is central to the concept of democracy understood as a way of life. This is a hard, demanding faith, a faith with no guarantees but only melioristic commitment to realizing new possibilities and overcoming old defects. In the face of world terrorism and the realization that it is not true that "war is over if you want it," the requirements of this faith are even more strenuous. The opportunities are also greater: a just peace in the twenty-first century. I argue that this requires not just military and homeland security but also a wider economic and social security that can promote democratic habits of thought and action.

To focus on habits of thought and action is to recognize that democracy is a personal way of life, and thus a faith in the possibilities of human nature. The possibilities of human nature, of course, are possibilities of different, plural human natures. Having powerfully developed this insight, John Lachs has brought it to bear against absolutism, narrowness, and intolerance. In chapter 4, I draw critically on Lachs's account of the relevance of philosophy to practice, the role of choice in the constitution of fact, the resulting possibilities for expanding human meaning and happiness, and the implications of all this for philosophy. In particular, I argue that pragmatism's tolerance and pluralism must acquire a more critical edge, an edge that will allow it not only to recognize and appreciate plural human natures, choices, and lifestyles, but also to assess critically what is better and what is worse in this plurality.

Accordingly, in chapters 5, 6, and 7, I explore the resources in the philosophies of Gilles Deleuze, Theodor Adorno, and Michel Foucault for developing both the form and the function of pragmatic criticism. Embracing Deleuze's philosophy of production rather than lack—what I term his "pan-machinism"—and his affirmation of immanence and surface rather than depth, as well as noting useful points of contact between his radical empiricism and that of James and Dewey, I ask whether Deleuze's thought provides resources for criticism and resistance to new forms of control and new self-inscription industries. Illustrating moves in part via the internet from Deleuze to government, corporate, and university development of information warfare and social control, I seek simultaneously to forge a Deleuzian surface pragmatism and to point out limitations and possibilities for cooptation that remain. Does critical theory provide a Herculean alternative to, or resources for, these remaining problems?

In chapter 6, reversing Adorno's criticism of popular culture by employing it (in the form of R.E.M. lyrics) against his philosophy, I show that his critical theory articulates a radically new account of the relations between theory and practice, an account that depends on a new understanding of the relation between immanence and transcendence, an understanding that in turn finally depends on a novel grasp of the relation of subject and object. This view, I argue, fails because of Adorno's commitment to an intellectual dialectics that mistakenly treats relations of difference as relations of non-identity. In its place, I set forth a non-dialectical view of criticism, a criticism without transcendental basis, a critical practice that is irreducibly genealogical.

In chapter 7, I graft this genealogical dimension of criticism to pragmatism through an analysis of the socially transformative capacity of Foucault's philosophy of non-positive affirmation. In part, from sources as different as a novel by Ernest Hemingway and a popular song by the Talking Heads, I seek to enact the modalities of genealogy identified by Foucault. At the same time, I explain that this genealogy contains no theoretical safeguard to guarantee that it can render problematic and regard critically its own operations and gestures, and that it can respond strenuously to its would-be assassins.

In chapter 8, I bring the results of these three chapters to bear on John Dewey's theory of logic and his account of inquiry. I argue that Dewey's logic, the logic of pragmatism, despite its many remarkable strengths, is marred by being depoliticized, depluralized, and decontextualized. In response, I argue that the practice of inquiry must be linked intrinsically to practices of power, the operation of interests, and the constitution of selves. Doing so transforms the task of inquiry from simply the determination of shared problems to also the proliferation of experiences and the creation of a more pluralistic universe.

The relation between pluralism and pragmatism is the focus of chapter 9. Drawing on Wallace Stevens's notions of "philosophic assassins" and "seasons of belief," I trace William James's and John Dewey's declining confidence that pragmatism will be the future of philosophy. I extend this line of thought, arguing that pragmatism is just one possible future for philosophy, just one season of belief, and one that must become more pluralistic if it is to avoid being simply one more philosophic assassin. To recognize this point is to take seriously the role of temperament in philosophy and the existence of plural temperaments; it is to insist, on behalf of pragmatism, that there should be as much plurality in philosophy as there is in life.

This view provides no consolation—no consolation to the critics of pragmatism, no consolation to pragmatist assassins who demand that pragmatism be the future of philosophy, and no consolations to those who insist on spirituality in all lives and transcendence in all philosophy. In the final chapter, with these issues in mind, I articulate a thoroughly pluralistic, thoroughly strenuous pragmatism, a pragmatism that makes possible new lives and philosophies without spirituality and transcendence. My concern, a pluralistic one, is to demand this philosophy of no one, but to evoke it as a possibility for everyone. It is an ordinary and hard possibility, a possibility of great love and great sadness, a possibility, long after the millennium in which pragmatism first appeared, for genuinely original relations with the universe.

CHAPTER 1

Thinking beyond the Twentieth Century: Democracy and Education after Liberalism

Thinking beyond the Twentieth Century

In 1836, Ralph Waldo Emerson critically demanded for, and from, his readers fresh, new, different thoughts and lives. He wrote movingly:

> Our age is retrospective. It builds the sepulchres of the fathers. It writes biographies, histories, and criticism. The foregoing generations beheld God and nature face to face; we, through their eyes. Why should not we also enjoy an original relation to the universe? Why should not we have a poetry and philosophy of insight and not of tradition, and a religion by revelation to us, and not the history of theirs? Embosomed for a season in nature, whose floods of life stream around and through us and invite us by the powers they supply, to action proportional to nature, why should we grope among the dry bones of the past, or put the living generation into masquerade out of its faded wardrobe? The sun shines to-day also. There is more wool and flax in the fields. There are new lands, new men, new thoughts. Let us demand our own works and laws and worship.[1]

Centuries after Emerson, are there today new thoughts? Are there new, different, living insights? Is there today even any desire for "an original relation to the universe," much less any will to do the work that creates such relations?

Certainly today, long after Emerson, there are problems that seem to cry out for new thoughts and lives, new ways of thinking and new ways of living. These problems are evident in lives marked by massive aggravation, anger, and selfishness without compassion. They are reflected in deep disillusionment, smug suspicion, boredom, and paralyzing cynicism. Information outstrips wisdom and even any commitment to the love and search for wisdom. There are big technologies, big science, big corporations, and forces and weapons with big consequences. There are suicidal policies and suicide bombers. And there are little gray people carrying briefcases with plans for terminal lives, virtual communities, and theme-parks. Loyalties are unstable and insecure, and fear, despair, suffering, terror, and violence are beyond chronicling. There is a severe shortage of genuine ambition, imagination, and vision. Old habits and old beliefs are maintained bitterly, stubbornly, and all too successfully. It is an age of apparent insanity.

In 1971, songwriter Ray Davies characterized the twentieth century this way, and begged "just give me some security":

> You keep all your smart modern writers
> Give me William Shakespeare
> You keep all your smart modern painters
> I'll take Rembrandt, Titian, Da Vinci and Gainsborough
> Girl, we gotta get out of here
> We got to find a solution
> I'm a twentieth century man but I don't want to die here[2]

Obviously, each person who reads this book has something in common: you did not die a twentieth-century death. You did not die with Charles Peirce, Charlotte Perkins Gilman, William James, Josiah Royce, W. E. B. Du Bois, Jane Addams, George Santayana, G. H. Mead, or Alain Locke. You and I did not die with John Dewey. So, having lived beyond, having *outlived*, Dewey and the American pragmatist philosophers of the twentieth century, the question now is simply this: Will you and I *outthink* them? Will you and I think beyond and go past them, become post–twentieth century men and women in mind as well as body? The twentieth century: like Davies, I didn't want to *die* there. The twentieth century: In the spirit of Emerson, I don't want any longer to *think* there.

To say this, Emerson realized, is to say "that we have come up with the point of view which the universal mind took through the eyes of one scribe; we have been that man [or woman], and have passed on. First, one, then another, we drain all cisterns, and waxing greater by all these supplies, we crave a better and more abundant food." No one who has lived, he concluded, "can feed us ever."[3]

The leading pragmatists of the twentieth century knew this. John Dewey, for example, would have been quick to agree with Emerson that his

(Dewey's) own philosophy could not feed the future, plural futures, forever. As a result, any effort to call forth genuinely new thoughts and lives—like any effort to make new and different futures of philosophy—is itself Deweyan. In this context, mere nostalgia—"you keep all your smart modern writers"—is no solution at all. By itself, looking backward provides no real security, even to those who would live in libraries and museums, or, more commonly, think in libraries and museums, free and untroubled by all those smart modern (or is it now postmodern?) writers and painters. To those who, in effect, sing "just give me John Dewey," I reply: I definitely don't want to die *there.*

So, think and live forward. Think and live prospectively instead of retrospectively. Call forth the strenuous mood and look forward in thought and life. Each generation must write its own books or, rather, the books for the next generation, Emerson instructed, and his point was that we really must act on this advice rather than merely quote it if we are to grasp it and renew it. Look forward—to the next generation, to the future. At their best, many American philosophers, especially pragmatists, have delivered this message of, and demand on, collective self-reliance.

Look forward—OK, yes, but to what? Look forward to your own death, to the end of your future, to the death that you don't want to die here, to the death that you will die here or someplace else. At its worst, American philosophy and American culture more broadly, have failed to deliver this message of individual impermanence and transience—and failed to deliver it honestly again and again. This message is, in effect, "Instant Karma" pragmatism: "Pretty soon you're going to be dead."[4]

Of course, books that look forward for this generation or the next generation are *re*constructions rather than wholly new constructions. Advance and preservation, insight and tradition, deep originality and deep attention to history are interwoven. The artist, Emerson observed, is not emancipated from time, place, tradition, and inheritance. But this historicity and tradition-bound character of all originality and creation provide no canonical permanence and no justification for mendicant and sycophantic readings and interpretations.[5] There is no permanent inoculation or in-principle immunity against cultural obsolescence or irrelevance. No book, art, or thought can be so vaccinated against change and transformation, undoing and doing over, passing by, time. This means, for example, that both in principle and in fact, earlier American pragmatists may become increasingly remote from the advance of global thoughts and lives in America and everywhere else, and, even importantly inadequate to present needs and implicit principles of successful action. And, it means that present needs may not be brought to consciousness, much less satisfied, merely by noting again and again, with Dewey, that any philosophy that fails to do this may be lost "to chewing historic cud long since reduced to woody fibre."[6]

For some thinkers, metaphysical and epistemological perplexities now may seem to arise. For example, what is the chewing-life of historic cud? What are the warning signs of undernourishment in philosophy? How can woody fiber be identified? Most directly: What should you do if you begin to suspect you have been chewing, or even still are chewing, woody fiber?

In response, this is my advice: Stop chewing; don't swallow; spit it out. As Emerson and Dewey have argued, the past is included in the "moving present" only when that present makes use of the past to direct its own movements. This is an irreducibly pragmatic point: The past lives only in the present's self-direction.

After the twentieth century, we have plenty of pasts, but too little self-direction. Davies was right: We've got to get out of here. Yes. Fine. However, which way is out—or on? In sum, how could and should you and I direct the present and, in doing so, what use could and should you and I make of the past? In effect, what does it mean—what could it come to mean— to be a pragmatist today, a pragmatist tomorrow, a post–twentieth century pragmatist, a new-millennium pragmatist? What is the pragmatic meaning of pragmatism now, pragmatism long after Dewey? What difference, practical difference, does it make whether one is, or is not, a pragmatist? What is the practice of pragmatism—not just the professing of pragmatism, or the writing about pragmatism in books, but the living of pragmatism? And can pragmatism help us "get out of here"? Can it help us at all?

The characteristically American reply remains: Show me.

Some Old Habits and Three Problems

In its broadest sense, the sense in which John Dewey claimed that all genuine philosophy is philosophy of education, these questions raise three crucial *educational* problems.

However, at this point, you know the routine, I know the routine, we all know the routine. You do know the routine: A writer steeped in pragmatism calls attention to, and bemoans, current educational problems; trots out favorite, familiar quotations; refers to favorite pragmatist authors as resources for dealing with these problems; concludes by urging that we make use of these resources, apply pragmatic theory to practice, render practice more intelligent and meaningful; and, everybody (with a home) goes home, happy that another chapter is done.

I don't want to do this anymore.

This routine constitutes a fixed habit, a habit so well established that it is always available when needed. Perhaps it is the results of this habit that you expected to encounter in this book. A book on pragmatism, postmodernism, and the future of philosophy? OK, I know just how to do this, just where to find that appropriate quote about experience, criticism, immaturity, growth, imagination, inquiry, the child and the curriculum, pedagogic creed, schools of tomorrow, just where to refer to Foucault, Deleuze, Lyotard, Adorno, and so on. This habit, like other habits once fixed, may become over time a merely routine habit, a bad habit, a habit that blocks the development of new habits, a habit that impedes further development, growth, and education, a habit that prevents new ways of thinking and new ways of living. "Habits reduce themselves to routine ways of acting, or degenerate into ways of action to which we are enslaved just in the degree in which intelligence is disconnected from them," Dewey wrote. He continued:

> Routine habits, and habits that possess us instead of our possessing them, are habits which put an end to plasticity. They mark the close of the power to vary. There can be no doubt of the tendency of organic plasticity, of the physiological basis, to lessen with growing years. . . . 'settling down' . . . means aversion to change and a resting on past achievements. Only an environment which secures the full use of intelligence in the process of forming habits can counteract this tendency. (*MW9*: 54)

Three important questions are suggested here. First, how can social life best renew itself? This is a fundamental *educational* question for any society, perhaps *the* fundamental, central pragmatic question. Of course, this is not a new question; it has been taken up before.

So, second, how could our thinking about this educational question, in turn, best renew itself? This is a fundamental *methodological* question for any pragmatist philosopher of education. Thinking about this issue would not take place, of course, in a cultural vacuum.

Thus, third, what cultural environment would best secure, and in turn be secured by, this renewal of thinking about this fundamental educational question? This is a basic *social* question for all members of every social group. It is a question that points to the critical evaluation of all cultural institutions, practices, and relations in terms of their direct contribution to the growth of their members and the creation and renewal of environments that make possible this growth.

In the face of these questions, it is not sufficient simply to provide a reading of Dewey's *Democracy and Education* (or a different "greatest hit" by a different "great pragmatist"). Instead, *Democracy and Education* must be thought and written anew, rebuilt for different times, addressed to, and for, different lives. Any new message, moreover, must be delivered effectively. No "Field of Dreams" strategy will work. If it is only built, they will not come. The routine habits of philosophers, I am afraid, do not look very good in this light. They are for the most part the habits of tradition, history, and retrospection. New thoughts, if there are to be new thoughts, will require and produce new, different habits of mind, further new thoughts, new philosophy, philosophy with genuine futures.

In the meantime, pragmatists may conclude their routine by urging that we make use of pragmatism's supposedly already-made resources, apply pragmatic theory to practice, render practice more intelligent and meaningful. OK. Last call.

Three Important Pragmatic Insights

John Dewey's philosophy of education contains three insights that demand attention and reconstruction today:

1. the distinction between education and schooling;
2. the identification of growth as the end of education, and the development of this notion of growth as a criterion for social criticism; and,
3. the recognition of the close and reciprocal relationship between education and democracy.

These insights are partial springboards for pragmatism to renewal and new thoughts.

In ordinary English, 1) the distinction between education and schooling is often erased, and it is overlooked even more often by "educators" who are employed by, and primarily concerned with, schools. As a result, educational problems and issues are often misinterpreted and viewed overly narrowly as schooling problems and school issues. Education, however, is a broader notion. School is one important means of forming the habits and dispositions of the immature members of a society, but it is only one means and, compared to other more powerful ones, a relatively superficial and ineffectual one. Dewey made this clear: "Only as we have grasped the necessity of more fundamental and persistent modes of tuition can we make sure of placing the scholastic methods in their true context" (*MW*9:7). In contrast to schooling, Dewey identified education with the processes of communication:

[Persons] live in a community in virtue of the things they have in common; and communication is the way in which they come to possess things in common. What they must have in order to form a community or society are aims, beliefs, aspirations, knowledge. The communication that insures participation in a common understanding is one which secures similar emotional and intellectual dispositions—like ways of responding to expectations and requirements. Consensus demands communication. Not only is social life identical with communication, but all communication, and hence all genuine social life, is educative. To be a recipient of a communication is to have an enlarged and changed experience. (*MW*9:7–8)

This means that a genuine community only exists when its members share more than physical closeness, and it means that relations and interactions among individuals are not fully communal unless they include communication and its results. Unfortunately, communication and meaningful association often fail to take place. When this happens, societies— even societies with democratic governments—fail to be communities, persons fail to be genuine individuals, and relations among persons fail to be more than mechanical, manipulative, and external.

This view of education makes clear that major social institutions— the government, the economy, the family, the workplace, the legal system, volunteer organizations, the military, terrorist organizations, and religious groups, for example—have broader and deeper educational consequences than the schools (even though these educational consequences may not be the immediate objectives or conscious mission of these other institutions). Accordingly, these institutions can be evaluated, criticized, and reconstructed in terms of their educational failures and successes. It may be said, Dewey wrote, that the measure of the value of any social institution—political, economic, domestic, legal, religious, or whatever—is its educational effect, its effect in expanding and improving experience:

In dealing with the young, the need of training is too evident; the pressure to accomplish a change in their attitude and habits is too urgent to leave these consequences wholly out of account. Since our chief business with them is to enable them to share in a common life we cannot help considering whether or not we are forming powers that will secure this ability. If humanity has made some headway in realizing that the ultimate value of every institution is its distinctively human effect—its effect upon conscious experience—we may well believe that the lesson has been learned largely through dealings with the young. (*MW*9:9–10)

Though the educational effects of schooling are small, few, and temporary in comparison with the effects of these more far reaching and powerful social institutions, there is an undeniable social need for schooling or formal education. In fact, as Dewey observed, the need has never been greater, and this has become more and more the case since Dewey wrote. The increasing complexity of our society and our explosive, fast-paced gains in knowledge immensely widen the gap between the learning capacities of the young and the learning possible through day-to-day, informal involvement with adults. Without such formal education, Dewey said succinctly, "it is not possible to transmit all the resources and achievements of a complex society" (*MW*9:11).

The chief danger here, of course, is that the activities and subject matter of the schools may become remote from actual social practice, that they may become abstract and merely artificial, irrelevant, dead. When this happens, theory and practice, thought and action, become separated. It is this separation that is noted by all students who find a gap between their schools and the so-called real world. This is not an insoluble problem, but it is a major problem for, and in, schooling, and it is a problem that frequently is not addressed, much less solved.

As to 2), the identification of growth as the end or goal of education, and the use and consequences of this notion in evaluating institutions and practices provides a basis for social criticism and makes possible a critical philosophy that is pragmatic, non-foundational, non-transcendental, and non-dialectic. Dewey argued, of course, that the goal of education—all education and not just schooling—is growth. In response to the obvious question, "Growth toward what end?" Dewey replied "further growth." In order to understand this, it is important to identify the conditions necessary for growth. The most important of these conditions is immaturity, the absence of routine and bad fixed habits, not simply the absence of maturity but the real presence of a power or potential to develop. While it may sound odd to treat immaturity as a positive capacity, the alternative is odder still: maturity as the absence of any capacity to develop further. The possibility for further development constitutes a kind of plasticity and imaginativeness, an ability to learn anew from experience and retain that learning for coping with later difficulties. This capacity to learn from experience and to use that learning in future experience signifies the capacity to acquire new habits. In this light, Dewey observed:

> A habit is a form of executive skill, of efficiency in doing. A habit means an
> ability to use natural conditions as means to ends. It is an active control of
> the environment through control of the organs of action. Education is not

infrequently defined as consisting in the acquisition of those habits that effect an adjustment of an individual and his environment. The definition expresses an essential phase of growth. But it is essential that adjustment be understood in its active sense of control of means for achieving ends. If we think of a habit simply as a change wrought in the organism, ignoring the fact that this change consists in ability to effect subsequent changes in the environment, we shall be led to think of "adjustment" as a conformity to environment as wax conforms to the seal which impresses it. But habits transform the environment and mean formation of intellectual and emotional disposition as well as an increase in ease, economy, and efficiency of action. (*MW*9:52–53)

Education, then, is the continuing development of the capacity to develop new habits, and also the continuing renewal of this capacity itself. Dewey called this "growth" and defined education as growth in just this sense. "Our net conclusion," he wrote, "is that life is development, and that developing, growing, is life. Translated into its educational equivalents, this means I) that the educational process has no end beyond itself; it is its own end; and that II) the educational process is one of continual reorganizing, reconstructing, transforming" (*MW*9:54).

This concept of growth supplies a criterion for evaluating and remaking social institutions, practices, and relations. How well does each create and sustain the desire for continuing growth, and how well does it supply the means necessary to satisfy this desire? This may sound nice and sweet, but it is morally and politically revolutionary stuff. Democracy has a moral, valuational meaning, Dewey argued, in making the supreme test of all social practices the contribution they make to the growth of every member of society. Consider, for instance, a nation's economy not in terms of its "gross national product," but rather in terms of its "growth national product." Consider, similarly, school systems, factories, prisons, legal tribunals, governments and shadow governments, religious groups, hospitals, armies, and public and private media in this same way. What sorts of dispositions, capacities, habits, and consummations do they produce? How did they come to have these consequences, how did they work? What sorts of subjects or selves do they constitute, and whose interests do they serve or fail to serve? What sorts of alternatives exist?

A critical social philosophy of growth makes evident 3) the close and reciprocal relationship between education and democracy. Education stands in a special twofold, reciprocal relation to democracy. First, education as growth is the means to democracy, the method of democracy, the process by which democracy operates. Second, at the same time, this growth is the end of democracy, the goal of democracy, the values at which democracy aims. Democracy, understood as a way of community life, is possible only through education. In turn, education, understood as growth aiming at further growth, is possible only through democratic, shared participation in the decision-making processes that affect this growth. Democracy is self-government; it requires selves. Education is the creation and growth of selves; it requires a social environment in which this is possible and realized.

For Dewey, philosophy itself is one with education, and education is possible only as a society is genuinely democratic. Only active education understood as growth creates and re-creates shared inquiries, activities, and meanings. Only active education creates the freedom needed to realize through shared inquiry shared ideals. Democracy as a way of life, rather than merely a form of government, seeks and requires its citizens to have freely shared lives and values.[7] As a way of life, democracy is also the measure of growth. Accordingly, Dewey's views of experience, education, inquiry, and democracy mutually imply one another. If Dewey's notion of growth is separated from his notion of democratic way of life, it is impossible to determine in practice the presence or absence of growth, and impossible to differentiate in practice lives marked by growth from those defined by fixation, fanaticism, fundamentalism, and fascism. Moreover, when this separation leads to a commitment to a pragmatic notion of democracy without commitment to a pragmatic notion of education as growth, then democratic theorists fruitlessly must seek a rational basis for democracy beneath (foundational for) or beyond (transcendent of) a democratic way of life. A renewal of Dewey's philosophy provides a way to avoid these problems and the pointless projects that respond to them, and it simultaneously sheds light on his claim that *Democracy and Education* is the fullest statement of his philosophy. In this context, he noted:

> If we are willing to conceive of education as the process of forming fundamental dispositions, intellectual and emotional, toward nature and fellow men, philosophy may even be defined as the general theory of education. Unless a philosophy is to remain symbolic—or verbal—or a sentimental indulgence for a few, or else mere arbitrary dogma, its auditing of past experience and its program of values must take effect in conduct. The reconstruction of philosophy, of education, and of social ideals and methods thus go hand in hand. If there is especial need of educational reconstruction at the present time, if this need makes urgent a reconsideration of the basic ideas of traditional philosophic systems, it is because of the thoroughgoing change in social life accompanying the advance of science, the industrial revo-

lution, and the development of democracy. Such practical changes cannot take place without demanding an educational reformation to meet them, and without leading men to ask what ideas and ideals are implicit in these social changes, and what revisions they require of the ideas and ideal which are inherited from older and unlike cultures. (*MW*9:338)

Education after Liberalism

Now, listen carefully to Dewey's words in his 1897 "My Pedagogic Creed":

I believe that the community's duty to education is therefore, its paramount moral duty. By law and punishment, by social agitation and discussion, society can regulate and form itself in a more or less haphazard and chance way. But through education society can formulate its own purposes, can organize its own means and resources, and thus shape itself with definiteness and economy in the direction in which it wishes to move. *I believe that when society once recognizes the possibilities in this direction, and the obligations which these possibilities impose, it is impossible to conceive of the resources of time, attention, and money which will be put at the disposal of the educator.* (*EW*5:94; italics added)

Teachers and students and administrators—persons involved in schooling—are likely to smile at this. Conflating education and schooling, they are likely to believe that society has *not* recognized the liberal possibilities that Dewey outlined. They are likely to view this as an explanation for why too little time, too little attention, and too little money is put at the disposal of the schools, their schools. They are likely to feel that we have not yet realized the liberal values that Dewey championed, that he was a bit too hopeful, a bit too rosy, maybe a bit too American. They are likely to feel that Deweyan liberalism, a liberalism committed to empowering freedom, communal individualism, and experimental intelligence, stands in front of us still. They are likely to feel that we are living *before liberalism.*

I confess that I would like to believe that this is the case. If it were the case, the agenda for social action would be clearer. But I just can't believe it fully any longer. Consider again Dewey's claim. What if we suppose that he was not overly hopeful or overly rosy? What if we suppose that he was right on target? What if we suppose that society in fact already has recognized the possibilities presented by education, and has recognized the obligations that these possibilities impose? In fact, isn't this the case? Doesn't American society—perhaps most societies globally—put vast, almost inconceivable resources of time, attention, and money at the disposal of its educators? Of course, the educators who have these resources are not the little teachers, students, and administrators in our relatively superficial schools. Instead, they are the big educators in American society, the educational heavyweights such as: international businesses and global forces of production, marketing, and consumption; media and entertainment giants; national governments and international legal groups; militaries, police, and organized crime and terror; systems of surveillance, information production, and information warfare; and, religious organizations. In all honesty, is it not virtually impossible to conceive of the time, attention, and money put at the disposal of these mega-educators, these other-than-school educators?

There is no question that these institutions are educators in the sense in which Dewey frequently used the term. They forge habits and dispositions, communicate meanings and consensus, and create desires and actions on their behalf. The result, however, is rarely and only incidentally growth. It is rarely the continuing development of the capacity to forge new habits and the continuing renewal of this capacity itself.

To the extent that the major educational forces in our societies no longer even aim at growth, no longer hold growth as an ideal, we are not living before liberalism. To this extent, rather, we are living *after liberalism.*

To the extent that these educators are successful, on their own terms, individual persons will no longer actively prize growth, even their own growth, and they will feel that this situation is just fine.

I'm Not Going to Disneyland

In many countries and in many societies, the political left (or what passes for the political left) and the political right agree in theory that their public schools are not working. They propose different solutions, of course—from higher teacher salaries and lower class sizes to voucher systems and new incentives, from better facilities and new technology to charter schools, from uniform academic testing for students and teachers to school uniforms and same-sex classes and metal detectors, and from more public funding to more private competition. Still, in theory they agree that the public schools too frequently do not work.

I'd like to believe that this too is the case, but I cannot do it any longer. These arguments and theories about how to fix public schools parallel arguments about how to fix all kinds of other institutions and practices that typically are viewed in theory as dysfunctional. How can we fix the prisons? How can we make federal and international drug policies work? How can we make the health care and health insurance systems work? How can we deal with AIDS? How can we end racism and sexism and other forms of discrimination? How can we create meaningful work and leisure opportunities for everyone? How can we fight and win wars against ignorance, terrorism and crime, drugs, disease, poverty, and injustice?

The concept of growth, Dewey made clear, supplies a criterion for evaluating and remaking social institutions and practices: How well does each create and sustain the desire for continuing growth, and how well does it supply the means necessary to satisfy this desire? From the standpoint of this concept of growth, public schools—and all these other institutions and practices—are not working. From the standpoint of growth, they can receive only low evaluations, and they desperately need radical reconstruction.[8]

However, after liberalism, after major educational forces in practice affirm ideals other than growth, there are alternatives (to the notion of growth) that might well be used to evaluate social institutions and practices. These alternative concepts supply other criteria for evaluating social institutions and practices. Why not take this seriously? Why not take it as seriously in theory as it is taken in practice? Why not turn all these issues around? Why not say that the public schools and all these other institutions and practices are working just fine? They create desires and, at a societal level, they provide the means necessary for a sufficiently large number of persons to satisfy many of these desires. The desires, however, are not for growth. Perhaps they are desires for material wealth or comfort, a policed or medicalized or drugged existence, ready entertainment and amusement park lifestyle, consumer choices, or a gated community free from difference in practice as well as theory. In any case, for the most part these desires are not desires for growth.

It is not simply that these institutions do not much produce actual growth. Rather it is that they produce habits that do not idealize growth— do not lead persons to value growth. As such, they are postliberal; they are after liberalism. The difference could not be more dramatic. Dewey argued that action on behalf of the ideal of a life of growth could move us closer to this ideal. Many institutions and practices that today play major educational roles produce habits inconsistent with the ideal of a life of growth. In terms of the goals internal to these habits, these institutions and practices work just fine. Indeed, they are wildly successful. For example, whoever thought—really thought—that the goal of the still ongoing "war on drugs" in the United States is the end of non-prescription drug manufacture, sale, and use? Whoever thought that the goal of penal institutions and their punishments is the end of crime? Whoever thought that the goal of public schools is education as growth? After liberalism, this can sound downright quaint. And to students in schools, it can sound like something very distant from their "real world."

"If we train our children to take orders, to do things simply because they are told so, and fail to give them confidence to act and think for themselves," Dewey movingly wrote, "we are putting an almost insurmountable obstacle in the way of overcoming the present defects of our system and of establishing the truth of democratic ideals" (*MW*8:398). Yes. But, now this logic must be completed: If we put almost insurmountable obstacles in the way of democratic ideals, including the ideal of growth, we will train our children habitually to value other ideals.

I believe that this now is happening. That schools, puny educational forces in comparison to other social institutions, now are swamped by a global business culture that produces habits of mind inconsistent with the value of growth is not new. What is new is the fact that schools themselves are now far along in internalizing this business culture, this anti–education-as-growth culture, and are becoming part of the production of habits of mind at odds with the ideal of growth. Schools now are taking on the structures and aims of business; schooling is becoming the education business, and students are becoming education consumers.[9] The impact of these developments is particularly obvious in the case of philosophy and other humanities fields. Once a required subject that stood at the core of a liberal arts education, philosophy today is irrelevant to professional education. In the United States, more students take courses in hotel management and leisure studies than philosophy. More important, few philosophers say or do anything to indicate that they believe there is something wrong with this. They are busy seeking professional tenure and post-tenure professional distinction.

This may be bad news for the business of philosophy and the humanities, but it is far worse news for the business of democracy. Democracy requires selves who have developed the critical capacities necessary for self-government. Of course, few persons habitually value in practice democracy as a way of life. And, in a global society in which persons obviously have unequal opportunities, schools committed to growth would provide a last line of defense of the opportunities of all. Of course, in the global education marketplace, it is also the case that few persons habitually value in practice equal opportunity. Indeed, most persons believe there are large groups of other persons who are simply superfluous. While "holy war" and "ethnic cleansing," so prevalent in practice, have a bad name at least in theory, "economic cleansing" is embraced openly in theory as well as practice. In education, as in everything else, the objective is to buy low and sell high. For our own children and ourselves we want better, not equal.

Dewey coldly observed that the formation of fixed classes is fatal to a democracy:

> There must not be one system for the children of parents who have more leisure and another for the children of those who are wage earners.... The democracy which proclaims equality of opportunity as its ideal requires an education in which learning and social application, ideas and practice, work and recognition of the meaning of what is done, are united from the beginning and for all. (*MW*8:403–404)

Yes, and so it is now time to make the last step in this reasoning: The formation of fixed classes is fatal to democracy, and it also is fatal to an ideal of democracy, an ideal of community life committed to equal opportunity and the growth of all persons. It has given birth, instead, to an ideal of democracy as the freedom to have opportunities and resources from which other persons are excluded but which are essential to their growth. Again, the point is not simply that educational forces today rarely produce actual growth. Far beyond this, the point is that they produce habits and lives that increasingly no longer even value growth, no longer hold growth to be an ideal.

Dewey's radical conception of growth as a democratic way of life has never been included in the goals of the big educators, the big educational forces, in any society. Getting it on their agendas requires in part stepping outside the schools, academic organizations, and the largely intramural debates that go on there, and scholarly books like this one.

At the same, today's agenda must not be merely retrospective, merely repetition of twentieth-century pragmatism. Instead, it must aim at new ways of thinking—new ways of thinking democracy, community, individuality, values, criticism and appreciation, power and inquiry, meaning, multiple meanings, pluralism, and death. It must aim self-reflectively at new ways of thinking about new ways of thinking—at new ways of thinking futures of philosophy. It must aim at new ways of living.

In the face of many constraints and difficulties for success, this remains the most important educational task, a genuinely Herculean labor, for anyone who professes anew pragmatism in the millennium after Dewey.

Notes

1. Ralph Waldo Emerson, *Nature* (1836), p. 181.
2. Ray Davies, "20th Century Man" (Davray Music, 1971).
3. Ralph Waldo Emerson, "Self-Reliance" [1837], in *Pragmatism and Classical American Philosophy: Essential Readings and Interpretive Essays*, ed. John J. Stuhr (New York: Oxford University Press, 1999), p. 24.

4. John Lennon, "Instant Karma (We All Shine On)" (Lenono Music, 1970).

5. Emerson, "Self-Reliance," p. 32.

6. All references to the writings of John Dewey are provided within the text of the chapters of this book. These references are to the following: *John Dewey: The Early Works: 1882–1898*, (Carbondale: Southern Illinois University Press, 1969–1972), ed. Jo Ann Boydston, 5 volumes; *John Dewey: The Middle Works: 1899–1924*, (Carbondale: Southern Illinois University Press, 1976–1983), ed. Jo Ann Boydston, 15 volumes; *John Dewey: The Later Works, 1925–1953*, (Carbondale: Southern Illinois University Press, 1981–1990), ed. Jo Ann Boydston, 17 volumes. References to these volumes of Dewey's writings are abbreviated in the standard form: by initials for the series, followed by volume number and, following a colon, page number. Thus, for example, reference to *The Middle Works*, volume 10, page 47 (from which this quote is in fact taken), would be abbreviated as (*MW*10:47), and reference to *The Later Works*, volume 2, page 119 would be abbreviated as (*LW*2:119).

7. See chapter 3 for an extended discussion of this point and its implications.

8. See the final section of my essay "Education and the Cultural Frontier: Community, Identity, and Difference" in my *Genealogical Pragmatism: Philosophy, Experience, and Community* (Albany: State University of New York Press, 1997), pp. 252–259.

9. See my "The Humanities, Inc." in *Genealogical Pragmatism: Philosophy, Experience, and Community* (Albany: State University of New York Press, 1997), pp. 3–20.

CHAPTER 2

The Defects of Liberalism: Lasting Elements of Negative Pragmatism

A Blind Date with a Negative Pragmatist

"There is no way of plotting a living thing upon a flat sheet," the American philosopher William Ernest Hocking wrote on the flat sheets of his 1926 book, *Man and the State*.[1] Hocking now is long dead and almost wholly forgotten. Despite the fact that he is no longer a "living thing," is there a way sensitively and accurately to plot what, if anything, remains living today in his thought?

Before addressing this question, I want to tell you that, the so-called problem of other minds notwithstanding, I know just what you're thinking. You're thinking: Is this chapter focused on a forgotten, dead American philosopher really worth my time and effort? You're thinking: What's this got to do with thinking and living differently in the future, and, more specifically, what's this got to do with me? You're thinking: This is going to be really bad.

Now, I admit that this sounds like a recipe for a tedious and unrewarding intellectual blind date. However, I think this obscure dead American philosopher, William Ernest Hocking, may surprise and engage you. Of course, I won't promise love at first sight; few blind dates are that easy or effortless.

Instead, let me promise only critical honesty and a thoroughly straightforward strategy. I begin directly with a statement of fact and a postulate. Moving from this fact and this postulate, I seek to establish a general conclusion. Let me begin with this statement of fact: William Ernest Hocking is today an obscure philosopher. Of course, to note that Hocking is an obscure philosopher is to engage in redundancy. In American culture (and most cultures) today, philosophers typically are unfamiliar, inconspicuous, and remote, and so to be a philosopher today typically is to be obscure. Even so, Hocking now is especially obscure, or doubly obscure, because his work now is unfamiliar even to most philosophers. It is simply a matter of fact that even professional philosophers rarely read, write about, or discuss Hocking's thought. Almost all of his many books now are out of print. There are hardly any references to his work in scholarly citation indices. Professional conferences do not include papers about him, and graduate students do not write dissertations about his thought. His views are very seldom taught, even in courses on American philosophy and even in courses on twentieth-century American philosophy. The 1990s *New Oxford Dictionary of Philosophy* includes no entry on Hocking, while the 1960s *Encyclopedia of Philosophy* devotes a single column to Hocking's life and work, a column squeezed between longer entries on the anything but familiar Leonard Trelawney Hobhouse and Shadsworth Hodgson. At Penn State University, most of Hocking's books aren't even housed in the massive main library; instead, they gather dust in a warehouse annex filled with books that aren't used enough to merit shelf space in the stacks. In short, it is a matter of fact that today Hocking's philosophy is very rarely read, analyzed, or utilized.[2]

This neglect of Hocking's philosophy is remarkable because it stands in sharp contrast to the serious and sustained attention devoted to, and the importance ascribed to, his philosophy during his long career, from his first published philosophical essay in 1898 at age twenty-five through some 300 publications right up to his death in 1966. During much of this time, Hocking was generally regarded as a major thinker of lasting importance and real originality, a philosopher mentioned in the same breath as James, Royce, and Dewey, a thinker one could not avoid.

As such, Hocking is a striking case study in the processes of canon formation within professional philosophy and the humanities more generally. How, why, and in whose interests has Hocking been so thoroughly marginalized, excluded, and erased? Just when did he move from professional philosophy's Top 40 playlist to its discount dustbins of genuinely alternative music? What are the consequences of this dramatic reversal of fortune? What follows from it? Who is implicated in it? How has it shaped our own thought?

I think these are very important questions. They are questions to which philosophers, despite their proclaimed interest in self-knowledge, devote surprisingly little attention. As a beginning, any adequate genealogy of the virtual disappearance of Hocking's philosophy from our intellectual horizons must include at least the following three concerns. First, Hocking has vanished in part because the sweeping *scope* of his thought stands in opposition to the present narrow specialization of most professional philosophy. Drawing on realism and mysticism, empiricism and Christianity, naturalism and intuitionism, Asian thought and Marxism, and modern philosophy and then-contemporary currents of reflection, Hocking ranged across problems in religion and politics, education and ethics, biology and psychology, and epistemology and aesthetics. In doing so, he displayed a stunning intellectual breadth and wide and generous sympathies that readily seem outdated in an era in which philosophical portfolios are considered diversified if they include, for example, both Quine *and* Davidson, or both Heidegger *and* Derrida, or both Peirce *and* Habermas. Moreover, Hocking's philosophy outstrips and undermines the intellectual partitions that professional philosophy now has established for itself. He attended seriously and carefully to the writings of American pragmatists, British analysts, Continental metaphysicians and anti-metaphysicians, and Indian mystics. As such, Hocking embodied in abundance the pluralism that is in such short supply in professional philosophy today.

Second, just as the scope of Hocking's philosophy stands in opposition to the intellectual specializations and subspecializations within professional philosophy, so too the *orientation* of his philosophy stands in opposition to contemporary professional philosophy. Like John Dewey, Hocking believed that philosophers should address the real, living problems of men and women rather than the artificial issues, formal methods, and retold histories and marginal comments of so many professional philosophers. Accordingly, Hocking wrote without the jargon, conversational name-dropping, nearly endless footnotes, and other trappings of the academy. He aimed at an educated public. Today, that public may not exist in sufficient numbers to provide him with readers. His books certainly have no place in the chain bookstores that fill their philosophy sections with bestsellers on new age metaphysics, cyber-power, and the healing properties of pyramids and crystals; the Zen of business downsizing; and the application of "total quality management" principles to intimate personal relationships and weight loss. In addition, this orientation now is largely ignored by scholarly audiences that judge such work insufficiently technical and instead demand that their philosophy be less public and more professional. Hocking, however, took seriously the view that philosophy is concerned with wisdom—and not just with knowledge. He took seriously the view that wisdom is a shared good, such that successful philosophy must be public philosophy. As a result, his writings are a virtual chronicle of public problems and transformations in twentieth-century America—from his books on nationalism and world civilization, experiential faith and living religions, and science and values, to his essays and articles on war and military psychology, diplomacy and the League of Nations, foreign relations with the East and Mideast, law and human rights, the atomic bomb and international responsibilities, the treatment of former enemy nations following World War II, the role of unions and labor strikes, the mission of public education, the Cold War, the meaning of the death of President Kennedy, and the public role of the free press—an analysis recommended to its readers by *Time* magazine. By contrast, professional philosophy today finds little time (or space) for this commitment to illuminate practice by theory and to test theory by practice.

Third, Hocking's philosophy is ignored today not just because of its broad scope and public orientation, but also because of its *content*. Hocking was an idealist, and idealism has long been out of fashion in philosophy. In the twentieth century, European phenomenologists, existentialists, hermeneuticists, critical theorists, and poststructuralists and postmodernists have attacked idealism. British and Anglo-American ordinary-language philosophers, positivists, analysts, realists, and materialists have rejected idealism. And American pragmatists, naturalists, and empiricists have criticized idealism to the point that they rarely bother anymore even to engage it. By itself, of course, none of this hostility toward idealism establishes that idealism is fatally flawed, or even flawed at all. To demonstrate that idealism is incorrect requires a detailed analysis of the validity and soundness of the arguments set forth by idealists and their enemies. It does, however, establish that idealism now seems to most philosophers to be something musty, something stored in library warehouses and metaphysical museums, something more important to the history of philosophy than to the present life of philosophy. For most philosophers today, idealism is no longer, in the words of William James, a "live hypothesis"—a hypothesis that stands in relation to an individual as a real possibility, a hypothesis that scintillates with credibility for that individual, a hypothesis on which that individual is willing to act and to live (and not just to sit passively while reading a chapter like this).[3] Hocking's own description of the movement of thought and the changes in philosophical climate seems to apply to idealism today. He wrote: "The formulae that were once potent here too begin to fail: ideas and phrases, gritty a generation ago, a decade ago, are already worn smooth and lend no more friction to any human work."[4]

Hocking surely tried to render idealism a live hypothesis, a potent, gritty philosophy. He recognized that this is not an easy task. Writing to a friend in 1954, he offered this observation about the present and possible future of philosophy:

I have for a long time been concerned over what we might call the "bad press" which idealism has been suffering under. In spite of the irrelevance of the notion of "fashion" to the world of ideas, there is no doubt that in this country, and to some extent in Europe, there has ruled an anti-idealistic fashion. And strangely enough in a field where care in the use of terms should rule, this current has been opposed less to idealism than to subjectivism with which it is too easy to identify idealism. . . . It is a matter of great importance to get idealism as a metaphysic presented as it is, and not as those who seek the air of novelty by an illicit contrast would like to present it. . . . I am giving myself to the same effort so far as circumstances permit—to write *that paragraph* in which the meaning of idealism is so transparent and radiant that it will compel its own attention and conviction, and spread through the whole network of human mentality. That may take a hundred years, but what does that matter?[5]

Hocking attempted to spread idealism by engaging tirelessly its critics— particularly pragmatists such as William James and John Dewey. Indeed, in many respects, Hocking's metaphysics and philosophy of religion constitute a sustained attempt to set forth an idealism that can not only withstand, but also incorporate, the insights of pragmatism. Hocking viewed pragmatism not simply as a challenge to idealism, but above all as an opportunity for idealism to release its forces, to render itself more complete, self-consistent, and ultimately reasonable. Thus, Hocking wrote that pragmatism had laid bare the weakness of classical idealism by demonstrating that idealism "does not do the work of religious truth" and, so, "is not the truth of religion." He continued:

The salvation [that idealism] offers men seems still to be, in effect, a salvation from the particular in the general, the *ideal*; even though it names the *concrete* as its goal, it has not yet been able in this matter of religion to accomplish union with the concrete. . . . so that when the pragmatic test comes, a religion which is but a religion-in-general, a religion universal but not particular, a religion of idea, not organically rooted in passion, fact, and institutional life, must fail. (*MGHE*, pp. x, xii)

Because Hocking accepted this pragmatic argument against traditional idealism, he endorsed what he calls "negative pragmatism"—the view that "that which does not work is not true." Hocking explained:

if a theory has no consequences, or bad ones; if it makes no difference to men, or else undesirable differences; if it lowers the capacity of men to meet the stress of existence, or diminishes the worth to them of what existence they have; such a theory is somehow false, and we have no peace until it is remedied. I will go even farther, and say that a theory is false if it is not interesting: a proposition that falls on the mind so dully as to excite no enthusiasm has not attained the level of truth; though the words be accurate the import has leaked away from them, and meaning is not conveyed. (*MGHE*, p. xiii)

Hocking did believe, then, that "negative pragmatism" serves a valuable critical function, a kind of self-help function for flabby idealists who need to get out of the universal and into the particular and "just do it." However, he thought that "positive pragmatism"—a view that he bizarrely understood as committed to the view that there is "No reality yet unmade" and simplistically summarized as the theory that "Whatever works is true"— served no constructive function at all. Throughout his life, Hocking continued to caricature pragmatism and to argue that pragmatism, (mis)conceived in this manner, is self-refuting.

Although Hocking made this argument over and over, it is a terrible argument. Hocking's argument does not establish that pragmatism is self-refuting. Rather it establishes that pragmatism is incompatible with certain idealist assumptions about human nature. This, of course, is hardly startling. Pragmatists themselves recognize that their views are incompatible with metaphysical idealism, and that their views instead must be coupled with radical empiricism, an account of experience as transactional and an account of the universe as pluralistic. Given his idealist assumptions, Hocking concluded that pragmatism is false and that idealism is true. However, this simply begs the question by using idealist assumptions to establish idealism.

For example, in his 1912 *The Meaning of God in Human Experience*, Hocking asserted that "the only kind of truth which in the end can comply with the pragmatic requirement . . . is a non-pragmatic truth, a truth which has an absolute aspect" (*MGHE*, p. xvii) Why? Hocking answered that only belief in the Absolute and ideal works in practice: "No religion, then, is a true religion which is not able to make men tingle, yes, even to their physical nerve tips, with the sense of an infinite hazard, a wrath to come, a heavenly city to be gained or lost in the process of time and by the use of our freedom" (*MGHE*, p. xiv). Only idealism, Hocking asserted, can make us tingle with the sense of infinite hazard. Only idealism, he thought, can give us "the unlimited right of Idea in a world where nothing that is is ultimately irrational" (*MGHE*, p. xii). Only idealism, Hocking wrote, can provide us "the mystical and authoritative elements of faith" (*MGHE*, p. xix). Beginning with a deep longing for the Absolute and the belief that "life is but a certain consciousness of the Absolute" (*MGHE*, p. 203), Hocking concluded that any philosophy which fails to satisfy this longing is not satisfactory. As he put it: "We could not live without the Absolute, nor without our idea of the Absolute.... Thus, accepting fully the pragmatic guide to truth, we conclude that the only satisfying truth must be absolute—that is, non-pragmatic" (*MGHE*, p. 206).

This argument may be revealing from a psychological perspective—it may tell us something about Hocking and his hopes and desires and needs—but it is not successful from a logical point of view. To presuppose that we—and just who is this "we" anyway?—require a mystical and authoritative faith, a world in which nothing is irrational or irreducibly plural, a sense of infinite hazard that makes us tingle, the companionship of God that renders us open to experience (*MGHE*, p. 225) is to assert, rather than argue for, idealism.

Hocking frequently repeated this question-begging argument, as though it might be made true if set forth sufficiently frequently. In his 1929 *Types of Philosophy*, for example, Hocking asserted that "pragmatism requires a non-pragmatic truth" and "fails by its own test."[6] Again, why? Hocking claimed that pragmatism views truth as humanly created, as intrinsically tied to our purposes and choices, as dependent on us and accessible to us. This, he continued correctly, makes impossible absolutely objective truth and makes non-existent any reality absolutely independent of human experience. But, he asserted, it is only this objective truth and independent reality "that can set us free" (*TP*, p. 170). Thus he concluded that humanism depends on idealism (*TP*, p. 450): "God is nothing if not that on which we depend.... We cannot swing up a rope which is attached only to our own belt" (*TP*, p. 170).

Pragmatists and radical empiricists, of course, deny that there are any other belts to which one might attach a rope. They deny that humanism depends on idealism. And they deny that there is, or needs to be, or could be any non-pragmatic justification or non-pragmatic foundation for pragmatism. Thus James noted that "*tho one part of our experience may lean upon another part to make it what it is in any one of its several aspects in which it may be considered, experience as a whole is self-containing and leans on nothing*" (italics in original).[7] Hocking's desire—a desire shared by many persons—to be able to "swing up" is no doubt real, but the mere existence of this desire does not establish the truth of his belief that there is an Absolute that satisfies this desire.

Hocking repeated this argument in his 1938–39 Gifford Lectures, "Fact and Destiny," summarized, revised, and published in 1966 as "History and the Absolute."[8] Here his target was not simply pragmatism but the whole "malaise of Modernity," a deep relativity and fragmentation in our science, philosophy, and lives. The self, Hocking claimed, desires and requires "some assurance of integrity in itself, of wholeness and truth in its vision of the world." Modernity, however, cannot meet this demand because it "suffers from an inability to find an objective and durable goodness in its many goods, a necessary unity in its aims, a radical bond between its best-justified wishes and the Facts" (*PRCWC*, p. 460). Modernity delivers only suffering, irrationality, the absurd, evil, and death—"the apparent finality of Tragedy"—and the relativity of our meanings and values. Once again, Hocking claimed this view is self-refuting: "Relativity, on being discovered, is already in principle overcome" because "the Relative can be known to be such only in contrast to an Absolute" (*PRCWC*, p. 461).

Once again, this is an expression of hope and longing, rather than a conclusion of fact and logic. Hocking believed that given modernity, multiple histories and finite lives lose significance by acquiring finality. We suffer and die. In contrast, Hocking asserted that given an Absolute, human life "acquires significance by losing finality." Thus he concluded:

> [The Absolute] includes the assurance of a continuing future, in which mean-ings as yet unimagined are to be proposed; and in whose fulfillment our Will-to-create and, with it our Will-to-suffer in creation, shall find its full scope. As realizing the presence of his Absolute, the word of the fully-living human being is "Lo, Thou art With me"; and because of that fellowship, problems alleged intractable—the rooted hatreds, calls for revenge, despairs—lose their finality, without losing their summons to develop within history the perti-nent empirical situations. (*PRCWC*, p. 462)

Here again the contrast with pragmatism, and the desires that underlie it, could not be sharper. For example, in his *Pragmatism*, James wrote:

> I am willing to think that the prodigal-son attitude, open to us as it is in many vicissitudes, is not the right and final attitude towards the whole of life. I am willing that there should be real losses and real losers, and no total preser-vation of all that is. I can believe in the ideal as an ultimate, not as an origin, and as an extract, not the whole. When the cup is poured off, the dregs are left behind forever, but the possibility of what is poured off is sweet enough to accept.[9]

Although James claimed that pragmatism is a new name for an old way of thinking, it is Hocking's message that is an old way of thinking in philosophy and also a long-standing message in religion. Hocking delivered this message in language that now seems dated and musty. More important, it is a message propped up by a question-begging argument. It is a message rooted in an unwillingness to recognize its own historicity or accept the finitude of life, the untranscended reality of suffering, and the finality of death. It is a message that in substance today need not be a live hypothesis.

Falling in Love with a Critic of Liberalism

I began with a statement of fact: Today Hocking is an obscure philosopher. I located the tripartite basis of this obscurity in the broad scope, public orientation, and idealistic content of his philosophy. In this light, I now introduce a postulate: Some obscure philosophers deserve to be obscure. I know that this postulate may trouble Ph.D. students combing the history of philosophy for writers and issues about which almost nothing has been written; I realize that it may upset untenured philosophy professors determined to identify a novel research agenda so as to publish rather than perish professionally; and I understand that this may offend senior faculty who have built careers by developing ever larger expertise on an ever shrinking subject matter. Still, for present purposes I assert confidently that some obscure philosophers fully merit their obscurity.

Given the fact that Hocking is an obscure philosopher, and given the postulate that some obscure philosophers deserve to be obscure, the question is obvious: Is Hocking an obscure philosopher who deserves to be obscure? More generally: What criteria must any obscure philosopher meet to deserve obscurity? For example, is it enough to write dense, unclear prose? To employ convoluted, invalid arguments? To address artificial or trivial problems? To make false or merely uninteresting assertions? To write too much or too little? To fail to exhibit originality or creativity?

It may be tempting to think that Hocking's caricature of pragmatism and his repeated question-begging argument for idealism are sufficient to merit obscurity. I admit almost complete hostility toward his idealism and the longing that gives rise to it. In doing so, however, I note Hocking's own advice on the treatment of one's philosophical opponents and enemies: Love your enemy as you love your friend. This advice, preached often but practiced seldom, is more familiar than clear. It is often understood as a call to treat friends and enemies just alike, to treat them indifferently. Hocking argued that this interpretation misses the point. To take up the task of love, Hocking explained, is to seek to transform an enemy, to enlist that enemy in a "cohostility" to its own evil, thereby to render it no longer an enemy at all. He urged: "The task of love is not mere amiability toward the right-minded; it is also creativity toward the wrong-minded: it is to effect this radical *change of will.* We thus reach *an ethical Absolute* which is the reverse of indifference—it is the *making* of difference" (*PRCWC*, p. 436).

It is in this spirit of love—"creativity toward the wrong-minded" (in this case the wrong-minded idealist)—that I approach Hocking, though I approach him without any ethical Absolute. Admittedly, this tough-love approach entails major surgery: specifically, I propose to detach as fully as possible Hocking's pragmatic social and political thought—his analysis of the state, liberalism, and individualism—from his idealist metaphysics. I propose to hold on to his requirement to effect a radical change of will and make a practical difference, but at the same time throw out his Absolute, both metaphysical and ethical. The importance of this task is itself pragmatic. The point of this operation is not simply to save Hocking from undeserved obscurity, but rather to make different and to renew Hocking's insights for persons living after Hocking.

Hocking's social and political philosophy is most insightfully and fully developed in his 1926 *Man and the State* and especially in his 1937 *The Lasting Elements of Individualism.*[10] (Hocking dedicated *The Lasting Elements of Individualism* to John Dewey, "comrade and opponent in debate through many years of deepening affection," and it is instructive to consider Hocking's now little-known books in light of Dewey's familiar, canonical 1927 *The Public and Its Problems,* 1929 *Individualism: Old and New,* 1935 *Liberalism and Social Action,* and 1939 *Freedom and Culture.*) Hocking described *The Lasting Elements of Individualism* as a study in the philosophy of history that attempts to look forward but not in any way that pragmatism looks forward. He explained: "It is hostile not to pragmatism, but to mere pragmatism: it believes that our experimentalism is destined to transform itself into a version of the 'dialectic method' whereby mere groping takes on rational direction and destination. *Out of the flux, certainty*" (*LEI,* p. xii–xiii).

Hocking did not achieve his goal. He did not transform experimentalism or pragmatism into a philosophy of certainty or idealism. In fact, what he did (or what may be done by transforming his work) is just the opposite. His penetrating criticism of liberalism makes possible a move from a philosophy of history as necessary direction or pre-determined destination to a philosophy of history as a contingent experiment or ongoing journey, constantly in need of piecemeal reconstructions on plural fronts. In short, in spite of Hocking's own intent, the lasting element of his *The Lasting Elements of Individualism* is its demonstration that *out of certainty, flux*—and the need to confront this flux with intelligence.

Hocking defined individualism as "simply belief in the human individual as the ultimate unit of social structures," belief that the individual person is more real than social groups and institutions generated by, and composed of, individuals (*LEI*, pp. 3–4). Hocking then claimed that the "plain facts of experience" do not support individualism. Rather, they support the view that "individuals are products of social groups quite as much as social groups are products of individuals." Like Dewey discussing the interrelations of individuality and community or Mead setting forth his view of the social self, Hocking observed that "dependency seems to run both ways," and so "if we are simply reporting the overt facts of society, we should say that Aristotle and Locke are both right—the state is prior to the individual, and the individual is prior to the state: there is an alternating current or cycle in which neither can claim absolute priority" (*LEI*, pp. 4–5).

Accept these "plain facts of experience"—the reciprocity and interdependence of individuals and social groups such as families, neighborhoods, universities, and states. Why then would anyone endorse individualism, the belief in the priority of individuals to social groups? Almost everyone in the modern Western world, Hocking thought, does endorse individualism. But why? Modernism is this passage of the locus of reality to the individual, "the turning point from the dominance of the formula, *To every group, numerous men and sets of men*, toward the dominance of the formula, *To every man, numerous groups, and possible groups*" (*LEI*, p. 30). This belief in individualism, Hocking explained, rests not on the surface facts of experience but rather on a liberal faith, a "faith or intuition which is *liberal* toward the individual." Hocking described this liberal faith as "an attitude or confidence toward the undemonstrated powers of the units of society; it means a faith that the welfare of any society may be trusted to the individuals who compose it." He continued:

> Liberalism maintains that the greatest natural resource of any community is the latent intelligence and good will of its members; and it seeks those forms of society which run a certain risk of preliminary disorder in order to elicit that resource. Since individuals can be developed only by being trusted with somewhat more than they can, at the moment, do well, liberalism is a sort of honor system. (*LEI*, p. 5)

Political liberalism, Hocking argued, is simply the result of this liberal faith in individuals.

The consequences of this faith, Hocking thought, constitute the three core tenets of liberalism: equality, liberty, and rights. A liberal faith in individuals, Hocking explained, leads to: 1) "an essential *equality* of men, since the respects which set a man apart from the group are the same for all men," and the necessity for each man to rely on his own reason "implies a native fund of reason qualitatively the same in all"; 2) "an essential *liberty,* since each individual, as chooser of his group, must mentally contain all these social possibilities in himself" because "what society is to be depends on him, rather than what he is to be upon society"; and, 3) "a set of *rights* which spring from his needs as a man," needs that "become the basis of his choice of his many possible groups" of equals, and, thus, the basis of political fraternity (*LEI,* p. 35).

Long before George W. Bush, Dick Cheney, Clarence Thomas, George Bush, Jerry Falwell, Pat Buchanan, Newt Gingrich, Ronald Reagan, Richard Nixon, George Wallace, and Barry Goldwater, Hocking, like Dewey, worried that liberalism is not working, or not working well enough, and needs to be revised, reconstructed, reborn. Proceeding just like a pragmatist, Hocking asked: What are the actual practical results of trusting the welfare of society to the individuals who compose it? He asked: What have we gained by implementing the honor system that is liberalism? The results, he asserted soberly, are mixed. Individuals have developed new energies under freer political conditions, and in this respect liberalism has been a great success. Hocking continued:

> But these energies have not infallibly been devoted to the welfare of the society; the individual has frequently seized the opportunity to make something for himself and let society take the consequences. He may be surprised and annoyed to be told that anything else is expected. For liberalism trains people to receive, and only hopes that they will give. If the group is to be liberal toward individuals, they must be recipients of its liberalty; and few habits are easier to develop than then habit of being recipients, especially if this receiving is connected with the idea of "rights." (*LEI,* p. 6)

As an honor system, as a political system rooted in a faith in individuals, Hocking concluded, liberalism needs "some kind of supplement" if it is to receive from individuals what it requires to succeed.

The pragmatic question, then, is this: What is the supplement that modern liberalism needs, and how and by whom, if at all, can this supplement be provided? Before one can offer a prescription for the ills of liberalism, Hocking thought, a more detailed diagnosis is required. What exactly is wrong with liberalism? In an analysis that is remarkably similar in many respects to Dewey's analysis in his *Liberalism and Social Action,* an attack on outdated and ahistorical earlier varieties of liberalism, Hocking claimed that liberalism suffers from three major defects that it alone cannot remedy.

These are, he argued, the permanent defects of liberalism. His analysis is instructive and very relevant today for persons who would think and live beyond the twentieth century. First, Hocking asserted, liberalism is incapable of achieving and maintaining social unity. Although some sort of social unity is desirable, this unity is neither guaranteed nor automatic. It has to be achieved. It has to be achieved because "society is not an organism; it only faintly resembles one and that least of all when it is analyzed into individuals, each of which can set up independent life, as the cells of a body never pretend to do" (*LEI*, p. 42). Moreover, the larger the social group, the more difficult it is to achieve this unity because "the less it is possible to conceive of it as a result of the conscious consent of its individual members." This lack of unity is evident everywhere in liberal political and economic social relations. In liberal democratic politics and government, do elected representatives represent the unified interests of a state? Can they represent the state, taken as a unified entity, when their political survival depends on satisfying a local electorate by producing local results? "In such a body," Hocking observed, "it is just the total-interest which is nowhere represented" (*LEI*, pp. 45–46). Liberalism may offer us fine theories of the unified, general will, but in experience this general will is extinguished. Hocking observed: "Our theory tells us that each individual is capable of thinking 'We' as well as 'I'; and that since human beings are born in groups, they will naturally put 'We' first and 'I' afterward. But if our individualism has trained them in the rightness and necessity of putting the 'I' foremost, it may well have brought us to a pass where no genuine political 'We' can get a voice" (*LEI*, pp. 46–47). In a time of special-interest and single-issue politics, Hocking's diagnosis rings true—even when a politician markets himself to a deeply divided electorate as "a uniter, not a divider." In economics and business, Hocking argued, we find the same lack of social unity. Have the economic transactions that liberalism has made possible resulted in a prosperous land? No, Hocking answered in alliterative excess: We have only some prosperous individuals in certain spots, only "pimples of prosperity on a visage predominantly pale." Changing metaphors, Hocking observed that these "private reservoirs of wealth" have no regular working relationship to unified public concerns. Instead, the "liberal theory of property terminates in the processes by which they [the privately wealthy] receive possession; individualism has no theory of the relation of private wealth to the working commonwealth, except through the taxing power, which appears as an unwelcome intrusion from a political arm not wholly above suspicion of self-interest, and not as the normal development of the owner's will" (*LEI*, p. 50). Accordingly, social unity is not built: "Action as a whole, and for the whole, is beyond the reach of a purely individualistic enterprise" (*LEI*, p. 51). In the time of a massive global gap between rich and poor, Hocking's point, if not his language, has never been more relevant.

Liberalism's second major defect, Hocking claimed, is its attachment to rights without duties, rights that are supposedly natural and inalienable, rights that thus become privileges. Hocking called this an infection of the Western mind, a moral toxin, once a "useful encouragement" but now a "pernicious flattery" (*LEI*, p. 53). "There are no unconditional rights," Hocking wrote. "For the conditions of all rights are moral conditions; without good will, all rights drop off (*LEI*, pp. 53–54). John Locke recognized that an individual's right to immunity from exploitation carried with it a duty to refrain from exploitation of others, but Locke's liberalism now lies in wreckage in the disposition to take without giving, to receive without acknowledgment or sense of debt. This modernist liberal disposition is omnipresent and is at work in our economic stereotypes: from the idle rich to welfare cheats and able-bodied food-stamp recipients, from sweatshop owners to their lazy employees, from neighbors who borrow without returning to parents who demand that society provide for the children they conceive, and from faculty desperately trying to reduce their teaching loads and minimize their office hours to "frequenters of colleges"— Hocking says that he will not call them students—who expect to graduate to positions of leadership without engaging in the hard work that leadership requires. Hocking concluded: "Liberalism has not merely shown a flaw, it has undermined itself and prepared the way for a general regime of dependence" (*LEI*, p. 57).

Hocking called the third defect of liberalism "the emotional defect" and identified it as the root of the other two defects. Liberalism's original emotional appeal lay in its cheerful, amiable view of human nature as, by nature, good. But, Hocking countered, this liberal faith in the nature of individuals has produced individuals unworthy of that faith. It has produced self-indulgent individuals now incapable of putting this faith into practice in their own lives. This group includes conservatives, reactionaries, fundamentalists, and absolutists who make use of the very liberal institutions, practices, and sympathies that they criticize, subvert, and seek to overthrow. But this group also includes fair-weather liberals who no longer really fight for liberal principles even though they are surrounded by suffering, injustice, violence, and terror—even though "there is plenty to be done before the world is even decently liberal." He wrote:

> The chief source of suffering and discontent regarding the passing Liberal age is not that it has evolved its own special brands of poverty, injustice, political ineptitude; it is the experience of a prevalent flabby mediocrity of mind

and character which begins, in our virile moments, to inspire a sort of moral loathing. To say that each man is as good as the next means only that the next is as poor a sort as the first. . . . Until Liberalism learns how to include in its hopeful program the provision for correction and the honorable severities of living, it will be no guide for the steps to be taken. (*LEI*, pp. 59–58)

Our liberal faith, then, has produced individuals who do not justify that faith and who are incapable of taking up that faith. Liberalism, Hocking concluded, has produced individuals, liberal hypocrites, politically correct but illiberal at the scratch, for whom liberalism itself no longer has emotional appeal. Liberalism's success, Hocking concluded, now has produced conditions that leave it vulnerable to attack from inside and outside, and so guarantee its failure.

Hocking's analysis of the defects of liberalism and modernism is informed and penetrating, and it remains timely and genuinely important. On this basis alone, it is a mistake to neglect Hocking. We permit and sustain the obscurity of his ideas and arguments at our considerable peril.

Breaking Up with an Incorrigible Absolutist

Can liberalism overcome these defects? Is there a solution? If so, what is it? How must liberalism be reconstructed or supplemented in the millennium after it arose? Hocking believed that liberalism can overcome these defects—perhaps even that there is a dialectical necessity that liberalism will overcome these defects. The defects of liberalism did not lead him to champion communism, fascism, anarchy, revolution, terrorism, or isolationism. A supplemented liberal state, Hocking argued, in the future must meet two necessary conditions. First, the liberal state can achieve social unity only in action, not in thinking alone—only in practice, not in theory alone. The liberal state must actively create, rather than passively reflect, political unity. The state must engage in uniting deeds, acts that "can embody the latent 'We' of the society or nation." Hocking explained that in most liberal democratic states this would constitute a breach with "the tradition of hampered government." But in this breach, he continued, "it may well be that democracy will for the first time exist, because for the first time a true general will exists and finds its way into action, or rather gains real existence by finding its way into action" (*LEI*, p. 106; see also *MATS*, pp. 14, 44, 157). The liberal state, then, must become an active state, a state uniting in action. Such a state must perform what Hocking called the "commotive function": the unending activity of a group's constituting itself as a group, making up its unified mind, and moving together, wills and emotions and ethical passions united in a shared mission. This need, Hocking observed (with some implicit references to America's post-Depression New Deal), has never been greater: we simply cannot "endure the same amount of division, dissent, obstruction, delay as was tolerable a century ago" (*LEI*, p. 142). In being commotive, the state supplies the social unity that Hocking claimed modern liberalism and its individuals lack. It actively must educate its citizens for liberal lives, and it must create, not just reflect, a liberal faith.

The liberal state, if it is to repair itself, must meet a second necessary condition. The individual in this state, Hocking claimed, must be "incompressible." What does this mean? Hocking explained that the liberal state can merge or unify individual purposes—be commotive—only when its public purposes are prolongations of, and derive life from, individual purposes. He summarized: "The individual thus remains mentally prior to the state; and the principle of every future state must be this: that *every man shall be a whole man*" (*LEI*, p. 133), that every state must establish the objective conditions for the exercise of the will of this whole man (*MATS*, p. 325). (I will interpret this charitably, presuming that Hocking wanted, or now would want, women to be whole women as well!) Hocking meant that the new, active, unified, and unifying liberal state must not be a totalitarian or dictatorial state. He thought that it must submit itself to the free judgment of its members, must risk its continuation to the free approval of its members, and must provide its free members the means to differ with it. In uniting incompressible, whole individuals, the state supplies the duties reciprocal with rights and the emotional foundation that Hocking claimed the liberal state lacks.

Is it possible to unite these two necessities, the commotive state and its incompressible members? Hocking asked: "How can the strong and unified state be compatible with this incompressible individual life and liberty, how can we have a strong state and strong individuals?" (*LEI*, pp. 138, 143).

The answer, Hocking thought, can be supplied by what he called a "co-agent state": a state "based on the unanimous action of free individuals," a state "whose primary function is the commotive function issuing in action, which is at once particular, history-making action, and unanimous action, an extension of every citizen's will" (*LEI*, pp. 150–151). A co-agent state, Hocking explained in conclusion, would differ from a liberal state in its foreign relations and diplomacy, its economic policy and educational arrangements, and its freedoms. Here is just one of Hocking's examples that illustrates this difference: The co-agent state would insist that "freedom to express thought is *for thinkers.*" It would recognize that many people who ought to think actually "imitate, absorb, pretend, rationalize, adhere, far more than they think" (*LEI*, pp. 173–174). Here, long before talk radio and trash television, is Hocking at his rhetorical best:

> Idea bearing should be as solemn a business as child bearing; and we have turned it into a public promiscuity in which every Hornblower, Influential Editor, National Clown mingles his say with that of Ambitious Priests and Leading Ladies to turn the General Will. . . . To the hideous perils and absurdities of the Censorship, we must join the equally hideous perils, hypocrisies and humbugs of No-censorship. . . . The new state must do two things where the Liberal state attempted but one. It must restrict liberty for the sake of liberty. (*LEI*, pp. 174–175)

Unfortunately, rhetoric aside, this is not Hocking at his philosophical or political best. Accordingly, I step sharply away from this line of thought in order to explore a different direction. In criticizing Hocking's supplement to liberalism, the co-agent state, it is crucial to understand that his introducing this co-agent state is something like pulling a rabbit out of a hat. It is a very good trick, but it is a trick nonetheless, and a trick that can be done only if the rabbit is secretly put in the hat before it is pulled out. Of course, the difficult part of this trick is putting and keeping the rabbit into the hat; once this is accomplished, pulling the rabbit out is very easy. I have no doubt that Hocking's co-agent state, once pulled from the philosopher's hat, in theory would repair the defects of liberalism. After all, it is a state that by definition is based on the unanimous action of free individuals, a state that is by definition a unity of responsible individuals with strong emotional attachment to their state, a state that by definition is engaged in unanimous action that is an extension of every citizen's will. It just doesn't get any better than this.

Or, at least if you are an idealist, it doesn't get any better than this—because this co-agent state is simply the ongoing realization of the Absolute in history. In this co-agent state, Hocking wrote, "it is not necessary to choose between the universal and the particular, the ideal and the real: every actual deed is a union of both" (*LEI*, p. 151). All varieties of defective liberalism, it seems, need the Absolute or a God on their side. The co-agent state, Hocking wrote, is a mortal and finite edition of God (*MATS*, p. 405). Hocking's supplement for the defects of liberalism is the God of his brand of idealism, Christianity, and mysticism. In this respect, Hocking does not differ greatly in theory from many other persons who now appeal to their particular God, religious principles, and ways of life to remedy the defects of liberalism. For Hocking, individualism has a lasting element to the extent that it provides conditions necessary for the realization of the meaning of God in human experience. His co-agent state is the political embodiment of the meaning of God in human experience.

Just as he does in his metaphysics, Hocking begs the question in his politics. The way he does this is instructive, but the consequences are dangerous, far-reaching, and concrete. As a result, his private, self-effacing admission that "I am stupid about organizations ... and trust in God for the outcome"[11] appears at least as ominous as it may be honest. Hocking does not ask, much less answer, any of the most obvious and pressing practical, as opposed to theoretical, problems. Consider, for example, these questions and issues:

- In the co-agent state, only those who express themselves responsibly have a right to expression. Who, then, determines what is censored in the co-agent state? A philosopher king? A charismatic leader? A government agency? Local boards of citizens? Publishers of major newspapers and magazines and producers of television and radio programs? The companies that sponsor these publications and programs? An off-shore military tribunal? Moreover, how is this censorship enforced?

- In the co-agent state, only those "who have a right to consume" determine what is produced (*LEI*, p. 166). Who, then, determines which persons have a right to consume what products? How will society identify "rightful demand?" Hocking wrote that there is nothing worse than a complex bureaucracy, and claimed that the economy needs only "the touch" of the co-agent state, but who directs this touch and what, if anything, prevents the light touch of a co-agent state from becoming the heavy-handed grip of a massive bureaucracy, an entrepreneurial global elite, or a fanatical sect?

- In the co-agent state, who secures the unanimous action of free individuals—free even if censored, free even if "touched" by the state? Just how is this done? By a philosophy class in critical thinking? By a national marketing campaign? By the military—be all that *we* can be (rather than "an army of one")? By political propaganda or religious indoctrination? Hocking said that the co-agent state requires the commotive equivalent of war. Besides war itself, what is the commotive equivalent of war? If the co-agent state gives a war, how does it ensure that everyone will participate? And in the commotive equivalent of war, are there casualties?

- In the co-agent state, if the state becomes an experimenter rather than a dictator, as Hocking said, does it really become justified in *dictating* its experiments (*MATS*, p. 409)? What experiments? Who experiments, and on what subjects are experiments conducted? Who dictates when these experiments are failures, when they are solutions, and, perhaps, when they are final solutions?

- In the co-agent state, rights are "conditional on good will" and "the criterion of good will is in general the disposition of the individual to submit to what is called discipline" (*LEI*, p. 172). Whose discipline? That of the co-agent state itself? Hocking did not say. He sidestepped the issue by claiming that "conscience tends to a certain universality" such that "there is a tendency to ethical agreement among men" (*LEI*, p. 171). At the same time, he asserted that the co-agent state provides for the possibility of an honest and competent opposition (*LEI*, p. 177), even though the actual exercise of this opposition is incompatible with the unanimous action that defines the very existence of the co-agent state.

To leave these questions unasked and unanswered is to supply only a theoretical remedy for the real and pressing defects of liberalism that Hocking insightfully identified. It is to abandon pragmatism in politics as well as metaphysics. Like Hocking, Dewey sharply criticized liberalism. Unlike Hocking, Dewey believed that the problems of liberalism and democracy can be addressed only by transforming and intensifying liberalism and democracy—by making them new and different. Dewey's philosophy has not been implemented to any significant degree, and so it is difficult to know if this course of action would repair the defects of liberalism, particularly the emotional defect, so astutely analyzed by Hocking. Is pragmatism so amiable, cheery, pluralistic, and flabby that it cannot deal with the divisions, hatreds, violence, and absolutism that it allows? Or is Hocking's prescribed treatment worse than this illness itself? Listen to Hocking, carried away from his usually saner judgment by his idealism and its Absolute:

> The failure of the Liberal civilization is at the top, not at the bottom. Contrast the moral condition of such a community with the fierce idealism which flames up here and there among the youth of Russia or of China, to whom the nation itself, with a task which appears glorious in proportion to its difficulty, has become the absorbing business of life. The puff-cheeked bombast of Mussolini, the narrow fanaticism of Hitler, are less attractive, because their national conceptions are still loaded with the primitive goals of bigness and self-importance: "Make Us Mightier Yet"! It is an inferior brand of national purpose. But crude as it is, it is still something–and in this something, superior to the ideal of a state whose ambition is to avoid entanglement and to hug in isolation the fragments of a disturbed national prosperity. (*LEI*, pp. 113–114)

If these are our only options—Hitler and Mussolini or Hoover and Roosevelt—then we would do better to pursue "disturbed national prosperity" without national purpose rather than puff-cheeked fanaticism and fascism, no matter how absorbing, idealistic, or co-agent the fanaticism may be. After the twentieth century, however, neither of these options will do.

This sort of idealism that pictures history on the side of its Absolute and, in turn, believes this Absolute "permeates the texture of history" (*PRCWC*, p. 463) simply does not work and simply must be abandoned. In the hands of Hocking, this kind of idealism may sound agreeable and well-intentioned; in the hands of dictators, propagandists, suicide bombers, and white-collar thieves, however, its consequences are terrible. As Hocking said, "if we are to follow a pragmatic philosophy, that which does not work is not true, and should be changed off for something else" (*LEI*, p. 64). Still if liberalism is to renew itself, it must confront the defects diagnosed by Hocking. This would require a liberal faith, a strenuous faith. Perhaps it requires a faith that is for some persons emotionally defective in practice because it is so strenuous and demanding, because it is a faith without guarantee or certainty, because it, unlike idealism, is a faith that discovers in human affairs no "power, self-consciously eternal, actively communicating its own scope to the feeble deeds, the painful acquirements, the values, the loves and hopes of men" and women.

Without this self-consciously eternal power, Hocking argued that "we have no right to such faith as we habitually assume." I think this is correct, and I take this point with complete seriousness. Without this faith, Hocking continued, "there is for us [idealists] no valid religion" (*MGHE*, p. 524). Again, I think Hocking is correct.

By contrast, for those without "valid religion," for those with only a pragmatic temperament and an insistence on new ways of thinking through a revitalized liberalism and a radically democratic meliorism, Hocking's philosophy constitutes a revealing, instructive illustration of another faith. As such, as Hocking himself knew well,[12] it constitutes an important opportunity for us to revitalize and reconstruct our own most important and sometimes obscure loyalties, an opportunity to become something different. Even if this now sometimes involves a trip to a distant library annex or dusty used bookstore, this is an opportunity well worth seizing.

Hocking's failure makes clear that illiberalism, in any form, is no real remedy of the defects of liberalism. At the same time, Hocking's insights into those defects make clear the challenges that face attempted liberal remedies for liberalism's defects. Can liberalism meet this challenge? Why should we not at least demand a politics, as well as a poetry and philosophy, of insight and not merely tradition?

Notes

1. William Ernest Hocking, *Man and the State* (New Haven, Conn.: Yale University Press, 1926), p. xv. Hereafter *MATS*.
2. Tiny in number in comparison to publications on Hocking's American contemporaries such as Dewey, Mead, and Lewis, and tinier still in comparison to publications on his European contemporaries such as Heidegger, Sartre, and Marcel, there are a few studies of his thought. They include: Margaret Lewis Furse, *Experience and Certainty: William Ernest Hocking and Philosophical Mysticism* (Atlanta: Atlanta Scholars Press, 1988); John Howie and Leroy Rounder, *The Wisdom of Ernest Hocking* (Washington, DC: University Press of America, 1978); Charles S. Miligan, "William Ernest Hocking's Philosophy of Religion Revisited," *American Journal of Theological Philosophy*, Vol. 17 (1996), pp. 185–209; Leroy Rouner, *Selfhood, Nature, and Society: Ernest Hocking's Metaphysics of Community in "On Community"* (Notre Dame, Ind.: University of Notre Dame Press, 1992); Leroy Rouner, "The Metaphysics of Community: William Ernest Hocking's Doctrine of Intersubjectivity," *Journal of Chinese Philosophy*, Vol. 15 (1988), pp. 255–267; Xavier J. Puthenkalam, *Religious Experience and Faith: A Critical Evaluation of William James' and William Ernest Hocking's Theories on Religious Experience in Relation to Faith* (New Delhi, India: Oriental Institute of Religious Studies, 1989); Catherine Barry Stidsen, *William Ernest Hocking's Theory of the Reconception of Christianity* (Bangalore, India: National Biblical Catechetical and Liturgical Centre, 1992); R. B. Thigpen, *Liberty and Community: The Political Philosophy of William Ernest Hocking* (The Hague, Netherlands: Martinus-Nijhoff Publishers, 1972); and, Bruce Wilshire, "Passion for Meaning: William Ernest Hocking's Religious-Philosophical Views," *Transactions of the Charles S. Peirce Society*, Vol. 33 (1997), pp. 985–1002.
3. William James, "The Will to Believe" in *The Will to Believe and Other Essays in Popular Philosophy, The Works of William James* (Cambridge, Mass.: Harvard University Press, 1979 [1896]), p. 14.
4. William Ernest Hocking, *The Meaning of God in Human Experience: A Philosophic Study of Relgion* (New Haven, Conn.: Yale University Press, 1912), p. ix. Hereafter *MGHE*.
5. William Ernest Hocking, 11 May 1954 letter to Daniel Sommer Robinson, in Daniel Sommer Robinson, *Royce and Hocking, American Idealists: An Introduction to Their Philosophy, with Selected Letters* (Boston: Christopher Publishing House, 1968), pp. 159–160.
6. William Ernest Hocking, *Types of Philosophy* (New York: Charles Scriber's Sons, 1929), pp. 164–165. Hereafter, *TP*.
7. William James, "The Essence of Humanism," *Essays in Radical Empiricism, The Works of William James* (Cambridge, Mass.: Harvard University Press, 1976 [1905]), p. 99.
8. William Ernest Hocking, "History and the Absolute," in *Philosophy, Religion, and the Coming World Civilization: Essays in Honor of William Ernest Hocking*, ed. Leroy Rouner (The Hague, Netherlands: Martinus Nijhoff, 1966), pp. 423–463. Hereafter *PRCWC*.

9. William James, *Pragmatism: A New Name for an Old Way of Thinking, The Works of William James* (Cambridge, Mass.: Harvard University Press, 1975 [1907]), p. 142.

10. William Ernest Hocking, *The Lasting Elements of Individualism* (New Haven, Conn.: Yale University Press, 1937). Hereafter *LEI*.

11. Hocking in Robinson, *Royce and Hocking, American Idealists*, p. 160.

12. William Ernest Hocking, *Living Religions and a World Faith* (New York: Macmillan, 1940), p. 274.

CHAPTER 3

Democracy as a Way of Life, Democracy in the Face of Terrorism

John Dewey set forth in relatively traditional language a remarkable and radical view of democracy. He wrote:

> The very idea of democracy, the meaning of democracy, must be continu-
> ally explored afresh; it has to be constantly discovered, and rediscovered,
> remade and reorganized; while the political and economic and social insti-
> tutions in which it is embodied have to be remade and reorganized to meet
> the changes that are going on in the development of new needs on the part
> of human beings and new resources for satisfying these needs.... Democ-
> racy as a form of life cannot stand still. It, too, if it is to live, must go forward
> to meet the changes that are here and that are coming. If it does not go
> forward, if it tries to stand still, it is already starting on the backward road
> that leads to extinction. (*LW*11:182)

There is today no shortage of complex social problems. Perhaps earlier generations confronted equal difficulties, some similar and some different, and now all more remote. In any case, there can be no question that our current social ills range across all aspects of our lives, and appear both already deeply entrenched and still multiplying and intensifying. These deepening problems include terrorism, fanaticism, and absolutism; hunger and homelessness; debts and deficits; illiteracy and illness; intolerance, ille-gality, and illiberalism; physical and psychic violence and scandal at both individual and institutional levels; environmental degradation and inter-national conflict; apathy, resignation, contempt, and selfishness. Even American presidents who think they see "a thousand points of light," proclaim a "new world order," insist that is not just wishful thinking to "keep hope alive," advocate "compassionate conservativism," or pronounce confidently who is evil and who is good must notice in moments of honesty the surrounding vast cultural darkness, despair, and disunity.

From the perspective of the past, these current problems are horrible reminders of the public and personal consequences of letting democracy "stand still." From the perspective of the future, these problems are also sobering reminders of the demands on our collective imagination, intelligence, and will. They are a challenge to extend, reconstruct, and renew democratic institutions, social practices, and individual lifestyles. They are a challenge to remedy the defects of liberal democracies. As such, these problems are a challenge to any commitment to democracy and to all democracies themselves.

Of course, some people may say that this view is too optimistic. These pessimists, self-styled realists, and Leninists of liberalism may say that democracy cannot meet this challenge. They may say that liberalism, pluralism, and democracy are luxuries that cannot be afforded in times of conflict, aggression, oppression, and weapons of mass destruction. On this view, these luxuries have made us soft, and we now must abandon them in order to defend ourselves. They may say that law and order are sufficiently robust social goals, cautioning that it is too much to hope or work for more. Or they may say that democracy must be sacrificed now, always just for the short term, of course, so that it can be reached sometime later in the supposed long and administered march toward democracy. For such persons, off-shore military tribunals are an answer to the question "What is to be done?"

At the same time, other people may say that it is alarmist and exaggerated to believe that democracy itself faces any real challenges. These optimists may deny that democracies today face problems that are this serious in character or wide in scope, particularly since the end of the twentieth century, when it appeared that the Cold War was over and democracy had won—so that now "the winds of democracy are blowing everywhere," through central and eastern Europe, Africa, South America, Central America, and elsewhere.[1] From this rosy perspective, even if democracy does not soon become the United States' largest export, it appears well established, within its own borders, firmly in place, and secure from fundamental attack—no matter how serious the passing problems of the day at home or abroad. After all, on this view, Americans pledge steadfastly—if practice imperfectly—allegiance to majority rule and minority rights, the separation of powers, government by law, equality and opportunity, broad suffrage and fair elections, and civil liberties and justice for all. This, it may be held, was the enduring achievement of the nation's founders. This is what they secured for future Americans. This much, this view concludes, is safe, sure, and settled.

In part, this view of democracy in America may arise from and reflect a much deserved (when not uncritical) recognition and appreciation of democratic accomplishments and traditions in American culture. At the same time, this view of democracy in America, no matter how reassuring, is rooted in myopia about the past, unjustified reassurance about the future, and superficial patriotism in the present moment. Borrowing a term now familiar in ecology, I would like to contrast this superficial or shallow patriotism to a "deep patriotism." In developing this notion at a time when American politicians and entrepreneurs rush to cloak themselves in the American flag—in a time when democratic symbols have become substitutes for democratic reality (*LW*13:301)—I am aware that many people may view social criticism as simply incompatible with patriotism. But patriotism must not be identified with complacency (*LW*9:161). Genuine patriotism requires social criticism—and perhaps, in former President Nixon's campaign rhetoric, "now more than ever." In short, the optimistic view of democracy in America as settled and secure, like the pessimistic view that it is a relic of safer centuries past, is mistaken in theory and dangerous in practice.

This view is mistaken in theory because it ignores both change and context. Change, not permanence, is a fundamental feature of individual and social life. The ongoing development of democracy in America is no exception and, in this regard, America is not exceptional. Moreover, this development is contextual. Change produces myriad particular demands and particular effects on institutions and ways of life in particular situations. To fail to recognize this fact of change-in-context is to render democracy a mere abstraction. It is to be blind to the sweeping actual differences of American democracy in the days of Jefferson from American democracy in the days of Dewey—as well as the differences of Dewey's America and world from today's America and world. It is to overlook within America today massive social differences of meaning and experience—differences of wealth, race, health, ethnic background, gender, age, religious belief, physical ability, sexual preference, power, and hope—that constitute plural and different "democracies." And, it is to cover up the precariousness of the present and the openness of the future with illusions of permanence (whether permanent reality or permanent impossibility), fate, destiny, historical inevitability, and an end of ideology. We recognize such illusions when offered by others—illusions that range from imperialist Manifest "Destiny" to a war that will "permanently" end all wars; from an "inescapable" triumph of Nazism to an "invincible" superiority of the

U.S. economy; and from the "chosen" character of racial apartheid to the "inevitable" global spread of communism. In recognizing these illusions, however, we must not manufacture, participate in, or sustain new fictions about the secure, uncontested, and complete character of democracy in America.

It is not only wrong in theory but also dangerous in practice to treat democracy in America as a done deed, finished and final. This view is dangerous practically because it fosters both complacency and absolutism. It wrongly turns the urgent need for ongoing, never finished amelioration of pervasive social and personal problems into justification for passive optimism. Armed with the mistaken belief that democracy in America once and for all is an accomplished fact, one may smugly turn away from the uncertain practical tasks of continually reconstructing global society in creative new ways. As pointed out by well-known critics like John Dewey and obscure ones like William Ernest Hocking, when this happens, Americans become mere spectators, unwitting agents, or hapless victims to an increasing lack of fit between new problems and needs and earlier democratic institutions and practices. We fail to renew and revitalize America's democratic inheritance, acting as though yesterday's hard-won investments and tomorrow's rosy projected earnings always will be adequate for needed social expenses today. We thus fail to bridge the growing gap in America (and elsewhere), for example, between new powers of inquiry and communication and their infrequent, haphazard actual employment for genuinely democratic purposes. Rather than exploring and realizing new possibilities for public inquiry, participation, and self-government, we instead achieve by default political, economic, educational, environmental, aesthetic, and religious exclusion of people from effective decision making about their own lives. At the same time, we fail to recognize that this increasing cultural disenfranchisement undermines and is incompatible with the ideals of American democracy itself. Here complacency fosters absolutism, both inside and outside of America. It converts social, economic, political, scientific, and moral arrangements that fostered democracy at earlier particular times and places into sacred, revered, timeless institutions, practices, and relations. It dogmatically turns once effective historical means into eternal ends—ends supposedly beyond the demands of progressive social reconstruction.

As a group, philosophers of course have been responsible for more than their share of this sort of ahistorical theory and complacent practice. There is, however, no reason to dwell on this fact here. To do so would only be to reduce philosophy to therapy for philosophers themselves, and substitute the often barren problems of professional philosophers for critical, philosophical examination of the problems that arise in the actual experiences and lives of people. Still, in this light, there is ample reason to suspect that philosophers have little to contribute to genuine cultural concerns and problems. Having recognized rightly that they have no special access to Truth, Knowledge, Justice, Goodness, Beauty, or Reality, they wrongly have retreated too thoroughly to merely academic sanctuaries and logically possible worlds with special professional vocabularies, techniques, and issues. Even when they deal with public issues, they too fully do it, iron-ically,largely only within this professional context or conversation.

In this situation, the philosophy of John Dewey stands as a striking exception. Throughout his long public career, popular writings, and many volumes of scholarly work, Dewey persistently sought to identify challenges to democracy and to articulate intelligent responses to these changing challenges. As he well knew, Dewey provided us no crystal ball, no ready-made solution, no blueprint, no formula, no formal decision procedures—not even a "Method," aside from the progressive development and application of intelligence in experience. As a result, it is not enough today to simply read and endorse, for example, *Democracy and Education* (*MW*9), *Experience and Nature* (*LW*1), *Liberalism and Social Action* (*LW*11), or *Logic: The Theory of Inquiry* (*LW*12). Instead, as Dewey recognized—and as American thinkers such as Jefferson, Emerson, and William James all knew—one must rewrite these books and reconstruct institutions to accom-plish democracy over again and again, new and different, for our own time. In taking up this never finished task of "creative democracy," Dewey's writ-ings on experience, inquiry, education, and democracy constitute an invalu-able and rare resource for us today. After the twentieth century, it is time that we recognize, utilize, and extend this resource.

For philosophers, this can amount to a recovery of philosophy (*MW* 10:3ff) through a retrieval of Dewey's insight that philosophy is inher-ently criticism (*LW*1:295ff; 8:29ff) and reconstruction (*MW*12:80ff, 187ff, 256ff). This point is badly missed even by many contemporary "neoprag-matists" and some postmodernists who construe Dewey's pragmatism as an effective escape from their peculiar, self-induced "theory-guilt"—their apparent guilt for having no absolute, infallible, transcendentally-justified philosophical theory.[2] This narcissistic concern, however, is irrelevant to the practical burden (or "guilt") that Dewey places on philosophers. The point of philosophy, he made clear, is not to make theory practical but to make practice intelligent.

In this light, what is democracy? What does democracy mean today in America? What can it mean? What should it mean? What is the value of democracy? What is its justification? How can we achieve it or more fully overcome its defects? What must we do and how can we at least begin to do it? Who has come to be empowered and permitted to ask, or to answer, these questions? It is not enough to fault philosophers for frequently failing to undertake the task of addressing these questions. The task itself now simply must be undertaken. In 1936, Dewey called this study "the outstanding task of progressive education" (*LW*11:190). It remains so today.

Two Meanings of Democracy

> Democracy is much broader than a special political form, a method of conducting government, of making laws and carrying on governmental administration by means of popular suffrage and elected officers. It is that, of course. But it is something broader and deeper than that.... It is, as we often say, though perhaps without appreciating all that is involved in the saying, a way of life, social and individual. (*LW*11:217)

"Democracy" is a vague term. It has many meanings and connotations, and it is used in a broad array of contexts for widely varying purposes. Nonetheless, it is now commonplace to understand democracy as a particular social organization or system for making decisions.[3] On this view, a decision is made democratically to the extent that it embodies the expressed preferences of the majority of the people, and results from a process in which the preferences of all people are included, informed, considered, contested, and counted equally. Democracy thus is both an adversary system designed to apply fair procedures to conflicting interests and opposing goods, and a system of public deliberation designed to create and promote common interests and shared goods. It is in this light, for example, that political theorist Robert Dahl formulated the criteria of an ideal democratic process as virtually universal adult suffrage; equality in voting; equal and enlightened understanding of the issues; effective participation throughout the decision making process; and final control over both the agenda of issues to be decided and the delegation of authority.[4] It is on this basis that democracy often is contrasted with other decision making systems, such as monarchy, oligarchy, theocracy, anarchy, and totalitarianism. And, finally, it is on this same basis that familiar contrasts often are developed among different forms of democracy, such as direct democracy and representative democracy.

Of course, democracies (like all social forms of decision making) are not mere generalizations or abstractions. Actual democratic decision making (like actual non-democratic decision making) always takes place within some particular context—at some time and place on some issues for some people. This context may be, for example, a family, a school, a research laboratory, an athletic team, a religious group, a neighborhood, a labor union, or a business. To the extent that any of these organizations, practices, or institutions embodies the characteristics of democratic decision making, then it is to that extent a democracy.

It is evident that today we think about democracy almost exclusively in the context of one social institution: government (and usually national government). From the standpoint of sheer authority and power alone, there may be good reason for this: Government frequently has been and is the final authority in society, and so often has, though it may not use, the power to determine partly the democratic or non-democratic character of decision making processes in other institutions and practices. Given this focus on government, historians have charted the emergence of democracy in small city-states and its complex transformation and development in larger nation-states. This transformation often has been situated first in nineteenth-century America. Given this focus on government, sociologists and statisticians have determined the real number of democracies that exist today. At the end of the twentieth century, that number typically was estimated by political scientists at 35 to 40, or 25 percent to 33 percent of the world total.[5] And given this focus on government, social theorists, economists, and politicians have considered and argued problems concerning participation in, freedom from, and control of democratic decision making processes. In short and in general, democracy is understood today as a form of government.

By contrast, John Dewey consistently understood democracy more broadly. For Dewey, democracy is primarily and most fully a form of *life* rather than a form of *government* alone.[6] Democratic government, he argued, is only a part—albeit an important one—of a democratic society or democratic culture. It is a means for realizing democratic ends in individual lives and social relationships. Although it is the best and most expedient means yet invented to achieve these ends, it is only a means. Accordingly, Dewey radically cautioned that one must not treat means— that is, institutions and practices of democratic government such as universal suffrage, recurring elections, and majority rule—as ends, final or complete in themselves (*LW*11:218). These structures of government are "external and very largely mechanical symbols and expressions" (*LW*13:295) of a fully democratic life. They are not the core of democracy. They are only its political dimension or phase.

Because democratic structures of government have a value that is instrumental rather than final, they must be dynamic rather than static if they are to continue to promote a democratic way of life under changing conditions. This means that democracy is not something fixed, "a kind of lump sum that we could live off and upon," something complete that can be simply "handed on from one person or generation to another" (*LW*13: 298–299), something so natural that it would simply maintain itself if once established. "I cannot rehearse," Dewey wrote, "the list of events that have given this naive faith a shock" (*LW*15:259). Accordingly, no one can afford passively to idolize practices and institutions that proved instrumental in the past; instead, there is a need continuously to appraise and be ready to revise them when necessary relative to their present and future contributions to a democratic way of life.

Dewey began to articulate the nature of democracy as a way of life by exploring the basis of democracy as a way of government. He located the basis of democratic government in the conviction that no person or group of persons is sufficiently wise and good to govern others without their consent, "that is, without some expression on their part of their own needs, their own desires and their own conception of how social affairs should go on and social problems be handled" (*LW*13:295). This conviction implies both equality, such that the "social will comes about as the cooperative expression of the ideas of many people," and opportunity, such that all people have both a right and a duty to form and express convictions about their own places and welfare in the social order (*LW*13:296; 11:219). This "expression of difference," inherent in a democratic way of life, is both a personal right and a means for public enrichment (*LW*14:228). This means that all persons involved in, and affected by, social practices should participate in their formation and direction. Dewey called this the "democratic idea in its generic social sense" (*LW*2:327) and termed it the "key-note of democracy as a way of life," "necessary from the standpoint of both the general social welfare and the full development of human beings as individuals" (*LW*11:217–218).

Throughout his later work, Dewey returned to this theme, developing an extended account of democracy as a way of life. In his 1926 *The Public and Its Problems,* he offered a succinct measure of a fully democratic form of social life:

> From the standpoint of the individual, it [the idea of democracy] consists in having a responsible share according to capacity in forming and directing the activities of the groups to which one belongs and in participating according to need in the values which the groups sustain. From the standpoint of the groups, it demands liberation of the potentialities of members of a group in harmony with the interests and goods which are common. . . . Regarded as an idea, democracy is not an alternative to other principles of

associated life. It is the idea of community life itself. . . . Wherever there is conjoint activity whose consequences are appreciated as good by all singular persons who take part in it, and where the realization of the good is such as to effect an energetic desire and effort to sustain it in being just because it is a good shared by all, there is in so far a community. The clear consciousness of a communal life, in all its implications, constitutes the idea of democracy. (*LW*2:327–328)

This idea of democracy and the consequences of implementing it are revolutionary. Writing for *Common Sense* in 1937, Dewey argued forcefully and passionately that, understood as a way of life, "democracy is radical":

> *The fundamental principle of democracy is that the ends of freedom and individuality for all can be attained only by means that accord with those ends. . . . The end of democracy is a radical end. For it is an end that has not been adequately realized in any country at any time.* It is radical because it requires great change in existing social institutions, economic, legal and cultural. A democratic liberalism that does not recognize these things in thought and action is not awake to its own meaning and to what that meaning demands. (*LW*11:298–299)

Two years later, in *Freedom and Culture*, Dewey linked satisfaction of these demands of democratic life to the development of a distinctively democratic view of human nature:

> No matter how uniform and constant human nature is in the abstract, the conditions within which and upon which it operates have changed so greatly since political democracy was established among us, that democracy cannot now depend upon or be expressed in political institutions alone. . . . Democracy is expressed in the attitudes of human beings and is measured by consequences produced in their lives. The impact of the humanist view of democracy upon all forms of culture, upon education, science and art, morals and religion, as well as upon industry and politics, saves it from the criticism passed upon moralistic exhortation. For it tells us that we need to examine every one of the phases of human activity to ascertain what effects it has in release, maturing and fruition of the potentialities of human nature. (*LW*13:151–152)

The ongoing development of these potentialities requires appropriate social conditions in which all share and contribute. Belief in the power of human experience progressively to identify and attain these conditions coupled with unflagging action on this belief is what Dewey, at the age of eighty in 1939, titled "Creative Democracy—The Task Before Us":

> We have had the habit of thinking of democracy as a kind of political mechanism that will work as long as citizens were reasonably faithful in performing political duties. . . . We can escape from this external way of thinking only as we realize in thought and act that democracy is a personal way of individual life; that it signifies the possession and continual use of certain attitudes, forming personal character and determining desire and purpose in all the relations of life. (*LW*14:225–226)

To the extent, then, that a given person does not participate consistently and fully in the consideration, formation, and implementation of social values, decisions, and policies, democracy as an individual's self-determining and self-realizing way of life simply does not exist. And to the extent that given social practices, groups, and institutions do not nourish shared interests, harmonious differences, and individual growth, democracy as a free community's way of life does not exist.

This understanding of democracy as a way of life rather than a form of government radically expands the idea of democracy.[7] That this is a conceptual expansion is obvious. Given a Deweyan view, people's actual lives and social relations may fail to be actually and substantially democratic even when their government surely and formally is democratic. That this conceptual expansion is a theoretical improvement or, more important, that it might make any practical advance at all, is at present less obvious. Moreover, although this expanded notion of democracy now should be clear in the abstract, its import and consequences for action may seem difficult to imagine and understand, much less achieve. What, then, is the practical meaning of democracy understood broadly as a way of life? And what is the pragmatic advantage of this view for us today?

Democracy as a Way of Life

> The question of what is involved in self-governing methods is now much more complex. But for this very reason, the task of those who retain belief in democracy is to revive and maintain in full vigor the original conviction of the intrinsic moral nature of democracy, now stated in ways congruous with present conditions of culture. We have advanced far enough to say that democracy is a way of life. We have yet to realize that it is a way of personal life and one which provides a moral standard for personal conduct. (*LW*13:155)

To view democracy as a way of life is not simply to substitute a broad account for a narrower one, a new definition for a familiar one, or a messy cultural notion for a neat political one. Instead, above all, it is to demand different personal conduct and far-reaching cultural reconstruction—deep changes in habits of thought and action, patterns of association and inter-action, and personal and public values.

These changes may be advanced at least a little, by a grasp of the theo-retical underpinnings and their implications of this broad view of democ-racy. For example, an understanding of democracy as a way of life overcomes and leaves behind traditional dualisms about self and society, autonomy and association, experience and nature, thought and feeling, and fact and value; compartmentalized views of social life that keep antisepti-cally separate the political, economic, legal, scientific, aesthetic, religious, and moral dimensions of life; and, essentialist, ahistorical conceptions of culture and cultural change. In their place, an account of democracy as a way of life recognizes the irreducibly social production and character of the self, its values, and its genuine individuality; the pervasive intercon-nections and mutual entanglements among all aspects of social life; and, the complex, varying historical efficacies of, and possibilities for, each of these dimensions of culture. These themes and concerns, when devel-oped at length,[8] establish a Deweyan pragmatism as a middle ground between the extremes of irrelevant transcendentalism, idealistic Absolutes, and desperate foundationalism on one side and quiescent neopragmatism, naive relativism, and theories of mere difference on the other side. These themes have been repeated many times, and they bear this repetition, for sustained attention to them could serve as an effective antidote to much that ails contemporary professional philosophy. I will not rehearse once more these concerns here, however, for my immediate objective is less democracy's intellectual beginnings than its personal and social ends.

Accordingly, I want to focus on the more immediately practical meaning and consequences of Dewey's broad view of democracy as a way of life. In doing so, I stress three points. In the first place, to view democracy as a way of life is to highlight the fact that *democracy as a way of life is an ideal.* To deny this is to strip democratic life of its claims upon our future conduct, while mistakenly treating it as a reality ready-made and antecedent to that conduct. In this regard, democracy as a form of government differs from democracy as a way of life. Though it may be impossible to identify an actual nation or state that fully embodies the criteria of a democratic government, there clearly are governments that regularly meet most of these criteria and significantly meet all of them. From this descriptive or empir-ical standpoint, some existing governments are actual democracies (though, again, this is not to say that they are fully democratic or that they do not need to do better even on this front).

By contrast, there appear to be no large nations, states, or cultures that significantly, much less fully, meet the criteria of a democratic way of life. Surely the present United States is not an example. From this standpoint, existing ways of life are not actually democratic. This, of course, is what Dewey meant by terming democracy a radical idea and an undertaking still before us. Moreover, there is no guarantee that this undertaking will succeed. A democratic way of life may never become a reality.

Does this mean, then, that democratic life is a mere fiction, wishful thinking, or utopian fantasy? Does it mean that the democratic ideal is wholly separate from, and without support in, any actual existence? No. First, to claim that democracy as a way of life is an ideal is not to deny that some existing ways of life are more democratic than others. As Sidney Hook pointed out, the fact that no man is absolutely fat does not prohibit us from determining that one man is fatter than another.[9] Second, and more important: as an ideal, democracy is not simply "unreal." As an ideal, it is— or may be or may become—a deep commitment, grasped by imagination, that draws lives together, makes meaningful our efforts, and directs our actions. As an ideal, it is generated through imagination, but it is not "made out of imaginary stuff." Instead, anything but "unreal" or "imaginary," it is "made out of the hard stuff of the world of physical and social experience—the material and energies and capacities that are the conditions for its existence (LW9:33–34; 13:174).

To describe democratic life as an ideal, however, is not so much to state a present fact as it is to recommend a future course of action, an admittedly radical course of action. To quietly favor, idly wish and hope for, or merely routinely assent to such a democratic course of action, however, is not thereby to make it an ideal. Today democracy as a way of life must become an ideal, a living ideal; it is not yet, if ever it was, such an ideal, and this fact constitutes one of its real defects. Thus, idealizing democracy is the first step in the task of realizing democracy. When, and if, our idealizing imagination actually does seize upon democracy as a way of life, personal life will express this ideal in action. In Dewey's terms, communication, freedom, and cooperation will become loyalties or values-in-action, instead of mere values-in-name only (LW14:275). As an ideal, democracy requires this committed expression and action from each person.

This makes clear, in the second place, that *democracy as a way of life is a moral notion*. Indeed, it is "moral through and through: in its foundations, its methods, its ends" (LW13:173); "We have to see that democracy means the belief that humanistic culture *should* prevail; we should be frank and open in our recognition that the proposition is a moral one—like any idea that concerns what *should* be" (*LW*13:151). In stressing the moral dimension of democracy, Dewey, like Thomas Jefferson, argued that the demands of democracy coincide with those of liberty, equality, and justice. Democracy as a form of government may be the best means to the fullest possible realization of human nature (*LW*13:155), but democracy as a way of life is that realization itself in process.

This means that democratic processes are not value neutral, consistent with all preferences, or tolerant of all loyalties—even when these loyalties are rooted in old habits or reflect the present desires of a majority. Instead, this explicitly moral formulation of democracy furnishes a basis in experience for criticism and reconstruction of experience itself. In fact, this is a defining trait of democracy. Democracy "is the sole way of living which believes wholeheartedly in the process of experience as end and as means; as that which is capable of generating the science which is the sole dependable authority for the direction of further experience and which releases emotions, needs and desires so as to call into being the things that have not existed in the past" (*LW*14:228). Recognition of the moral character of democracy directs one to assess and revise institutions, practices, and social relations in terms of the extent to which they yield and embody democratic concern for the free, intelligent, and harmonious development of individuals. It leads to repeated questioning concerning the extent to which social arrangements promote "living together in ways in which the life of each of us is at once profitable in the deepest sense of the word," profitable to the individual and to the individuality of others (*LW*13:303). And it leads to repeated questioning and contesting of this very notion of living together.

If this questioning is successful in theory, it undercuts worries about egoism, emotivism, subjectivism, and irrationalism, as well as demands for foundations, absolutes, a priori justifications, and final proof. If it is successful in practice, it enlarges and secures the democratic character of people's lives. But it is not an easy task. For the most part, it has not been achieved, and it will not be achieved by armchair philosophizing or speculative theorizing. Dewey put this nicely: "Not all who say Ideals, Ideals, shall enter the kingdom of the ideal, but those who know and who respect the roads that conduct to the kingdom" (*LW*3:151). The roads to the kingdom of democratic life are inquiry and communication; they are prerequisites of democracy as a way of life, prerequisites of what Dewey called the formation of the Public and the transition from a Great Society to a Great Community (*LW*2:324, 345, 350). It is hard to satisfy these prerequisites. The roadblocks to inquiry and communication are many:

exclusion from participation and denial of access; power over inquiry[10] and control of publicity and the dissemination of knowledge; manipulation of opinion and thought; interference with experimentation and dishonest research; ignorance and inarticulateness; distance, time, and cultural difference; conservative habits of belief and emotion; fear, greed, and selfishness; specialization and mediation; and, illusions of intellectual freedom in the absence of known external oppression. These are immense obstacles to a democratic way of life, and the weight of history is on the side of those who are cynical about the prospects of overcoming them.

This situation is a measure of the enormous cultural distance, evident in the life of each person, between what morally should be and what actually is. It highlights, in the third place, another key characteristic of democracy as a way of life: *the central role of democratic faith.* This faith carries no overarching or advance guarantees. It provides no specific assurances about the future existence or expansion of democratic life. Indeed, it provides no general warrant for any complacent expectation of progress. It finds nothing in human history, human nature, or the world situation today to support a rosy or comfortable vision of the future. Such mistaken visions merely treat present hopes as future realities. As Dewey often noted, it simply is no longer possible to hold the happy Enlightenment faith in the assured advance of science and its production of free institutions and fulfilling lives. This democratic faith, then, supports neither utopian thinking nor even optimism in the abstract.

At the same time, it stands in opposition to all pessimism, cynicism, and fatalism. It opposes every uncomfortable (but still in consequence complacent) dystopian future vision. Such mistaken visions merely treat present contingencies—for instance, social relations of power and personal traits of stupidity, selfishness, impatience, and laziness—as future, eternal necessities. There is every reason to recognize soberly the serious problems that these realities pose for democracy, but there is no reason to treat them as fixed and impossible to change.

Instead, democratic faith is melioristic faith in possibility. It is the conviction that associated human imagination, intelligence, and will, if exercised, can fashion progressively a more fully democratic existence. It is the belief that these things, if given a show, "will grow and be able to generate progressively the knowledge and wisdom needed to guide collective action" (*LW*11: 219).

This faith, Dewey said, must be the basis or motive for democracy and its ongoing self-renewal. Democracy is a way of life—that is, ways of lives—controlled by and infused with this faith. Is this faith warranted? The pragmatic answer is neither a final "yes" nor a final "no." Instead, it is only that "experience so far indicates that it is not unwarranted, but let's find out more fully." That is, despite the best efforts of clever political theorists and traditional epistemologists, there is no advance theoretical foundation or justification for democracy. There is no transcendental basis, no non–question begging deduction or procedural commitment, no final, binding empirical proof. (Similarly, there is no advance theoretical foundation or justification against democracy.) This sort of "epistemological" justification in advance of trial is impossible, and search for it is philosophically misguided. The matter can be decided only by experiment, not by argument. This experiment, in turn, would both require and make possible a changed cultural climate, changed ways of thinking and living.[11]

Democracy requires faith to sustain the action necessary for its fuller realization. Accordingly, this faith may be warranted only through experimental trial, only after the fact or eventually, only by means of its consequences, only in relation to its results (rather than its origins). At present, as Dewey noted, this trial stands before us because faith in democracy has emerged only recently and has been adopted only partially, haphazardly, and infrequently (*LW*11:219). Even under democratic governments today, thoughts and feelings are saturated with earlier preferences for authority rather than community, experimentation, and publicity. In fact, persons yet lack a common vocabulary to articulate the values involved in the realization of democracy (*LW*13:178). Still, results of adopting this democratic faith have broken the "hypnotic spell" (*LW*14:250) of earlier, failed alternatives (*LW*11:144; 14:250) and now warrant the extension of democracy. Those who "do their best to make the extension actual" expect no speedy victory: "They are however, buoyed by the assurance that no matter how slight the immediate effect of their efforts, ... they are projecting into events a large and comprehensive idea by experimental methods that correct and mature the method and the idea in the very process of trial" (*LW*11:145). And if experience and history teach anything at all, Dewey added, it is that this is the surest possible promise of practical advance (*LW*6:68).

Democratic Challenges and Democratic Methods

Democracy is the faith that the process of experience is more important than any special result attained, so that special results achieved are of ultimate value only as they are used to enrich and order the ongoing process. Since the process of experience is capable of being educative, faith in democracy is all one with faith in experience and education. (*LW*14:229)

Can a genuinely democratic culture be produced? Can democratic ideals be achieved directly in persons' lives—in your life and in my life (LW6:48)? Is democracy as a way of life possible? These are open questions, still open long after Dewey's death. Their answers depend on and await our action. Still, these questions point directly to the central pragmatic issue facing democracy today: *How and by whom* can a genuinely democratic way of life be produced? To sidestep this question is to demonstrate greater concern for the problems of philosophers than for the problems of women and men.

A *first* important, straightforward way to answer this question is to attempt to identify particular obstacles to a democratic way of life, formulate specific strategies to remove these obstacles, and then implement these strategies (making revisions in light of successful and unsuccessful results, new problems, and the need for new approaches). All of this, it should be remembered, requires pragmatic inquiry (and not just neopragmatic "conversation")—including inquiry into the values and power relations of particular inquiries. Dewey frequently pursued democracy in just this critical way. He tirelessly advocated far-reaching changes in, for example, American politics, political parties, and political action; international relations and foreign policy; labor, business, and the production and distribution of economic opportunities and material wealth and profit; divisions and relations of race and class; social welfare programs; entertainment, propaganda, and the direction of what passes for public opinion; and, of course, schooling and education administration. "The struggle for democracy has to be maintained on as many fronts as culture has aspects" (LW13:186), he summarized simply.

This same struggle confronts anyone concerned with democracy today. In some respects, of course, recent events, fresh concerns, and new knowledges have refocused this struggle on, for example, terrorism and absolutism; feminism and gender; internationalism and multiple cultures; information and new technologies; and environmentalism and nature. The struggle for democracy has to be carried to these and other new battlegrounds.

Sadly, in many other instances and details, the struggle for democracy remains much the same generations later as it was for Dewey. Worse yet, some of the conditions that Dewey recognized and analyzed as most threatening to democracy now appear even more pervasive and pernicious. Two problems stand out here. The first is economic, and concerns what Dewey called "the scandal of private appropriation of socially produced values" (LW5:95), the emergence of the "business mind" (LW5:69) and spread of a "corporate mentality," and the narrow use of intelligence for selfish ends and class interests (LW9:111). Today outdated ideas of economic liberty and free markets—the same ideas that Dewey debunked repeatedly in *Individualism: Old and New*, *Liberalism and Social Action*, and *Freedom and Culture*—still grip our minds and conduct. But these ideas now have little basis in social life. Instead, the gaps between wealthy and poor, idle and meaningfully active, and powerful and powerless have never been greater in the United States and throughout the world. The poverty and insecurity of much of the economic underclass has never seemed more permanent or hopeless. Institutionalized disregard, intolerance, abuse, and waste of the welfare of the sick, the weak, the hungry, and the homeless have never been more far-reaching. And the cynical equation of maximum material consumption, private prosperity, and pecuniary profit with the good life has never been more commonplace. Unlike Dewey, we almost must "admit that our outer civilization is attaining an inner culture which corresponds to it, however much we might disesteem the quality of that culture" (*LW*5:69). This situation is pathetic and outrageous, and it must be intolerable to anyone committed to democracy. In short, we must invent ways to make our economy democratic.

There is a second problem that seems to threaten and undermine democratic life much more now than when Dewey confronted it. It cuts across our culture and concerns what Dewey called propaganda, cheap amusement, and the control of opinion (*MW*11:118; *LW*2: 321, 348; 3:141; 7:361; 13:168). Today naive beliefs about "freedom" of thought and "free" expression, "public" opinion, and "self-determination"—the same beliefs that Dewey thoroughly criticized in *The Public and Its Problems* and many subsequent essays—still shape our images of ourselves and our society. But these beliefs now have little correspondence to reality. Instead, we are the unwitting, usually unconscious, targets of powerful public relations techniques and subtle marketing campaigns that promote everything from automobiles to philosophies, luxury cruises to news magazines, and domestic wines to foreign wars. We are inundated by influential sound bytes and carefully controlled images that wash over us but do not wash us clean. We have become habituated to institutionalized restrictions and private economic influences on the gathering and dissemination of information. And we are happy consumers of entertainment, constantly craving and everywhere institutionalizing it (rather than criticism)—even in our schools. Unlike Dewey, we almost have given up concern for the eclipse of a community or public and effective publicity, for the ideals of democracy and growth. Still, we must realize that this state of affairs is incompatible with a democratic way of life. In short, we must find ways to transform mass communications and mass media into public communications and public media—communications and media of, by, and for a public.[12]

There is a *second* related important way to answer the question about how to create a thoroughly democratic way of life. This second approach does not concentrate primarily on specific existing obstacles to democracy. Instead, it articulates the general preconditions or requirements of democratic life, and then inquires as to how to satisfy these conditions. Not surprisingly, Dewey frequently proceeded in this way too, explaining how inquiry and communication are intrinsically and reciprocally related to democracy:

> The prime condition of a democratically organized public is a kind of knowledge and insight which does not yet exist. In its absence, it would be the height of absurdity to try to tell what it would be like if it existed. But some of the conditions which must be fulfilled if it is to exist can be indicated.... An obvious requirement is freedom of social inquiry and of distribution of its conclusions.... The highest and most difficult kind of inquiry and a subtle, delicate, vivid and responsive art of communication must take possession of the physical machinery of transmission and circulation and breathe life into it. When the machine age has thus perfected its machinery it will be a means of life and not its despotic master. Democracy will come into its own, for democracy is a name for a life of free and enriching communion. It had its seer in Walt Whitman. It will have its consummation when free social inquiry is indissolubly wedded to the art of full and moving communication. (*LW*2:339, 350)

It is important to emphasize that this relation between democracy and both inquiry and communication is in practice a reciprocal, circular relation. Democracy as a way of life both requires and is required by inquiry and communication. This, of course, creates no logically vicious circle; it does not force us to decide whether chicken or egg came first. Instead, it indicates that a democratic way of life is not a separate entity or by-product of inquiry and communication. Instead, the progressive development of culture by, in, and through inquiry and communication constitutes fully democratic social life.

This progressive development is an educational matter, in the broadest sense of that term, and it is for this reason that, as explained in chapter 1, Dewey characterized democracy as a challenge to education. This suggests an important *third* dimension or way to address the question of how to create democracy as a way of life. On this view, education must be the practical or strategic focus. In its broadest sense, education is the creation of habits of mind and character (*LW*11:44), and in this context all social institutions and arrangements—not just the schools—"are educational in the sense that they operate to form attitudes, dispositions, abilities and disabilities that constitute a concrete personality" (*LW*11:221). In this light, democracy simply stands for a particular sort of education; it is a particular educational principle, measure, and policy (*LW*13:294, 304). What principle? Democracy as an educational principle is this: The social aim of education is the production of democratic attitudes, dispositions, and abilities—the free interaction and participation of individuals and their mutual interpenetration of interests in and through shared community life (*MW*9:92: *LW*2:327). This democratic educational principle receives little more than lip service from the most powerful educational institutions in America today—the economic system, the government, the military, the media, the family and neighborhood, and the school.[13] To this extent, remarkably, America is committed neither to democratic education nor to democracy.

Any democratic reconstruction of American society and society more globally is one with the democratic reconstruction of these institutions. And this, in turn, involves nothing less than the thoroughgoing change and adoption on all cultural fronts of democratic educational principles and their democratic social aims.

This demand for democratic educational principles is doubly radical: It is the pursuit of radically democratic *ends*, undertaken through radically democratic *means*. As a way of life, democracy cannot be achieved, sustained, or expanded in any other way. To employ on behalf of democracy means of social change other than those of intelligent inquiry and communication is, to the very degree in which those other means are used, to postpone and undermine democracy as a way of life. Experience supplies ample evidence of this, for in the past we regularly have depended on non-democratic means (*LW*11:170, 299)—whether explicitly violent, authoritarian or totalitarian, or implicitly coercive, elitist, or merely bureaucratic. In new situations, in response to new crises, we may do so again in the future, as Tatyana Vorozheikina, writing about late–twentieth century democratic changes in Russia, points out: "And if winter does come, the pressure for an alternative [to democracy] will become increasingly urgent because, unlike nature, society cannot expect the automatic arrival of spring. Whenever people who call themselves democrats embrace the 'objective necessity' of an authoritarian regime, democracy is dead."[14] Our first defense from this, Dewey wrote, "is to realize that democracy can be served only by the slow day by day adoption and contagious diffusion in every phase of our common life of methods that are identical with the ends to be reached" (*LW*13:187).

There is nothing flashy or catchy about any of this (and, for this reason, it is easy to miss the thoroughly radical character of democracy as a way of life). At best, democratic means of social change will extend democratic life only slowly and bit by bit. As a result, democracy is an unsure and difficult path to follow. On the other hand, it is a path open to us all. As a way of life, democracy has personal (as well as institutional) meaning and message. The message is straightforward: Democracy exists only on paper and in statute unless individuals enact it in their own transactions day by day and face to face in local communities. That is, a society of individuals can become a democracy only as those individuals act democratically. This is the *personal* (but not private) challenge of democracy to each person—as parent and child, teacher and student, friend and lover, neighbor and citizen, in recreation and work, and in relation to the rest of nature. In our various personal relations and associations, throughout our lives, even recognizing social limits and constraints, we each must seek to expand democracy, to invent new ways to extend free inquiry and full communication on behalf of shared values. We must realize in thought and action that democracy is a personal way of individual life (*LW*14:226), and we must rededicate our lives to its realization—now.

Democracy in the Face of Terrorism

"Seeing is believing." On September 11, 2001, unimagined horrific possibilities became unspeakable horrific realities.

Images of these realities have been broadcast worldwide over and over and over: the hijacked planes crashing into New York City's World Trade Center towers, the Pentagon, and rural Pennsylvania; explosions, fire and smoke, and collapse; people fleeing, trapped, and jumping; police, firefighters, and emergency services providers doing their duty, saving lives, and, in doing so, risking their own lives and, in many cases, losing them; and the piles and truckloads of stone and steel, the bodies recovered and missing, the ash and smoke and the long work ahead.

Americans, with persons all around the world, have looked at these images over and over and over. But *what did we see?* And, in seeing, *what did we believe and what do we now believe? What did others see and what did and do they believe?*

Observing these images, different persons saw and believed different things. The answer to this question about what we saw and believed depends on who "we" are, on who is authorized or permitted or compelled to answer this question. Proponents of democracy and deliberation and civil society and civic virtue often fail to realize this fact. They end up talking to themselves in terms that are unreal and impractical. This failure cannot be afforded any longer. The realization of this fact is essential to the future of democracy and it is essential to any effective deliberation about this future.

Stated most simply, what most Americans and many other persons saw and believed as a result of the terrible events of September 11, 2001, is this:

- there are evil people who do evil things in the world;
- America was and is very vulnerable to this evil; and,
- American values, like American buildings and bodies, are vulnerable and under attack in many places in the world.

After September 11, most Americans did *not* believe there is an effective moral order in the world, a "new world order" as announced by the first President Bush: the world is in disarray. After September 11, most Americans did *not* believe America is invincible or even sufficiently secure. Super powers obviously now have become super victims—and may become so again. And, after September 11, most Americans recognized that complacency is *not* enough and that they must reaffirm and deepen, rather than renounce or just take for granted, commitments to democracy, pluralism, community, individualism, and freedom. Without dedicated action on their behalf, democratic values are fragile, and American patriotism is empty.

This is an important part of what most Americans, with many other persons, saw and came to believe in the images and events of September 11, 2001. But even now, the meaning of these events is not complete or finished or fixed. The significance of what happened on September 11, 2001, depends in part on what *will* be done and *will not* be done in the future—on what is not yet done.

It is important, and perhaps also importantly American, to look forward in this way. But it is just as important to look forward in a way that is not blind or oblivious to the past. (The second) President Bush said that each death on September 11 was a world that went out of existence. This is something that *is* finished and fixed and final. Individually, we never again will have those worlds, those family members and friends and workers and neighbors, that life. Collectively, we never again will be the America or be the selves that existed before September 11, 2001, a younger America less aware of its vulnerabilities in a world that has always been dangerous. That this is so is not difficult to understand in the abstract; in the concrete, *what* this means is impossible to communicate. To look forward effectively and with dedication from this past will require resisting the fashionable and incessant demand for closure. It will require resisting the temptation, for example, to read past or ignore the daily "portraits of grief" that were published in the *New York Times*. It will require reading, going back and reading, every one of them. Slowly. It will require noting each world that has gone out of existence, and recognizing what cannot be imagined.

The destruction is real, finished, fixed. Any reconstruction—physical, social, or moral—remains an open question awaiting action. The question is this: How will America act after September 11, 2001, and what will it become? How will you live after September 11, what will you do, and on behalf of what values will you make big and little choices each day? It is only in light of this action still to be undertaken that it will be possible to understand more fully what has been seen and, in being seen, what is believed.

"What if they gave a war and nobody came?" In the late 1960s and early 1970s, many American opponents of the Vietnam War asked this rhetorical question. What did they mean? In general, they meant that if no one fought wars, there would be no war. But more particularly, they meant that if American citizens refused to participate in the Vietnam War—refused the military draft, refused to pay taxes that funded the war, refused to invest in companies that made Napalm and earned profits from military contracts, refused to let die the causes of Martin Luther King Jr. and Robert Kennedy, refused to jail war protesters, refused to elect and reelect pro-war representatives, and refused to believe that Lyndon Johnson or Richard Nixon had a secret plan to end the war (with the possible exception of Curtis LeMay's proposal to "bomb Vietnam back to the Stone Age")—that then this particular war could and would have ended. Unconsciously echoing American philosopher John Dewey's insight that democracy is a *personal* way of life, they meant that making or not making war is a matter of *personal* responsibility. They meant that every individual had a personal moral responsibility to not make war, to end the war, in Vietnam. They meant, as John Lennon and Yoko Ono declared in a full-page ad in the *New York Times* on December 21, 1969, "War Is Over If You Want It."

A copy of this page, framed but yellow and increasingly fragile despite my best efforts, hangs in my study by the desk where I prepared for my honors ethics course on September 11, 2001. My students told me that we should go on as planned and that terrorists should not be permitted to hijack their education. Lack of permission aside, the terrorist attacks simply did change education and American life more broadly. In 1969 I believed "war is over if you want it" was true, and after September 11, 2001, I still believe it is true—but, like all truths, only within definite limits. Yes, a war-making nation or organization can end war by refusing any longer to make it. If they want it, that war is over. And, yes, individuals in war-making nations or organizations—if significantly democratic—can help bring an end to a war by refusing to participate, refusing to show up, and refusing to come even when they give a war.

War is over if you want it—yes, but only if you are the attacker or aggressor, the only one giving the war. If you are not the attacker or the aggressor or if you are an overpowered victim or innocent, then war is *not* over just because you want it or as soon as you want it or the moment you'd like to stop. Instead, in this case, war is over only when the attacker wants it—or when the attacker can no longer attack. What if they gave a war and nobody came? When those on whom war is made refuse to fight to defeat the war-makers, and when the war-makers have no interest in democracy, a deliberative citizenry, uncoerced consensus, pluralism, or freedom, then the war will go on and on. Moreover, it may well get worse, and the war may come to you even if you do not come to it. This is a truth known to all innocent victims of aggression, and it is a truth that marks the limit of sane and responsible anti-war and pacifist commitments. In a dangerous world, no one can afford to forget this truth. To do so is to oppose war in theory without supporting peace in practice.

Almost immediately after the September 11, 2001 attacks, the president of the United States, his administration, and the American news media announced that the United States now was involved in the first war of the new century, the first war of the twenty-first century. This war, it has been claimed, is the very first war of the new millennium, a brand-new kind of war, a war against terrorism rather than countries, a military and financial and scientific and information war on multiple fronts around the world, a war for civilization itself.

Perhaps this sort of claim helps rally or sustain public support and political unity for wars, old and new. Perhaps it helps forge international alliances. Perhaps it has a therapeutic value for persons with new anxieties or with nostalgia stronger than knowledge. Perhaps it even increases television ratings or sells advertising or restores consumer confidence. It is, however, both false and a missed opportunity.

It is false because terrorism and wars against terrorism are old and ongoing stories. In Cambodia, the Philippines, Tibet, Japan, Chechnya, Zimbabwe, Algeria, Uganda, South Africa, Peru, Colombia, Chile, Nicaragua, Mexico, Cuba, Indonesia, Israel, Egypt, Spain, France, England and Ireland and Northern Ireland, even Oklahoma City, and throughout most of the world, terrorism and counterterrorism, frequently state-sponsored, were twentieth-century, not new twenty-first-century, stories. In fact, they have been, and continue to be, the norm as much as the exception. It requires immense inattention to history, even recent history, and massive myopia toward the rest of the world to fail to register this fact. Perhaps in part it also requires unfounded attachment to American exceptionalism and the belief that if someone gave a war and America did not come, then that war really did not happen or did not matter (to Americans) or did not have victims that matter (again to Americans).

However, the view that September 11, 2001, marked the start of a brand-new war for the United States is false. A terrorist war had been fought against America for some time prior to this date, and the fact that it was not recognized as such does not mean that it was not under way. There were, for example, American hostages, attacks on U.S. embassies, the first bombing of the World Trade Center, and ineffective weapons inspections and trade embargoes. America largely looked away. There was support for the Afghans fighting the Soviet Union. The Soviet Union left without victory, and America pulled out. There was U.S. military defeat and death in Somalia. Again America pulled out. There were attacks on American military bases, tourists, commercial interests, and the bombing of the USS *Cole.* America still did not adequately recognize or enter the terrorist war being waged against it. Attacks against and by Israel continued across agreements and cease-fires before and during this time. America asked for understanding and moderate response. Then on September 11, 2001, in part because they had given a war and America had not come, some terrorists brought the war to the United States. The battlefield was new. The resulting loss, fear, and insecurity were new. The American response was, and is, at least in part, new. But the war itself was not new. If American response is to be effective, it must not mistake this fact. It must not pretend that history vanishes when ignored.

Just as important, to proclaim the post–September 11, 2001 war on terrorism as the first war of the new century is to miss an important opportunity. Precisely because terrorism is an old story, America responded by fighting an old war, the last war of the twentieth century. What was new was something else: the opportunity to help establish the first *just peace* of the twenty-first century. America's "Operation Enduring Freedom" will not succeed unless it fosters a new, twenty-first-century justice, a more complete and more enduring justice. The only alternative is to fight each generation, over and over, ever more terrible wars on ever more fronts to make the world safe for democracy for a little while longer while somebody somewhere reloads.

Was John Dewey right that democratic ends require democratic means? In the face of unrecoverable losses, massive suffering, and real vulnerabilities, the post–September 11, 2001 obstacles to justice and peace are immense. But they are not all or wholly insurmountable. In the abstract, American objectives may seem clear enough, and so it is tempting simply to say:

- In response to evil actions against America, evildoers must be pursued, fought, captured, disarmed, and punished appropriately;
- In response to American vulnerabilities, homeland and international security must be improved in a manner consistent with basic American values; and,
- In response to attacks on America's basic values of democracy, pluralism, and freedom, these commitments through deliberation must be strengthened, deepened, and expanded.

Stated this abstractly, however, these objectives mask a complex practical problem. To recognize this problem, return to the images of September 11, 2001, and again ask: What did *we* see and, in seeing, what did *we* believe and come to believe?

In these images from New York City, Washington, D.C., and Pennsylvania, Osama bin Laden has said that he saw death and destruction that surpassed his expectations and hopes. Like many other persons, including the children who danced and sang and celebrated the events of September 11, he saw revenge for decades of humiliation and degradation and injustice. He saw the world divided clearly into two camps—his camp of faith and a camp of unbelief—and he saw his camp engaged in holy war. He saw the work of Allah in the death and destruction, and he praises Allah for striking America and for killing Americans. A month after the attacks, he said he saw more to come: "What America is tasting today is a small thing compared with what we have tasted for decades. For eighty-something years our nation's children are killed, its blood is shed, its holy places are defiled, it is ruled contrary to God's revelation, and nobody listens or responds. . . . They have come out wanting to wage war on Islam and falsely calling people 'terrorists.' . . . I swear by Almighty God that America and those who live in America will not dream of security before we live it as a reality."

Just as Bush labeled bin Laden "the evil one," bin Laden saw Bush as the evil "world leader of unbelief." Just as Bush asked that "God bless America," bin Laden offered praises and prayers to Allah. Just as Bush said that America will win, bin Laden said that he will prevail over the Americans and the Jews. The mutual identification of one's enemies as evil, the mutual belief that God is on one's side, and the mutual belief that one's cause will triumph: this is a recipe for radical disagreement without any possibility of solution by deliberation. Contrary to a belief that many Americans treasure, not all things are possible at all times, and not all problems have solutions. And sometimes the way a problem is conceived or stated is part of the problem.

Here there are no shared basic values. In particular, there was no shared commitment to democratic, pluralistic, free and open deliberation, and so there was no real opportunity for any such deliberation. Traditional proponents of deliberative democracy and responsible citizenship have nothing to contribute at this point—at the point that deliberation itself is not a shared value. This is not an intramural disagreement, like those between liberals and conservatives, or Democrats and Republicans, or socialists and capitalists. It is not the sort of disagreement that arises only because of common presuppositions and shared commitments that underlie different answers to the same, shared questions. It is a more radical disagreement that includes not only different views on particular issues but also complete disagreements on the proper way to characterize and resolve those differences. When theorists of democratic community and deliberation duck these radical disagreements, they reduce themselves to mere theorists.

Similarly, when Americans refuse to examine the ways in which their own government policies and actions and interests and individual lives have contributed to the impossibility of deliberation with a particular enemy, they sacrifice both understanding that enemy and understanding themselves. This sacrifice may bring some mistaken assurance that American actions never undermine American values, or that America's policies played absolutely no part in fostering the hatred and ignorance and evil so manifest on September 11, 2001. This mistaken assurance that the world really is just as it seems only to Americans, however, repeatedly has proven itself a strategic liability. This is not going to change. Thus, it is not going to be enough to say simply that the Arab children who celebrated and rejoiced on September 11, potentially the next generation of Osama bin Ladens, are simply "evil" or part of an "axis of evil." For the same reasons, it would not be enough for these children in turn to say that the Americans who have bombed their countries, or the children of these Americans, are simply "evil."

Given such radical disagreements, however, there is no incompatibility in principle between a commitment to democracy and a commitment to use force—even to go to war. To observe, again with American philosopher John Dewey, that democratic ends require democratic means is not to proclaim that force is never necessary to advance democracy. In the real world, it has been necessary and it was so after September 11, 2001. Instead, it is to recognize that force and military success cannot by themselves lead to democratic ends. It is to realize, in the terms of logicians, that democratic means, even when they are *not sufficient, are always necessary.*

It may be possible (which is not to say advisable) to bomb a country back to the Stone Age, but it is *not* possible to bomb a country forward to democracy and pluralism. Similarly, it may be possible through force to punish past wrongdoers and to better prevent security failures and future harms, but it is *not* possible simply through force to extend or deepen or renew the values of democracy, pluralism, and freedom. By itself, no war, even a new kind of war, can make the world safe for democracy.

Paradoxically, the world will be safe for democracy only when the world is genuinely democratic, only when individuals' ways of life (and not just their governments) are largely democratic. A world with totalitarian, fascist, absolutist, fundamentalist, genocidal tyrants and bullies and murderers is a world that is *not* safe for democracy. Democracy is safe only in a world that does not oppose, subvert, or attack democracy. This requires military and domestic security, of course, but it also requires economic and social security for all across a wide range of fronts, including health care, nutrition, child care, job training, environmental protection, workplace safety, decent wages, and retirement security. To fail to meet these requirements is to join an axis of short-sightedness. Accordingly, the task of enlarging and spreading basic democratic values remains ultimately an educational task, and it is a task that cannot be wholly outsourced and should not be privatized in ways that favor the wealthy. Above all, it involves the creation of democratic habits of thought and action. America must use not only its military power to punish and protect; it must use all of its cultural resources to foster living and felt commitment to methods of intelligence and deliberation, values of pluralism and freedom, and practices and institutions of democracy and self-criticism.

Does this mean that arguments for democracy beg the question by employing pro-democratic premises? Yes, just as arguments on behalf of holy wars against America also beg the question. This is why deliberation has its limits, and this is why there is absolutely no strategic value in identifying one's enemies simply as "evil." Does action on behalf of democratic values—for example, the education of women in Afghanistan—entail a kind of cultural violence against organizations and societies that now reject democratic values? Yes. However, America, like every other country, has no option *whether* to use or not use its power; the only options concern *how*, and on behalf of what ends, this power will be used. There is no shortage of errors from which to learn, and there can be nothing unpatriotic and everything strategic about trying to do better. Finally, in all honesty, this same power must be directed at opportunities to enlarge democratic values and more fully realize democratic aspirations in America itself—in schools, doctors' offices, newsrooms, courts, workplaces, neighborhoods, and bedrooms.

Of course, it is not possible to make the world, or even America, *permanently* safe for democracy. That there is change and that the future is not fixed is not a defect for theory to remedy through some dialectic that leads to absolutes. Rather it is fact for practice and a never-ending demand for ameliorative action. Democratic culture contains resources that always can be directed against democracy itself. That this is possible is not a permanent defect in liberal or pragmatic or any other kind of theory; that this should happen as little as possible is an ongoing challenge to pragmatism in practice. Moreover, the meaning of democracy must change continually with changes in lives and cultural conditions. As a result, the task of creating a just peace in the twenty-first century is a task on multiple fronts, and it is a task, like education and personal growth, that is its own end.

With strong resolve, smart thinking, and *personal* action, in part the meaning of September 11, 2001, can become the attainment of more fully democratic, pluralistic, and free lives throughout the world. *If you want it.* Before September 11, 2001, there may have been acceptable alternatives. There are none now.

Notes

An earlier, slightly different version of the first four sections of this chapter appeared as "Democracy as a Way of Life" in *Philosophy and the Reconstruction of Culture: Pragmatic Essays after Dewey*, ed. John J. Stuhr (Albany: State University of New York Press, 1993), pp. 37–58. Parts of this material subsequently were excerpted for publication under the same title in *The Kettering Review*, Vol. 18 (spring 1998), pp. 30–40. The final section of this paper, in slightly different form, appeared as "Democracy in the Face of Terrorism," *The Kettering Review*, Vol. 20 (winter 2002), pp. 51–57.

1. Oldemiro Baloi, Mozambique's vice minister of cooperation, as quoted by Rick Lyman, *Knight-Ridder News Service*, 2 December 1990. Days later, in a speech in Argentina, President Bush echoed his own 1988 Inaugural Address, proclaiming that "the day of the dictator is over," *Los Angeles Times*, 5 December 1990. More soberly, conservative Irving Kristol argues that modern democracies have gotten what they wanted, producing a new malaise in America: "The new, distinctive feature of our modern democracies is the contempt of this citizenry for their governments and politicians. They demand more and more of their governments, since they have been taught that this is their democratic duty, but at the same time they expect less and less." "America's Mysterious Malaise," in *The Times Literary Supplement*, 22 May 1992, p. 5. For an analysis that is less conservative and grimmer still, see Noam Chomsky, *Deterring Democracy* (New York: Verso, 1991).

2. This term, "theory-guilt," coined by Thomas C. Grey in his "Hear the Other Side: Wallace Stevens and Pragmatist Legal Theory," is expanded by Richard Rorty in his "The Banality of Pragmatism and the Poetry of Justice." Both

these essays are part of the "Symposium on the Renaissance of Pragmatism in American Legal Thought," *Southern California Law Review*, vol. 63, no. 6 (September 1990). My criticism is directed not at Grey but at Rorty's work in his *Consequences of Pragmatism* (Minneapolis: University of Minnesota Press, 1982) and *Contingency, Irony, and Solidarity* (Cambridge: Cambridge University Press, 1989). I discuss Rorty's thought and its important differences from a pragmatism that draws on James and Dewey in my *Genealogical Pragmatism: Philosophy, Experience, and Community* (Albany: State University of New York Press, 1997). See particularly chapter 6, "Rorty as Elvis." See also my review of Rorty's *Contingency, Irony, and Solidarity* in *The Personalist Forum*, vol. 5, no. 2 (fall 1989). In significant contrast, much of Rorty's later work recovers and extends both the spirit of meliorism and the characteristically Deweyan concern to fuse individuality and community. See *Philosophy and Social Hope* (London: Penguin Books, 1999) and *Achieving Our Country* (Cambridge, Mass.: Harvard University Press, 1998).

3. See, for example: David Truman, *The Governmental Process* (New York: Alfred A. Knopf, 1951); Alan Altshuler, *Community Control* (New York: Pegasus, 1970); William Alton Kelso, *American Democratic Theory: Pluralism and Its Critics* (Westport, Conn.: Greenwood Press, 1978); J. Roland Pennock, *Democratic Political Theory* (Princeton, N.J.: Princeton University Press, 1979); Robert A. Dahl, *Democracy and Its Critics* (New Haven, Conn.: Yale University Press, 1989); Jane Mansbridge, *Beyond Adversary Democracy* (New York: Basic Books, 1980) and *Beyond Self-Interest* (Chicago: University of Chicago Press, 1991); Sara M. Evans and Harry C. Boyte, *Free Spaces: The Sources of Democratic Change in America* (New York: Harper & Row, 1986).

4. Robert A. Dahl, *Dilemmas of Pluralist Democracy: Autonomy vs. Control* (New Haven, Conn.: Yale University Press, 1982), p. 6.

5. For example, Frank Bealey, *Democracy in the Contemporary State* (Oxford: Clarendon Press, 1988), p. 2.

6. By focusing on democracy as a way of life, by no means do I mean to suggest that democracy as a form of government is established in full in the United States. Problems and issues raised by the American 2000 presidential election—from the partisan activism of the Supreme Court to ballot-counting and voting-place irregularities linked to income, race, and political differences—demonstrate that even the task of establishing a fully democratic form of government in the United States is far from complete.

7. It is interesting to note similarities between Dewey's philosophy and the work of political theorist Robert Dahl. Although Dahl defined democracy as a kind of government rather than a way of life, he is quick to caution that democracy in this restricted sense may be necessary but not sufficient for sound policy. At the same time, like Dewey, he also was quick to point out the need to reconstruct our political order, values, and beliefs:

> For the most powerful ideologies of our age all suffer from having acquired their shape and substance in the eighteenth and nineteenth centuries, or very much earlier, before the world in which we now live had come fully into view. They are like medieval maps of the world, charming but dangerous for navigating unfamiliar seas. . . . Liberalism, conservativism, capitalism, socialism, Marxism, corpo-

ratism, anarchism, even democratic ideas, all face a world that in its form and thrust confounds the crucial assumptions, requirements, descriptions, predictions, hopes, or prescriptions they express. *Dilemmas of Pluralist Democracy: Autonomy vs. Control*, p. 3.

Although they seem wholly unaware of Dewey's work and its parallels with their own, see also Carol Pateman's discussion of a "participatory society" in *Participation and Democratic Theory* (New York: Cambridge University Press, 1970); and Anne Phillips's analysis of the implications and uses of feminism for democratic theory in *Engendering Democracy* (University Park, Penn.: Pennsylvania State University Press, 1991).

8. See my discussion of the temperament of pragmatism, politics, education, and wealth distribution in *Genealogical Pragmatism: Philosophy, Experience, and Community*, chapters 5, 13, and 14.

9. Sidney Hook, "The Democratic Way of Life," in his unfortunately now generally neglected *Reason, Social Myths, and Democracy* (Buffalo, N.Y.: Prometheus Books, 1991 [1940]), p. 285.

10. See the critical discussion of Dewey's theory of inquiry in chapter 8.

11. See the account of pluralism and cultural climate in chapter 9.

12. In this vein, Hook wrote: "A political democracy cannot function properly where differences in economic power are so great that one group can determine the weal or woe of another by non-political means. Genuine political democracy, therefore, entails the right of the governed, through their representatives, to control economic policy." He continued succinctly: "A further consequence of 'freely given consent' is the absence of a monopoly of education where education includes all agencies of cultural transmission, especially the press. . . . Not many years ago this would have been a commonplace. Today apologists have so muddied the waters of truth that its reaffirmation must be stressed." *Reason, Social Myths, and Democracy*, p. 286–287.

13. In this reconstruction, the schools, and intellectuals within them, have a special role to play in fostering critical inquiry and cooperative communication. At the same time, however, this role and its effectiveness are limited by external (*LW*3:273; 9:110, 207, 11:222, 414; 13:296) and internal (*LW*5:103) forces. See also Boyd H. Bode, " 'The Great American Dream,' " in *American Philosophy Today and Tomorrow*, ed. H. Kallen and S. Hook (Freeport, N.Y.: Books for Libraries Press, 1968), pp. 65–79.

14. Tatyana Vorozheikina, "Why Not Try Democracy?" in *The Nation*, 4 May 1992, pp. 594–596.

CHAPTER 4

Relevances, Realities, and Rat Races: Democracy as a *Personal* Way of Life

The Personal, the Possible, and the Plural

Calling democracy a way of life that we have not yet created, eighty-year-old John Dewey immediately added, as stressed in the last chapter, that we must realize in thought and act that this democracy is "a *personal* way of individual life." By emphasizing that democracy is a personal task that confronts every individual, Dewey sought to stress that "it signifies the possession and continual use of certain attitudes, forming personal character and determining desire and purpose in all the relations of life." He continued: "Instead of thinking of our own dispositions and habits as accommodated to certain institutions, we have to learn to think of the latter as expressions, projections and extensions of habitually dominant personal attitudes." Democracy, he said concisely, "is a way of life controlled by a working faith in the possibilities of human nature" (*LW*14:226).

Now, presumably this pragmatic faith in the possibilities of human nature is faith that our nature's possibilities are large, faith that we can do better, and faith that understands itself as realistic rather than utopian or blind. After the horrors of the twentieth century and the new horrors at the start of the twenty-first century, are any such democratic faith and any such melioristic pragmatism warranted or still warranted? Should we take seriously this faith, or just cry, laugh, or seek shelter?

Even if a working faith in the possibilities of human nature indeed turns out to be a faith that works, in exactly what is it a faith? What are the possibilities, or at least the better possibilities, of human nature? How are these possibilities sufficiently clearly determined before the fact so as to motivate personal action on their behalf? In whose nature and in what possibilities for human nature do pragmatists profess faith?

Here is another question: What is the relation between, on the one hand, democracy understood as a working faith in the possibilities of human nature, and, on the other hand, pluralism understood as a working belief in the multiplicity of human natures? Is it possible to hold a working faith in democracy not as *a* personal way of life, but rather as plural and different personal ways of life, multiple ways of life?

More than any American philosopher since Dewey, John Lachs consistently has expressed both this working faith in the large possibilities of human nature and a working commitment to the plurality of human natures and their fulfillments.[1] Arguing for tolerant concern, the virtue of accepting the alien, and loving someone whose values we do not share, Lachs echoes Peirce's fallibilism, James's pluralism, Santayana's individualism, and Dewey's focus on social intelligence:

> The epistemic foundation of such openness is doubt about one's ability to discern the good for everything that moves. Its ontological basis is the multiplicity of natures that surround us, every one of which demands its own proper fulfillment. . . . [o]bjections to a wholesome pluralism of perfections constitute only a philosophical rearguard action on behalf of intolerance. Both long-term social developments and the best thought point in the opposite direction.[2]

Lachs claims an experiential basis for this faith in the possibility of our fuller fulfillment and this insistence that there are multiple human natures and, thus, plural perfections. When philosophy turns from its own words to the world and its contingencies, it may provide, illuminate, and enrich this experience. In so doing, Lachs holds, philosophy becomes relevant to life.

At a time when most philosophers ignore or debate John Dewey's advice that philosophers should focus on the genuine problems of men and women rather than the artificial problems of philosophers, John Lachs simply demonstrates the value of doing so. Like Dewey, Lachs's ultimate goal is not to make philosophy more relevant and practical but, rather, to make life more intelligent and meaningful.

This sort of pragmatism must be evaluated on pragmatic terms. In this light, does this philosophy itself make life more intelligent and meaningful? For angry, victimized, and resigned persons who may be in no mood for "a celebration of life,"[3] what use is this philosophy? Can it help people living after the twentieth century and "thinking in the ruins" of modernism?[4] Can it even be relevant?

Relevance and Plural Relevances

Is this, or any other philosophy, relevant to life? Or is philosophy relevant only as an irrelevance, in the same way that some postmodern philosophers have stressed that something may be present as an absence? Can philosophy be relevant to life? If so, upon what conditions does relevance depend, and how can we create or sustain these conditions? Whether or not philosophy now is relevant to life, *should* it be relevant to life? And, is it possible to answer this question without begging the question?

Surely no philosophy is relevant to life in the abstract. Even pragmatists who seek the unity of theory and practice demand the relevance of theory to some concrete practice. Accordingly, any relevance to life first must be relevance to some particular life, some actual, concrete, real life, some group's or individual person's life. Any relevance of philosophy to life must be relevance to my life, your life, the life of some specific somebody somewhere and sometime. Second, any relevance of philosophy must be the relevance of some particular philosophy, some determinate philosophy, this philosophy rather than those other philosophies. Any philosophy relevant to life must be my philosophy, your philosophy, the philosophy of a specific someone. Third, any philosophy relevant to life must be relevant to life in some particular way, constitute some particular relationship rather than other relationships between philosophy and life. Any philosophy/life relevance must be a relevance of illumination or instrumentality or synthesis or analysis or genealogy or faith or suspicion or some other specific relation. In short, if the gospel of the relevance of philosophy to life is to succeed—succeed in life and not just in philosophy—then its message must be couched in terms of the multiple particulars of multiple lives. This means that when one considers the relevance of philosophy to life, and when one asks whether philosophy is, or can, or should be relevant to life, one must always at once ask three additional questions: First, *which* philosophy? Second, *whose* life? And third, *what* relevance?

Anyone who considers these additional questions when raising the pragmatic issue of the relevance of philosophy to life will be a pluralist. Rather than contemplating the relevance of philosophy to life, pluralists focus on the multiple relevances of philosophies to multiple lives and their multiple situations—the plural and different relevances of plural and different philosophies to plural and different lives. Moreover, pluralists will not simply assume that only one philosophy is, or can be, or should be relevant to all lives. They will not assume that a philosophy relevant to some life is, or can be, or even should be relevant to all life. They will not assume that philosophies are, or can be, or should be relevant to lives in only one way. Instead, pluralists concerned with the practical relevance of their philosophy will insist that their philosophies, always fallible and always unfinished, take seriously the full diversity, and the possibilities for fuller diversity, of our lives. And they will understand equally that lives may draw successfully on the full diversity of philosophies. There is no reason to insist on the importance of any smaller number of different philosophies than there are different lives that give rise to them and in turn are illuminated by them.

This pluralism is a crucial component of any effective pragmatism.[5] Pragmatism, William James wrote, is a new (though not so new anymore) name for an old (now older still) way of thinking. This way of thinking, I believe, is one in which philosophy is understood not simply or primarily as a body of knowledge—the presence or absence of which can be measured by final exams, conference presentations, and book publications. Rather, this way of thinking is one in which philosophy is understood as a way of life—love of wisdom—the presence or absence of which can be exhibited only in character, practice, and action.

When philosophy is understood as a way of life, it is obvious that the consideration of the relevances of philosophies to lives is not what it may have seemed at first. The pragmatic issue ultimately is not about how *two* different things—philosophies and lives—are, or can be, or should be relevant or related to one another in some specific ways. Rather, the issue is about *one* integrated thing—a philosophical life, a lived philosophy—and our large responsibilities to achieve it. To insist, with John Lachs, on "the unity of theory and practice in practice" (and not just "the unity of theory and practice in theory") is to insist that we live our lives in certain ways rather than others (*RPL*, p. 10). Some of the possibilities for human life are not fulfillments and perfections. There is a difference between being different and being better. Not every difference is a betterness, and so philosophies and lives that aim for mere difference do not aim high enough.

In what ways, then, should we live our lives? Lachs tells us that we should lead our lives in unified ways, in ways that manifest, or at least strive for, the unity of theory and practice in the world, not just in words. "We can all come near it," he writes, "by acting on what we believe, by making our books the authors of our deeds" (*RPL*, p. 10). To read John Lachs—the author of words—is to discover the unity of theory and practice in theory, to discover the relevance of philosophy to life in elegant philosophy. One would have to know John Lachs—the author of deeds—to experience firsthand the unity of his theory and his practice in practice, to know the relevance of this philosophy to that life in energetic life itself.

Like James, Dewey, Santayana, Hocking, and other American philosophers on whom he draws, Lachs has written that this unified life cannot be captured or demonstrated in words. In what ways, to repeat, should we lead our lives? Turning away from words and turning toward the world, Lachs responds:

> To questions of this sort there is no general answer. Typically some things we do are more satisfactory than others, but so much depends on context and individual preference that universal claims should arouse suspicion.... Human nature is so diverse that generalizations invite counterexamples and blanket prescriptions prove futile. In the place of a universal hierarchy of values, we must be satisfied with identifying the factors that affect sensible choice. Ability, opportunity, satisfaction, social standards, and variety are the five most important considerations to take into account when we choose what activities to enjoy.... Unfortunately, the skill of making sensible and timely choices cannot be taught by explaining its principles.... Those who are sensitive and smart eventually learn to choose by choosing, and that often means by making mistakes and then not making them again. (*ILWL*, pp. 58–59, 69)

Because I believe that the world toward which Lachs would have us turn is irreducibly (if only partially) a world of words and meanings, I have some reservations about the word/world dualism that underlies his sane advice. This dualism, manifest in Santayana's materialism, was dealt a deathblow by James's radical empiricism and Dewey's transactional account of experience.[6] Pragmatists would do well to abandon Santayana's ontology, just as they would do well to embrace his pluralism and relativism and his historicism about values. Moreover, I suspect that Lachs is not really advising us to turn totally away from words, especially his own words and understandings and uses of them. However, stripped of its dualistic metaphysical baggage (as it readily can be), Lachs's pluralistic advice is sound and, embodies "tolerant concern" and "good sense." As such, it is essentially Emersonian in nature. For Emerson's "American Scholar," action is essential, duties cannot be ducked, and books and words are for idle times and rainy days.

Professional philosophy today, of course, would have us believe that we live in a perpetual downpour, an unstopping monsoon season, a never-ending deluge that requires equally unending words and articles and books—a massive conceptual shelter from the storm. Lachs rightly tell us to put away the puzzles and clever theories that preoccupy us while we sit out the storms that rage around us and, instead, to venture outside. This pragmatic advice is both true and timely: If we don't risk getting a little wet, our philosophies will dry up.

This advice to act on what we believe and make our books the authors of our deeds, however, does not go far enough. We must employ pluralism not simply in the service of the relevance of philosophy to life, but also in the service of criticism of philosophies and lives, theories and practices, our books and our deeds—even when they constitute a unity. Our goal cannot be the mere unity of theory and practice, even in practice; rather, it must be the unity of critical theory and critical practice, a critical unity of sound theory (not just any theory) and sane practice (not just any practice). Consider—there is no need to imagine—racists or sexists, persons who hate Jews or Bosnians or single mothers or lesbians; rapists and terrorists and criminal accountants; the advocates of ethnic cleansing; the self-styled guardians of cultural purity, the announced enemies of supposed perversion, lifestyle police; and persons working tirelessly to make everyone else more like themselves. If these persons make their philosophies relevant to their lives, if they act on what they believe, as Lachs may seem to be urging, there may be an increase in the unity of theory and practice in practice. However, there surely will be no increase in practice of tolerant concern and good sense. In such cases where persons do not preach virtue, we are fortunate if they do not practice what they preach and if they are unable to engage in the activities that they have chosen to enjoy. The aim of a philosophical life is not just the unity of practice and theory, but rather the unity of practice and theory that result from critical inquiry and scrutiny. The point, then, is not the mere relevance of a particular philosophy to a particular life; rather it is the relevance of good philosophies to lives and, in turn, the relevance of good lives to philosophies. Pluralists must make judgments.

Realities and Human Natures

Consider, then, the relevance of good philosophies to good lives. It is at this point, of course, that most philosophers (and other theorists) abandon pluralism. They set forth a narrow, non-pluralistic account of the good life—the good life rather than good lives—and base this account on a theory of a single human nature, one that typically is suspiciously similar to the theorist's own nature (or understanding of it). As a result, in order to defend in theory moral pluralism—pluralism in both philosophy and life—it is necessary to set forth a pluralistic, anti-essentialist, anti-"natural kinds" view of human nature. And, in order to defend in practice moral pluralism, it is necessary to engage in broadly educational action that creates and sustains practices, institutions, and outlooks that form a pluralistic climate of belief.

Lachs has set forth just this sort of view in his account of plural "human natures."[7] This view rests on three major claims. First, Lachs argues that there are three kinds of facts: objective facts wholly independent of human interest and activity; conventional facts, wholly dependent on human purposes and practices; and, most important, a large class of choice-inclusive facts "whose constitution involves both objective elements and human decisions" (HN, p. 229). In the case of choice-inclusive facts, it makes no sense to ask about what *really* is the case, because in these cases there is no reality independent of our choices and decisions. In these cases, instead of asking whether a particular designation or classification or theory captures the supposedly independent facts, we instead should ask whether particular purposes are best served by one or the other "widely divergent ways of sorting and grouping the bounty of nature" (HN, p. 230). This, I take it, was the genealogical point Dewey frequently made when he urged us to convert ontological dualisms into functional distinctions, and examine the history of their formation, the work they do, and the interests they serve. In doing this, pragmatists recognize that epistemology is a subset of political philosophy.

Second, Lachs argues that the categories of biology and human nature are choice-inclusive facts (rather than objective facts as commonly thought). Within "the outer and rather fuzzy boundaries" of objective facts, the facts about human life "that surround us do not mandate any particular classification; they are rich and flexible enough to permit a variety of organizational arrangements" and to include "significant differences in the desires, activities, and satisfactions of people." Lachs summarizes: "Humanity is not a[n objective] feature that stares us in the face, but a coveted designation we award on the basis of complex criteria and shrewd assessments" (HN, pp. 233, 240, 236).

Third, this metaphysical pluralism returns Lachs to moral pluralism. He concludes that "expanding membership in the human family ... the full legitimacy of our fellows so long as they cause no harm," and broad tolerance are justified (HN, pp. 238, 241). In a telling passage, he writes that this view "makes it impossible for people to claim that one and only one style of behavior is natural and right or that certain desires and activities and satisfactions are unnatural" (HN, p. 241). Behavior unlike our own may be unusual or surprising or disconcerting or uncomprehended, but it is behavior that in the end is merely different. In being different, it is no less human and no less natural, and it need not necessarily be less good.

In an age of many kinds of fundamentalism, fanaticism, absolutism, and shrill small-mindedness, this is a refreshing and wholesome message, and one that we desperately need to establish in our philosophies and in our lives today. Like the doctor who offered Lachs's children an oral polio vaccine, Lachs offers us a conceptual vaccine for narrow-mindedness, self-righteous intolerance, and desperately inhumane action undertaken on behalf of so-called facts of human nature.

My eagerness to swallow this medicine, however, is offset somewhat by two pragmatic reservations about its side effects and its effectiveness. First, the trinitarian classification scheme—objective facts, conventions (is this just proper names?), and choice-inclusive facts—is full of problems that pluralism might well avoid. Lachs addresses this question in a particularly effective way: Are there any, or more than just a few, choice-inclusive facts? In answering in the affirmative, Lachs in effect takes a step away from Santayana and toward Dewey. He does not address as effectively two additional questions: Why believe there are any objective or choice-independent facts (and why hold on to an objective/subjective metaphysics)? And what is the status of facts that are intrinsically related to aspects of human experience other than, or in addition to, choice?

In effect, these are questions about whether a step toward Dewey on this issue—Lachs's admission of choice-inclusive facts—requires at once a larger step away from Santayana and supposedly objective facts. Indeed, referring to Dewey and Santayana, Lachs writes that his own "theory of human natures rests on a foundation that incorporates both of these views" (*RPL*, p. xvi). He continues that "good sense indicates that there are objective realities independent of us," but he does not explain what it is that is "good" about this sense. Perhaps if one had to pick between the objective realities of a materialism or a naturalism, on the one hand, or the subjective mind-dependencies of an idealism or personalism, on the other hand, then it might be good sense to pick the former. However, pragmatism undercuts both of these alternatives by rejecting the presuppositions that they share. As a result, the development of a more thoroughly pluralistic pragmatism does not require the return to a pre-pragmatic metaphysics. For example, when Lachs explicates this notion of a class of objective facts by instructing his readers to view the Gulf of Mexico "from its perspective," I have to confess that I do not think this is possible (even when I am swimming in it). Similarly, the fact that the gulf would continue to exist even though a mad dictator might choose to deny its existence does not show that the gulf exists independently of human experience (though it does show that the gulf does exist independently of the particular dictator's choices and pronouncements). To fail to note this fact is to fail to distinguish idealism from radical empiricism, to fail to recognize that pragmatism is not a form of anti-realism or a form of realism or some middle path between the two. Consider another example: Lachs writes that

although we may debate whether or not to choose to include in our classification of persons women, children, barbarians, Jews, Africans, Indians,
Christians, patients in comas, or dolphins, we may not debate whether
clouds and waves should be included in this classification. This is, Lachs
writes, because as a matter of objective fact, clouds and waves simply are
not human beings and cannot reasonably be so considered (HN, p. 234).
Now, although I have no pressing desire or purpose to classify clouds as
human beings, I see no argument or evidence why this would contradict
objective facts, or why different persons might not make different choices
and might not hold different notions of reasonableness. Similarly, I suspect
that only a couple of centuries ago it would have seemed to many Americans that women, American Indians, black-skinned slaves, and dolphins
simply "objectively" were not full human beings. The various classifica-
tions made by characters in stories and novels by Borges may be unusual
or useless for many common purposes, but on what basis could they be
shown to be wrong—and *objectively* wrong? What would this even mean?
Has Lachs really identified an outer-limit objective fact about human
nature, or has he simply assumed one particular choice-inclusive classification system and its particular standard of reasonableness? Because this
is a classification system that is familiar to us—more familiar, say, than the
classification of animals offered to us by Borges and cited by Foucault—
it may seem natural or objective or reasonable. But our standards of reasonableness, like our views of objectivity that result from these standards,
are themselves choice-inclusive and culturally situated. To designate a
fact as objective or material is to make implicit reference to a choice or
experience. Different choices and different experiences may reflect or
give rise to different facts. This is the lesson of Lachs's own pluralism: "the
virtue of accepting the alien."

From the standpoint of how we lead our lives, however, none of this
really matters much. The sheer fact—whether it is an objective fact or a
choice-inclusive fact—that some entity is or is not a person, does not by
itself wholly determine in any way our treatment of that entity. Even if it
is a fact, again whether objective or choice-inclusive, that dolphins or whole
ecosystems or clouds are not humans, what constitutes moral action toward
them is still unsettled. And even if it is a fact, once more whether objective or choice-inclusive, that Africans, women, paraplegics, gay and lesbians,
and philosophy professors are humans, what constitutes moral action
toward them is still up for grabs.

This leads to my second reservation. Lachs is a tolerant, enlightened
fellow, and so the prospect of his settling these issues is not overly fright-
ening. But if we believe that membership in the class of humans is deter-

mined by choice, we must not fail to notice that this determination is always a political matter, always a matter of power. Who makes this choice? Lachs? Osama bin Laden? Hitler? Cortez? The Irish Republican Army? Rebel leaders in Zaire? Homophobic legislators? Illegal immigrants? Small groups of militia? Large groups bent on ethnic cleansing? Middle Eastern death squads? Middle American taxpayers? College deans? Abusive husbands? The CIA? CEOs of large international businesses? You? History should give us pause—very long pause. It is not enough to point out that the classification of persons or human natures rests on choice; it must be made clear how and why some choices are better than others—and better in the absence of objective facts in which to ground that betterness. The logic of tyranny is the logic of exclusion. The justification for this exclusion is not independent fact but human choice. As a result, the recognition of the plurality of human natures and the role of choice (often contested choices) in this recognition is no guarantee of inclusivity, tolerance, and good sense. And, as a result, concern for plural human natures must pass into concern for the education of those natures in the practices of making wise choices. If it is to be pragmatic, pluralism must avoid the defects of liberalism and must effect through education a broad pluralistic climate of belief.

Rat Races

At a minimum, making wise choices requires that, to the extent possible, persons avoid the so-called "rat race," a busy but empty life. This is a life constituted by actions that have only instrumental value and connection, a life without consummations and satisfying completeness, a life of running through mazes in search of food to provide nourishment for further running. It is a life filled with means that lead not to ends but only to other means to still other means to yet other means and finally to death (itself a termination but not an end). Education consumers who read books just to write papers to pass courses to graduate to go to the next school to get a job to make money to retire early may acquire at an early age lifelong membership in the rat race. The rat race, as Lachs employs this term drawn from laboratory experiments, is a life of process, a life of processes undertaken in order to secure some end or goal other than the process itself.[8]

The pragmatic question is obvious: Is there an alternative? The pluralistic pragmatic question is also obvious: Are there multiple alternatives? If so, how can the rat race be avoided? Most generally, an alternative, at least in theory, is a life of activity rather than a life of process—a life constituted by actions that are undertaken for their own sakes and thus are their own ends. This is a life in which an action is its own end, a life in which means and ends are united through aims that include no goals beyond the actions themselves. Aristotle identified this life as a life of activity, *energeia*, rather than a life of motion, *kinesis*, and believed that such a life is as godlike as is humanly possible. It is a life in which, as Lachs puts it, process and product are one.

Like Lachs, I think this notion of activity (or the good life as activity) is one of the most powerful ideas in philosophy. However, is it relevant to lives in the ruins, lives after the twentieth century? If relevant, then certainly it is relevant as an ideal rather than an actuality. Our lives typically fall substantially short of this ideal. We may engage in brief moments of activity, but these moments are surrounded by long stretches of process, of doing things we'd not do if only we could get the results without engaging in the action. Some philosophers have thought that this is the best we can do. Aristotle, for example, believed a whole life of activity an impossibility for human beings. We cannot even contemplate continuously, he noted, for the simple reason that we get tired. In *Nicomachean Ethics*, Aristotle developed an account of the good life that moves our real lives in the direction of this ideal. It is a move, Lachs says, that "rests on the claim that there is an essential incompatibility between ends-in-themselves and means, between ultimate value and utility" (RR, pp. 87–88).

Can we do better than this unpragmatic dualism? Can we overcome this incompatibility? Lachs sketches two possible strategies for doing better. The first is what he calls the "Stoic gambit," a philosophy of attitude adjustment, a philosophy that tells us that whether an action is a process or an activity depends simply on how we look at it. For the Stoics, a life of activity awaits those who get their minds right. The Stoic, Lachs suggests, accepts the process/activity dichotomy, and then forges a strategy for converting processes into activities. If, for example, you will only view reading this chapter of this book as you view making love, then you will achieve happiness as you read. The Stoic message is easy: Let the rat embrace the race, and so transform it. The rat race? Expressing supposed Herculean strength, the Stoic replies: Give me more.

Though easy in theory, this message is notoriously difficult in practice. For this reason, Lachs suggests that pragmatism is an alternative to Stoicism, and so calls our attention to an idea set forth by John Dewey. Dewey argued that means and ends do not designate ultimately different kinds of values but, rather, different temporal relations within experience. There are no ends-in-themselves, Dewey claimed. To be an end is simply to be an end relative to a particular means—and thus what Dewey called an "end-in-view." Similarly, to be a means is simply to be a means relative to some other, future end, itself no end-in-itself but only an end-in-view. As a result, an action may be an end relative to other actions needed to achieve it, and at the same time a means relative to other goals for which it is a prerequisite. The result, then, may be a means-end integrated action.

In critically assessing this view, Lachs makes three major points: Dewey's view is an alternative, and stands in opposition, to Aristotle's view of activity; very few of our undertakings actually are means-end integrated actions; opportunities for creating more such integrated actions are extremely rare. If these points are correct, then pluralists need to look some-place other than pragmatism in their effort to distinguish "plural perfec-tions" from other ways of life.

Lachs extends an invitation to friends of Dewey to "set him right," and I want to accept this invitation because I think all three of these impor-tant criticisms miss their mark in important ways. First, Dewey's view is not so much a complete alternative to Aristotle's views as it is a post-Darwinian reconstruction of them. Lachs is right to think that there is a conceptual difference between ends-in-themselves and means, but it does not follow that there is an existential incompatibility between an action's being an end and a means at the same time. Dewey simply accepted Aris-totle's notion of activity, transformed the Greek dualism of ends and means into a pragmatic temporal distinction between an end-in-view and the means to it, and recognized that if we are to lead a life of activity then two conditions, rather than one, must be satisfied. The first condition is that good lives consist of actions that are worthwhile for what they them-selves are and not simply for what they may bring about later. The second condition is that good lives consist of actions that enable us later to take up other actions that also are worthwhile for what they themselves are. On this view, a good life consists in actions that are intrinsically worthwhile experiences and at once instrumentally valuable for producing future worthwhile experiences. This is an integration of means and end, a life rather than a moment of activity.

Are there precious few such integrated actions? Do kissing (and other acts of love) and dribbling basketballs (and other acts of play) pretty much exhaust the class of these integrated actions, as Lachs suggests? If so, our pluralism will not be very robust: confined to these cases, talk of "plural perfections" will be little more than talk of multiple ways of bouncing balls. However, at this point, it seems to me that Lachs's faith in the possibili-ties of human nature is uncharacteristically small in scope. Can't talking with friends, reading a book (say, *Pragmatism, Postmodernism, and the Future of Philosophy* or *The Relevance of Philosophy to Life* and *A Commu-nity of Individuals*), singing songs with one's children, helping a friend or meeting someone new, teaching a class or becoming a student again, painting in the open air or watching the sun set over an ancient cemetery, solving a math problem or just being lost in a math problem, eating a papaya or planting trees, driving no place in particular or remembering one's grandparents—can't any of these or countless other commonplace actions be means-end integrated actions? Though many persons engage in many actions that lack this character, still it seems to me that many persons lead lives frequently and substantially of just this sort. These realities need to be multiplied in practice, not restricted in theory.

That said, the notion of an entire life of means-end integrated actions surely is an ideal, and it was an ideal for Dewey as much as it is an ideal for Lachs. There is, however, nothing unreal about ideals. This ideal points to needs for social changes—tasks that are ultimately educational in the largest sense of that term. This is not an optimistic call, but it is melioristic and it is the call of those with faith in large possibilities for human lives.

Is it not possible to realize more often and more fully, if never wholly or perfectly, the goals of persons who lead lives that are hungry, poor, violent, abused, unimaginative, and lacking respect, joy, and hope? Is it not possible to fashion better means to ends? And is it not possible to act so as to forge values and meanings and goals that are more consonant with the conditions of lives, the plural conditions of different lives? Is it not possible to pursue ends that are more reasonable and to appreciate the alien pursuit of alien ends that are not more reasonable for us? Lachs certainly is right that "socialization has its limits," but philosophy should not pretend that we have come anywhere near these limits, that we cannot more fully, deeply, and lastingly spend our days making love to life (RR, pp. 97–98). This must be the message of any philosophy relevant to lives and attentive to their plural perfections. It must also be the message of any philosophy relevant to the plural perfections of lives in time, short lifetimes. Is it a message learned from children? Lachs writes: "They spend the day at the beach building things that will not survive the next tide. They enjoy the process, give themselves to their activity with total devotion, take pride in what they build, and then leave it all without regrets. Adults, by contrast, want everything saved, everything to last. We seem to forget that playing for keeps is not *playing* at all" (*ILWL*, p. 110). But the children at the beach who give themselves to their activity with total devotion *are* playing for keeps, even though they cannot keep playing forever. *While* they are playing, they are playing for keeps and playing for one of many kinds of perfection. To play for keeps, though, is to play for just a little while. And when the children realize this, they will awaken to Lachs's insight that "mastery of life is to remember death and yet live joyously" (*ILWL*, p. 125), playing for keeps because there is nothing to keep beyond the playing.

Relevance Again and Philosophy

I dreamed I was awake, and woke up only to find myself asleep.

—Stan Laurel

Running their own races, professional philosophers today do too little to educate children to live joyously while remembering death. They do not nurture an active faith in large and plural possibilities of democracy as a personal way of life. Individual philosophers may or may not be pragmatists in theory, but collectively philosophers surely are not pragmatists in practice. "There is no fate that cannot be surmounted by scorn," Camus wrote in *The Myth of Sisyphus.*[9] How, if at all, is it possible for philosophers to surmount their present fate? At a time in which pragmatism is not so much a new name for an old way of thinking, but instead an old name for new ways of not thinking very much, how can pragmatic philosophy actually be pragmatic?

This question, of course, will not interest most philosophers. They have reduced pragmatism to an occasional topic in their professional journals and scholarly books like this one. The question won't interest anyone else much either. In our commercial culture, even in higher education and higher virtual education, philosophy just isn't selling—and very few people are troubled by this fact. The demand for philosophers, pragmatists included, is only marginally higher than that for, say, cobblers, ice miners, alchemists, and certified phrenologists. As Ivan Klima wrote movingly in another context in *The Spirit of Prague*: "The more passionately we cling to [false hopes], the more we will come to resemble condemned men who await a miracle while marching towards their own destruction."[10]

So, what is, or might be, the role—the *personal* role—for a pragmatic philosophy that does not await a miracle? In the abstract, it might seem the answer to this question is clear: Give up false hopes, stop marching toward destruction and cultural irrelevance, and begin the hard work needed to imagine, think, and live differently, the hard work needed for philosophy to play different roles in the lives of different persons. But hard work is, well, hard work. It is, well, hard. And sometimes it is unprofessional. In practice, less strenuous projects have proven attractive—so attractive indeed that professional philosophers in effect regularly declare their own peculiar march toward the destruction of the cultural relevance of philosophy to be the very essence of philosophy, to be philosophy at its best, to be the salvation of philosophy.

Recall John Dewey's well-known demand in 1917 for a recovery of philosophy from chewing historic cud, apologetics for lost causes, and scholastic formalism. Incredibly—literally, incredibly—it seems that for most of the rest of the twentieth century, professional philosophers took Dewey's view about how philosophy can be lost as a blueprint for what philosophy should be. Endless textual explication and historical comparison, tireless policing of the borders and purity of philosophy, and ceaseless cleverness without consequence—this pretty much captures most of what professional philosophers do as professional philosophers. By itself, this has so little to do with philosophy understood as the love of wisdom and the art of existence that one almost must conclude that a lobotomy, memory loss, and diminished will are benefits of membership in the American Philosophical Association and other professional philosophical societies. How could the APA and professional philosophers have allowed professional philosophy to devolve in this way? Worse, how could it and they have administered this devolution? I pose these questions, I want to be clear, not as a prelude to recounting a tragedy, but as the background for possibly doing better. My concern is with hope.

Of course, to observe that philosophy has virtually no role in the education of persons to lead joyous personal lives is to note a fact about *professional* philosophy. Non-professional philosophy, non-technical philosophy, one's views about the nature of reality and the meaning and conduct of life—philosophy in this sense plays major roles in the lives of persons. As William James noted in essays such as "The Types of Philosophic Thinking," "The Present Dilemma in Philosophy," and "Philosophical Conceptions and Practical Results," the philosophy that is important in practice is not a technical matter at all. Instead, "it is our more or less dumb sense of what life honestly and deeply means ... it is our individual way of just seeing and feeling the total push and pressure of the cosmos"; and it is one's vision of "the whole drift of life, forced on one by one's total character and experience and on the whole *preferred*—there is no other truthful word—as one's best working attitude."[11]

There can be no question, I think, that this "more or less dumb sense of what life honestly and deeply means" occupies a central, major role in the lives of individuals and their associations with others. However, if philosophy in this non-technical sense plays a *large* role, it frequently does not play an *intelligent, successful* role. The problem with non-technical philosophies is that they too often are more, rather than less, dumb. Our best working attitudes and faiths too often just don't work very well. Instead, they guide, and reflect, lives filled with isolation, desolation, misunderstanding, emptiness, alienation, apathy, and anger. These non-technical philosophies run through relationships with self, others, and nature that are desperate, suicidal, abusive, broken, or just plain boring and petty. They sustain policies and institutions that are unreflective, unimaginative, destructive, unjust, and marked by massive opportunity costs and spectacular short-sightedness.

In this context, technical philosophy, professional philosophy, always has professed a love of greater wisdom and a commitment to a finer art of existence and a fuller liberation and actualization of the multiplicity of selves. And, in this sense, the goal of professional philosophy always has been educational in the broad, pragmatic sense. This intention, however, is not enough. Ask for more: How does professional philosophy seek to play this educational and liberating role? What does it do? What are its consequences? For whom? Does it succeed? The answers to these questions seem as clear as they are depressing. Professional philosophy seeks to play an educational role through formal schooling at the college and university level. Who provides this instruction? Certified philosophy professors, persons accredited by graduate schools and the educational bureaucracy that James called the "Ph.D. Octopus." What are the topics of this instruction? This seems like a stupid question because the answer seems obvious to professional philosophers. The answer is philosophy. But what is philosophy, professional and technical philosophy? This too seems like a stupid question to professional philosophers. The answer, in practice, is the thought of past philosophers—courses on Plato, Aristotle, Aquinas, Descartes, Hume, Kant, Hegel, Wittgenstein, Peirce, and Heidegger, to use common examples—and the subjects of contemporary philosophers, courses on systematic fields such as logic, metaphysics, epistemology, ethics, aesthetics, to use common examples once again.

This is both troubling and curious for anyone who takes seriously Dewey's claim that there are no properly philosophical problems but only philosophical approaches to genuine human problems. It is more than that for anyone who takes seriously Emerson's call for a philosophy of insight rather than mere tradition. And so, I am trying to think differently.

Suppose philosophy is not a subject matter or discipline (with its own problems and texts and authors) separate from and independent of other fields of study—suppose it isn't any such *thing* at all. Suppose philosophy, like consciousness for pragmatists, is a function: cultural criticism. There is, after all, nothing *inherently* philosophical about any given subject matter, and there is nothing *inherently* more philosophical about any given subject matter (say, epistemology or Hegel) than any other subject matter (say, agriculture or international business). It is time for pragmatists to define philosophy in terms of its consequences. To fail to do this is to become frozen in time—frozen in, or perhaps before, the twentieth century. Just as persons in the past concluded radically that a liberal education really is possible in languages other than Latin, and that there are more than three learned professions that would benefit by higher education, so too pragmatists might do well to conclude that there are multiple new sites of, and for, any philosophy relevant to real ways of living.

If this does not happen, philosophy increasingly will cut itself off even more from the lives of individuals and cultures. And philosophers, no matter how many articles they publish or how many professional honors they amass, will just be sleepwalking. Moreover, and far more important, the lives of persons may be cut off from critical (and self-critical) understanding and direction. Recalling Dewey's observations about the difference between the so-called liberal arts and a genuinely liberating education, I say: A philosophy with renewed relevance to lives should use the resources provided by the humanities, the social sciences, the natural sciences, and the professions and vocations so as to foster the ability to critically evaluate the demands and issues in the world today and tomorrow. To continue in Deweyan terms, such an education would be philosophical not *in spite of the fact* that it would depart widely from philosophy as it was conceived in medieval and modern periods. Rather, it would be philosophical *exactly because* it then might do for our contemporary world what earlier self-conceived philosophies tried to do for the worlds in which they arose.

To leave things here, however, is to leave them too general. So, with a working faith in large and plural possibilities and a pragmatic commitment to the creation of a pragmatic climate of belief, here are some specific and thoroughly modest sample targets at which to take aim:

- Ph.D. programs in philosophy should reinstate and require graduate minors in some field other than philosophy. Have political philosophers study law or economics, metaphysicians study physics or cognitive science; ethicists study psychology or anthropology. Philosophers must reject the narrowness of a single discipline.
- Ph.D. programs should require practice, a laboratory-like experience, an internship, some field work. Have political philosophers work with a government office, a legislator, or a community group, metaphysicians with a scientific team or a religious organization, ethicists with a corporation, foundation, policy organization, or newspaper. Philosophers must reject the narrowness of mere theory.
- APA meetings should no longer be philosopher-only events. Philosophers can talk with themselves one day. On the second day, meet with others each year in another discipline—political theory, biology, or comparative literature. On the third day, meet with leaders outside the academy—business executives, movie makers, labor unions, judges. Philosophers must

reject the narrowness of their own associations and relations. At the same time, the APA needs a correspondingly broader vision and fresher imagination. Most of what it now does could be handled by a conference planner and a computer webmaster. The APA needs to function primarily as a public—not just a professional—advocate for philosophy and for wiser lives and higher arts of existence. James's "Ph.D. Octopus," the omnipresent tentacles of professionalism, has created and given way to the "Philosophy Anemone"—a timid tidepool and backwater creature that draws within itself at the merest hint of contact with the rest of the world. Today, it is the anemone, not the gadfly, that serves as the de facto logo for professional philosophy. Philosophers should reject their own narrowness.

- Finally, in doing so, philosophers need to exhibit and embody a good deal of humility. The temptation is to believe that philosophers have much to contribute to personal ways of life, if only individuals will recognize the relevance of philosophy and the brilliance of philosophers. Perhaps so. However, at this point, other individuals and groups have at least as much to offer professional philosophers as philosophers have to offer in return. Accordingly, in a spirit of humility and openness, philosophers need not only to speak up but also to listen up. This is a necessary condition if philosophers are going to think and live differently—think and live for keeps—and wake up to the need for clear analysis, historical understanding, imaginative alternatives, and critical insights.

These proposals are rooted in a pragmatic and pluralistic philosophy that surely is not for everyone. However, perhaps those who do not share or appreciate its values will be able, as John Lachs has advised, to love it rather than take up philosophical rearguard action against it. Such at least is a source of working faith in the future, working faith in the possibilities of plural human natures and their plural joys. Such too is a source, more darkly, of anxious suspicion about the future, anxious suspicion about the possibilities of multiple forms of control and their multiple joys. As a result, John Lachs's observation is right on the mark: "In the place of a universal hierarchy of values, we must be satisfied with identifying the factors that affect sensible choice" (*ILWL*, p. 58).

At the same time, any pluralism that is genuinely pragmatic and fully awake must make possible criticism of what passes for sensible choice. After all, pluralism requires recognition of the fact that the rats give themselves with total devotion to their races through the mazes. In turn, the maze makers surely seem to enjoy the entire action, and they definitely play for keeps.

Notes

1. John Lachs, *Intermediate Man* (Indianapolis, Ind.: Hackett, 1981). John Lachs, *Mind and Philosophers* (Nashville, Tenn.: Vanderbilt University Press, 1987). John Lachs, *The Relevance of Philosophy to Life* (Nashville, Tenn.: Vanderbilt University Press, 1995). John Lachs, *In Love with Life: Reflections on the Joy of Living and Why We Hate to Die* (Nashville, Tenn.: Vanderbilt University Press, 1998). John Lachs and Michael Hodges, *Thinking in the Ruins: Wittgenstein and Santayana on Contingency* (Nashville, Tenn.: Vanderbilt University Press, 2000). John Lachs, *A Community of Individuals* (New York: Routledge, 2002).

2. Lachs, *The Relevance of Philosophy to Life*, p. xiv. Hereafter *RPL*.

3. Lachs, *In Love With Life*, p. xii. Hereafter *ILWL*.

4. Lachs and Hodges, *Thinking in the Ruins*, pp. 1–14.

5. See chapters 9 and 10, and also my "Pragmatism vs. Fundamentalism," *Genealogical Pragmatism: Philosophy, Experience, and Community* (Albany: State University of New York Press, 1997), pp. 63–86.

6. I assess the Santayana-Dewey exchange on this issue in "Experience and the Adoration of Matter: Santayana's Unnatural Naturalism," *Genealogical Pragmatism*, pp. 131–146.

7. John Lachs, "Human Natures," *The Relevance of Philosophy to Life*, pp. 228–242. Lachs expanded this account in his 1997 Presidential Address to the Metaphysical Society of America. Hereafter HN.

8. John Lachs, "Aristotle and Dewey on the Rat Race," *The Relevance of Philosophy to Life*, pp. 83–97. This essay appeared earlier in *Philosophy and the Reconstruction of Culture: Pragmatic Essays after Dewey*, ed. John J. Stuhr (Albany: State University of New York Press, 1993), pp. 97–109. Hereafter RR.

9. Albert Camus, *The Myth of Sisyphus and Other Essays*, trans. Justin O'Brien (New York: Alfred A. Knopf, 1955 [1942]), p. 90.

10. Ivan Klima, *The Spirit of Prague*, trans. Paul Wilson (New York: Granta Books, 1994 [1974]), p. 81.

11. William James, *A Pluralistic Universe, The Works of William James* (Cambridge, Mass.: Harvard University Press, 1977 [1909]), pp. 14–15; *Pragmatism, The Works of William James* (Cambridge, Mass.: Harvard University Press, 1975 [1907]), pp. 24–25.

CHAPTER 5

From the Art of Surfaces to Control Societies and Beyond: Stoicism, Postmodernism, and Pan-Machinism

Instructions for Assembly

> We're moving toward control societies that no longer operate by confining people but through continuous control and instant communication. . . . Compared with the approaching forms of ceaseless control in open sites, we may come to see the harshest confinement as part of a wonderful happy past. . . . Maybe speech and communication have been corrupted. They're thoroughly permeated by money—and not by accident but by their very nature. We've got to hijack speech. Creating has always been something different from communicating. The key thing may be to create vacuoles of noncommunication, circuit breakers, so we can elude control.[1]

This chapter differs in three ways from most published work in the humanities. First, it does not explicate, interpret; or represent anything. Instead, it experiments, inhales hard, and, in doing so, mutates. Second, it makes no claim, explicit or implicit, to truth. Instead, a metamorphosis, it takes apart, scatters and imports, and reconstructs. Third, it is not assembled for print—for the pages of this book—or for live authorial voice of visible author, the standard format for academic address. Instead, it is designed for a) an audience that accesses through the Internet projected on a large forward screen or monitor the author's printed words and the spliced tape-recorded speaking of these words by the author and the American writers John Barth and William Burroughs, while b) that audience is presented simultaneously both a series of connected Internet sites (see now site 1: www.google.com/search?q=Gilles+Deleuze)[2] and large monitor broadcast of real-time videotaping of the audience's own activity (also viewed live by the author from another location), all while the author and the audience (play recording now) listen to Frank Zappa's May 1968 recording of "The Chrome Plated Megaphone of Destiny."[3] As John Barth noted in 1968, this sort of thing, admittedly unusual, may be called pretentious.[4] In response, it could be said, with Barth, that form must follow, or emblematize, function. However, this would miss the point. There is no function independent of form, and one cannot read all the instructions before beginning assembly. (See site 2: www.uta.edu/english/apt/d&g/d&gweb.html)

Three Tool Parables

> A theory is exactly like a box of tools. . . . It must be useful. It must function. And not for itself. If no one uses it, beginning with the theoretician himself (who then ceases to be a theoretician), then the theory is worthless or the moment is inappropriate. We don't revise a theory, but construct new ones; we have no choice but to make others. . . . I leave it to you to find your own instrument, which is necessarily an instrument for combat.[5]

My father-in-law had a drawer filled with objects that he calls tools. Often when I visited during the years in which I first knew him, he undertook in front of me some small household project with these tools, hoping, usually correctly, that some combination of sympathy and scorn would lead me to complete the task for him. One day I painfully watched him pound in some finishing nails that had popped out of the base molding in his study. To pound these nails, he used a tool—a tool commonly known as a crescent wrench. After several minutes and a lot of bent nails and small dents in the wood molding, he began more successfully striking the nails with the flat front of the tool instead of its rounded end. "This works, doesn't it?" he said in my direction with some satisfaction. "Maybe," I replied with some irritation, "but you know that isn't a hammer." With an air of self-evidence, he responded, "It is now."

The nature (or being) of a tool is relative to a practice.

Some years later, my father-in-law gave this tool to my son, then five years old. It was pockmarked, bent, and would not maintain the size to which one set it, slipping always more open—as if someone had used it to pound nails into molding, close paint can lids, and dig holes for tulip bulbs. Seemingly eager to master the implements of carpenters and mechanics, my son practiced with this tool for some time after he received it. One afternoon he asked me to watch. Adjusting the wrench to fit some hex-head screws, he began to turn them into some scrap softwood. After a few turns, the wrench began to slip, stripping the screw heads. My son persisted, shaving slivers of metal off the top of screw after screw. "Gramps wrecked that wrench," I volunteered. "You can't get those screws into the wood. With that wrench all you'll do is strip the screw heads." My son looked puzzled by my exasperation. "I know, Dad, I know. That's what I'm doing— I'm stripping screw heads. This tool works great."

The effectiveness of a tool is relative to a purpose.

On his seventh birthday, my son received some new tools from my in-laws. He spent the next Saturday in top-secret (at least from me) construction. It involved a lot of hammering. The hammering was very loud. At lunch, I asked him what he was making. "You'll see," he answered. The hammering continued and then, just before dinner, it finally ended. He asked me to guess what he had made. I guessed a birdhouse, a sailboat, a coat rack, and, finally, a bed of nails. "No," he said triumphantly, "I made myself a hammerer."

The product (rather than the origin) of a tool's use is a tool user.

Can one philosophize with a hammer if one uses a wrench? Can one philosophize with a hammer if one is only trying to strip screw heads? And can one philosophize with a hammer and become anything other than a hammerer?

What Is a Pervert?

> This is a reorientation of all thought and of what it means to think: *there is no longer depth or height.* . . . The staff-blow philosophy of the Cynics and the Stoics replaces the hammer-blow philosophy. The philosopher is no longer the being of the caves, nor Plato's soul or bird, but rather the animal which is on a level with the surface—a tick or louse. . . . What are we to call this new philosophical operation, insofar as it opposes at once Platonic conversion and pre-Socratic subversion? Perhaps we can call it "perversion," which at least befits the system of provocations of this new type of philosopher—if it is true that perversion implies an extraordinary art of surfaces.[6]

What is a pervert, an artist of surfaces, an artist at the surface, at new and different, changing and original surfaces? What is this philosopher-pervert (no philosopher king), this philosophizing, this becoming-perversion-philosophy?

Most university professors, of course, will view this hammer-less philosopher much as they view Gilles Deleuze—as first and foremost an author. (See site 3: http://perso.wanadoo.fr/minerva/Biblio_Deleuze/Gilles_ Deleuze.htm) Gripping tight to their hammers, gripped tight by the practice of philosophy as hammering, most professional professors desire depth or height, roots or sky, groundings or transcendences, the primordial or the complete, emptiness or wholeness, self-denial or self-realization, origins or eternal returns. (Despite this commonplace desire of theorizing professors, theory consumers and other culture shoppers face a policy at the surface of no exchanges, no layaways, and no returns.) Desiring and manufacturing histories of philosophy as truth rather than histories of philosophy as desires, they neglect to preface their tales of Plato, Augustine, Hegel, and the like with "Once upon a time in a far-away make-believe land ... " or "One dark and stormy night ... "—Plato, Augustine, Hegel, and company as masters of horror fiction, the Stephen Kings of philosophy, so gripping that we cannot put them down. Gripping tight to their profession, Philosophy Inc.,[7] they view philosophy first and foremost as a kind of writing—and the more of it the better. (See site 4: http://www.dc. peachnet.edu/~mnunes/guattari.html)

But suppose love of wisdom is life—living, becoming-alive—at the surface, a kind of being rather than a kind of writing (or a kind of writing only incidentally). Why view the philosopher-pervert as someone who, above all else, writes rather than, above all else, walks with a staff, cooks, raises children, plays piano, makes prank phone calls, tends a garden, buries family members, makes love, or jumps out a window? There are multiple arts of surfaces, and there is nothing especially perverse about writing. At present, writing, or publishing writing, may be especially unperverse.

PROBLEM IV. How do nomads *use* their weapons as weapons, and are they weapons if they can't be so used?[8]

PROPOSITION XV. Which comes last?: Writing necessarily adopts war as its object when it is appropriated, whether or not it grants permission to be appropriated, by the state apparatus.[9]

At present, writing is also realistic, materialistic, capitalistic: Publish or perish! Yes, of course. Still, faced with this option, would it not be perverse, philosophically and genuinely perverse, to choose to perish—to perish at the surface, to perish as an event, to perish as an environmentally correct nomad who leaves no trace and assassinates no one, who lives life without transcendence, life without inscribing any crimes.

Deleuze, the voluminous writer, hinted at this. In *The Logic of Sense*, for example, his philosopher of the surface, the Stoic hero, is not a philosophy professor with a long résumé. Instead, it is Hercules, and the Herculean pervert-philosopher of the surface keeps quiet or delivers a blow with his staff when asked questions or addressed abstractions. "We don't suffer these days from any lack of communication," Deleuze noted in "On Philosophy," "but rather from all the forces making us say things when we've nothing much to say."[10] (See site 5: http://www.mythosandlogos.com/Deleuze.html) Perhaps, on the one hand, recovering philosophers of both the infernal abyss and the celestial height, as part of their twelve-step recovery programs, and, on the other hand, state-captured philosophers of the surface all need access to the sort of public library described in Richard Brautigan's novel *The Abortion*—a library that allows authors to catalogue and shelve their books, but does not ever allow anyone to check out or read any of its books.[11]

What, then, is this "new philosophical operation," this pervert-becoming, this surface Hercules? Shall we say it is a rhizome? A body without organs or abstract machine that deterritorializes and reterritorializes? A dice thrower? A maker of cogs in extratextual practices? A minority voice? A maker of maps of lines of flight? An assemblage that opens and multiplies connections? A smooth space? Shall *we* say any of this, and if so, *how* shall we say it—in what tone, in what style, and in the silence of what others? Shall we say it in a tone of imagined transgression and in a spirit of left-wing liberation? (See site 6: http://www.arts.monash.edu.au/visarts/globe/teaks.html) This is the tone of farm boys in the big city for the night and the response of self-satisfied children who, having played with animals or played with themselves, delight in having disobeyed rules. These rules exist *not* to be obeyed but rather to be used as tools by those who disobey them in order to inscribe and striate themselves as disobedients and transgressors—disobedients whose very existence as such requires and supports, rather than undermines, these very rules. Shall we say it this way? No, say Deleuze and Guattari: "Of course, smooth spaces are not in themselves liberatory.... Never believe that a smooth space will suffice to save us."[12] The point of staff-blow philosophy, Deleuze observed, is to *sadden*[13]—to sadden and disillusion those who would disobey, transgress, and hammer rather than live and love more than all the world at/as/among the surfaces.

INTERRUPTION 1: THEORY IN PRACTICE, IN THEORY. Here is one of many entry points into the pointless and particularly tiresome exchange between self-styled critics (including many pragmatists) of Deleuze, much recent French philosophy more generally, or "postmodernism" more generally still—typically these critics are Anglo-American philosophers, conservative social contract "liberals," and universalistic critical theorists—and advocates, defenders, and fans of all things Deleuze, French, and postmodern. (See site 7: http://muse.jhu.edu/journals/postmodern_culture/v002/2.3 mccarthy.html) The form of this exchange is not complicated; it can be continued ad infinitum; it already has been continued ad nauseam. The critics charge that philosophy as art of surfaces is impotent for, or in, political practice. They claim that it undermines all justifications for social criticism; it relativizes and implicates all values in systems of powers, desirings, bodies, and knowledges; it offers no untainted ideals or even any prospects for such ideals; and it provides no support or hope for actual struggles without contradicting itself in so doing. Deleuze and Guattari admit, the critics proclaim, that "if abstract machines open assemblages they also close them."[14] (See site 8: http://substance.arts.uwo.ca/44/01dele~1.html) The defenders reply, usually in learned and serious scholarly essays and books, that Deleuze, French philosophy, or postmodernism really may be politically valuable. They claim it really can demystify; it can historicize and destabilize institutions and practices of domination and violence; it can make us aware of ways in which our values and meanings are implicated in these institutions and practices; and it may help create space, assemblages, and new maps of territories for change and future difference. When successful, all this establishes *in theory* the practical value of Deleuze (or French philosophy or postmodernism), just as it unifies theory and practice *in theory*. (See site 9: http://slought.net/toc/about/mission.php) At this point, of course, the critics repeat their charge, and this theoretical exchange begins another cycle. There is a need for a new sort of reply to these critics, a new and different kind of negotiation with these powers, a creative rather than interpretive response. A theory about theories as instruments is not necessarily an instrumental theory, just as a book about practice is not necessarily or automatically practical—at least not practical or productive in the way it intends. (See site 10: http://www.iath. virginia.edu/pmc/text-only/issue.592/add-ext.592)

Shall we then say that the perverse philosopher of the surface is a rhizome, an abstract machine, a mapper of lines of flight, a smooth space— you know, the whole party line—in a tone of overcoming, leaving behind, or evading, a style of not knowing *sadness*, perhaps even unwritten sadness, say it in the spirit of delivering, rather than receiving, a staff blow? To paraphrase Richard Nixon, we could do this, but it would be wrong—wrong not because it would be untrue, but wrong because it would be irrelevant, pointless. The point of a statement, Deleuze wrote (with little real novelty), is its novelty: "the problem isn't that some things are wrong, but that they're stupid or irrelevant. That they've already been said a thousand times. The notions of relevance, necessity, the point of something, are a thousand times more significant than the notion of truth."[15] Has *this* been said before? (Consider Deleuze as Emerson writing in his journal: "I hate quotations, tell me what you know.")

In what tone or style, from what place, and with what power, can one speak the nature of philosophy at the surface, at new surfaces? Hercules, the artist of surfaces, is silent. But, the traditional thinker, the thinker supposedly deep below or high above surfaces, will ask for something more, will ask the traditional questions.

For example, what exists, what is reality, what is substance, why is there being? Here the response must be: Be sad; do not ask. No more ontologies, just surfaces and their arts. If we must speak, let us say only that difference repeats and that every repetition is different. With William James, let us take apart the Problem of Being in just a few paragraphs.

But how does, or can, one know, be justified, gain the truth? In response: Be dismayed and forlorn; do not ask. No more epistemologies, just Stoics out for Herculean walks. If we must speak, say only, as Deleuze says, that we are empiricists, pluralists, radical empiricists, neutral monists. With John Dewey, let us retool and close down the epistemology industry and melt down its machines.

But, what is the being of an anti-ontology, the epistemic status of an anti-epistemology, the philosophical criteria of the adequacy of philosophical theory? In response: Be heartbroken and crushed; do not ask. No more meta-philosophies. If we must speak, let us say only that concepts of concepts are just concepts, just more concepts still at the surface, still among the surfaces. With George Santayana, let us set aside diversionary dreams of supposed self-reference and pretenses of interruptions of theory that are not just more theories still.

In short, no more ontology, no more epistemology, no more meta-philosophy. Let us take off these masks when we do politics. Jimi Hendrix at a Nietzschean surface: May you never hear surf music again. Instead, at the surface we have to say about Deleuze's perversion-philosophy just the sort of thing Deleuze himself said about progress in philosophy: There's no point at all doing philosophy the way Deleuze did (or Emerson did, or Dewey did, or others did), not because we've superseded Deleuze but because you can't supersede Deleuze, and it makes no sense to have another go at what he's done for all times. There's only one choice: doing the history of philosophy, or transplanting bits of Deleuze (or Emerson or Dewey or others) into problems that are no longer Deleuzian.[16]

Becoming-Transplanting-Deleuze

> The object of philosophy is to create concepts that are always new.... They must be invented, fabricated, or rather created and would be nothing without their creator's signature.... What would be the value of a philosopher of whom one could say, "He has created no concepts; he has not created his own concepts"? ... We always come back to the question of the use of this activity of creating concepts, in its difference from scientific or artistic activity. Why, through what necessity, and for what use must concepts, and always new concepts, be created?[17]

So here is a new Hercules, a perverse artistic Hercules, Hercules beyond heavy lifting, Hercules the Deleuzian creator, Hercules the different philosopher of the future. Isn't this Hercules, the philosopher of the surface—now the staff blow is readied—a person *for* whom an other cannot speak? Shall we speak *about* this philosopher, then, in a tone of not speaking *for* this philosopher?

Shall we speak this way: Deleuze refers not to an essence but rather to an operative function, to a trait. He endlessly produces. He does not invent from scratch: there are all kinds of materials imported and reconstructed from the Stoics, Spinoza, Leibniz, Nietzsche ... Yet Deleuze twists and turns, transforming them all the way to ... finitude.[18] (See site 11: http://www.techgnosis.com/muds.html)

1. Deleuze manufactures. He creates, recycles, melts down metals, forms anew, produces endlessly. He is a conceptual entrepreneur, eyeing new markets, new insertions, new serrations, plotting new ventures and product lines of flight, always creating new concepts, always producing anew, always reproducing. He is a reverse-Duchamp machine: instead of putting tools into museums as art, Deleuze removes museum pieces—paint, stone, music, words, signifiers—and makes them tools; not art found, but tools produced. What would be the value of an industrialist of whom one could say "Produced nothing"? Deleuze is a concept machine, a concept industry, a thought capitalist, the Henry Ford and Andrew Carnegie of concepts, Paris—the Pittsburgh of the mind, Deleuze the philosopher-capitalist of the modern industrial age, an age in which all artists need business plans and production schedules, an age in which major magazines owned by international communications, entertainment, and "edu-tainment" ventures chart the sales of "alternative" music, an age in which public university professors write in code to one another about subversion and transgression and the design of

information technology. (See site 12: http://www.altx.com/ebr/ebr2/
r2kirsch.htm)

2. It is an age that demands new products, more products, bigger, better,
today's creations, fresh, always new, cutting-edge, the latest creations.
Deleuze thus expresses the logic of capitalism—novelty, new creations,
always more and newer creations. The marketplace must expand, must
have new products. There must always be new creations. It is a supply-
side age, a supply-side philosophy: Invent new concepts, and new desires
and demands will follow. You've grown tired of yourself and all of your
creations? Of course. Yesterday's creations will not do today; you require
something new, something different. Deleuze with Kevin Costner in
the Iowa cornfields, in the field of dreams, the field of concepts. A new
creation? I must have it. An old creation? I must have a newer one. It is
a supply-side age, creating new needs, manufacturing new desires. The
product exists; therefore, I must have it. A new book? I must read it! I
consume; therefore I am. Descartes at the mall, at the warehouse store,
at Concepts-Я-Us, at Gilles's Club. Novelty is the point. Deleuze at
the MIT Artificial Intelligence Laboratory. (See site 13: http://www.ai.mit.
edu/)

3. But the point of modern industry and its culture is also that it is better
to be a producer than a consumer, better to be a creator, an artist, than
a ticket-taker (and better to take tickets than to sit in the audience). It
is age of classes. Better to be a hammer than a nail. Better to be an
exporting than an importing state, better to be an exporting than an
importing machine. A new book? I must not be captured by it. The great
machines are great exporters. Let me live in a state with a high gross
national product. Let me work in a humanities department with a high
gross conceptual output. Let me be a productive scholar. Who has not
read a cv like a balance sheet, or regarded scholarly citations like money
in the bank? Deleuze was/is rich, a strong balance of trade, a First World
machine with a clear message: Don't run a trade deficit; make sure that
others use your products, your concepts, more than you use theirs. Make
their products your own, retool endlessly: Deleuze's Stoics, Deleuze's
Hume, Deleuze's Kafka. Concepts are tools. You must create your own
concepts. You must own the means of your own production. Masters
depend on slaves only in the abstract dialectic, only in the works of the
great fiction writers, only "once upon a time . . . " At the surface, masters
dominate slaves. At the surface, the real concrete surface, the master
recognizes that being master is a power (relation) to produce and
inscribe, independent of any recognition by the slave, to inscribe on
the slave, on the body of the slave. Be all the abstract machine that you

can be, or (in their later slogan) be an army machine of one. Join the bourgeoisie. Create the concepts. Own the production process. Be the production process. Drink Coca-Cola. Philosophy, Deleuze and Guattari note, "has not remained unaffected by the general movement that replaced Critique with sales promotion" and turned concepts into products that can be sold, product displays.[19]

PROBLEM V. When is a concept not a product display? Have Deleuze and Guattari remained unaffected, alone escaped?

PROBLEM VI. What are the consequences of a dream of pure, smooth concepts that are not product displays. For what products is this dream an advertisement?

PROPOSITION XII (Again). Capture.

4. Deleuze produces concepts. Concepts are machines. Deleuze manufactures concepts of machines, concepts of concepts as machines. He is a machine, a machine-producing machine. He produces assemblies, assembles endlessly. Everywhere there are new assembling machines, new assemblages of machines, rhizome machines, modern transnational industries crisscrossing borders and making new borders, invading and reterritorializing, surface weeds, imperialist rhizomes, concept kudzu, spreading into new markets, merging into new machines, resonating across government-military-industry-education multiplicities, linking to human intelligence and covert action resources on the Internet. (See site 14: http://www.fas. org/irp/wwwspy.html) There are machines everywhere: machines, linked endlessly to other machines, following lines of flight, shaping events, linked by movable bridges between surfaces, always reterritorializing, always reproducing, always creating. Pan-psychism is an old (and not very good) story in philosophy. *Pan-machinism* is a newer story; Deleuze is a *pan-machinist.*

On the Superiority of American Philosophy

It is the same in philosophy as in a film or a song: no correct ideas, just ideas. . . . You should not try to find out whether an idea is just or correct. You should look for a completely different idea, elsewhere, in another area, so that something passes between the two which is neither in one nor the other.[20]

Despite the Deleuzian demand for novelty, pan-machinism is not a brand-new story. It is a repetition, if, of course, a difference. Pan-machinism is pragmatism, a minor philosophy (is this phrase redundant yet?). Deleuze is a pragmatist, he repeats/differs pragmatism. Recognizing the superiority of American literature, remarking on the fact that American philosophy is so poorly understood in France[21] (and by American "French" philosophers), recognizing that American philosophy had no need to detour through Nietzsche, Deleuze embodies American pragmatic philosophy. He is a pragmatist. Here is a largely unscratched site, a dissertation-free surface, territories for vast future research programs that develop this linkage:

1. Deleuze as Emerson: Philosophy as creation, self-reliance, and an original relation with the universe; the repudiation of travel and the view of the nomad as one who settles into place, refusing to disappear;[22] the intimate connections between philosophy and nationality, philosophy and place, surface and striations—a geophilosophy that delivers history from necessity to contingency and transcendence to differences and ordinariness.
2. Deleuze as James: Pan-machinism as empiricism, as radical empiricism; empiricism as pluralism, as neutral monism—"I have always felt that I am an empiricist, that is a pluralist";[23] anti-Hegelianism, and the recognition of idealism and dialectics as illness; the focus on consequences, last things, productions, and concrete multiplicities; relevance, not truth.
3. Deleuze as Dewey: Philosophy as criticism, as the attempt to dissolve and get behind old problems rather than provide better or final answers; philosophy as reconstruction and reterritorialization, and evaluations as ways of being; the focus on the art of constructing or determining a problem, and philosophy as the elaboration of a question and its implications;[24] the contrast between philosophy and the history of philosophy; the subject as a product, a self that does not have a history but is a history; the rejection of dualisms; the awareness of links between reconstruction in philosophy and reconstruction in society, pan-machinic pragmatism as instrumentalism.

And yet . . . pragmatism surely has been a philosophy of communication. It has been a philosophy of community, of community as the principle of democracy. It has appeared to be a repudiation of Stoicism in its demand to remake the world and in its insistence that to be different is not necessarily to be better. As Deleuze wrote in the context of his own conception of philosophy as creation rather than philosophy as communication, as guerrilla campaign rather than community, and as Stoic rather than recon-structive, "philosophy needs a nonphilosophy that comprehends it."[25] Today, classical American pragmatism has no such nonphilosophy, no such larger cultural climate. Instead there are the guerilla campaigns of information warfare, information security, and dominant battlefield knowledge, new forms of communication based on a new premise: "The world isn't run by weapons anymore, or energy, or money. It's run by little ones and zeros, little bits of data. It's all just electrons. . . . There's a war out there . . . and it's not about who's got the most bullets. It's about who controls the informa-tion. What we see and hear, how we work, what we think, it's all about infor-mation." (See site 15: http://www.fas.org/irp/wwwinfo.html)

Memo from the NRA (National Reterritorialization Association): Con-cepts don't communicate to people; people communicate to people. Still, as Deleuze observed chillingly, and as publications of the Institute for the Advanced Study of Information Warfare frequently echo (see site 16: http://www.psycom.net/iwar.1.html): "A concept always has the truth that falls to it as a function of the conditions of its creation."[26] Communica-tion, community, anti-Stoicism always have this truth, and this is some-thing that future pragmatism would do well to acknowledge and incorporate.

However, it is also something that pragmatism should transform. Imagine William Burroughs, staff in hand, playing back these words on one of his *Ticket that Exploded*[27] tape recorders. Imagine Hercules no longer listening, having given up, walking on, walking past it all, Hercules the concept junkie, strung out on Spinoza or Nietzsche or Deleuze, looking to himself for a connection, howling in the dawn and looking for a fix.

Masters without Control/Self Inscription

> You can always replace one word with another. If you don't like that one, if it doesn't suit you, take another, put another in its place. If each one of us makes this effort, everyone can understand one another and there is scarcely any reason to ask questions or to raise objections.[28]

All pan-machinist production is local; all production is geo-production. Producing concepts, perhaps replacing a word with another, where are we? What territory do we inhabit? A land of human rights, a particular state-site of the universal capitalist market, a place of immigrants and workers with dreams of democracy and socialism—dreams that Deleuze and Guat-tari say lead to the same disappointment?[29] A land in which the temptation of viewing philosophy as Western democratic conversation able to produce a consensus ethic and aesthetic makes possible the take-over of the creation of concepts by product design and marketing? A surface on which philosophers are left to conceive of revolution as self-referential and self-positing, "apprehended in an immanent enthusiasm without anything in states of affairs or lived experience being able to tone it down, not even the disappointments of reason" as this concept calls weakly for "a new earth, a new people."[30] A territory in which there are machines everywhere, machines warring (see site 17: http://www.ndu.edu/inss/actpubs/act003/ a003.html), machines producing, reassembling, rhizoming, machines producing . . . but what is this? Who's rhizoming who? Just say it isn't so, Gilles, say it isn't a land of machines producing *a lack*? Listen: "We lack resistance to the present"; we lack the new earth and people of the future; capitalism and democracy lack becoming, and becoming always eludes a majority.[31]

Amidst machines and products everywhere, we *lack*? Does not pan-machinism require courage, more courage: No more lacks, no more repressions, no more absences, no more interruption, no more deferments, no more loss—only creations, productions, assemblages. Even the rusted machines of a silent factory produce silence, as capitalist markets produce unemployment, schools produce drop-outs and the unschooled, and churches produce sinners. Is it any wonder that the Stoic staff-blow philosopher, summoning but unable to create a people, must have the strength of Hercules—the triple strength to endure a) the present, b) one's own lack of resistance to the present, and c) the lack of resistance to one's own concept of resistance, the concept of utopian becoming that is not of history?[32] If we keep in mind this feat of triple endurance, then with Deleuze and Guattari, we can grasp "that people whose preconscious investments of interest do not, or should not, go in the direction of capitalism, can maintain an unconscious libidinal investment consonant with capitalism, or that scarcely threatens it."[33]

"We lack resistance." Isn't the dream of resistance the dream of subterranean depths, a call to pre-Socratic subversion (and inversion: our depths as our skies, our hammers as our wings)? Is it any wonder that, at the surface, Hercules, busy stripping screw heads as young executives rush by, if he hears this call, must be stoic? Does he hear from the depths this call to resistance? "We moved too quickly," Deleuze admits importantly, "as we presented the Stoics challenging depth. . . ."[34] Noting that there are things within our power and things beyond our power, Epictetus outlines the depth of resistance, advising: "Demand not that events should happen as you wish; but wish them to happen as they do happen, and you will go on well."[35] Similarly, Aurelius says, "Things cannot in themselves touch the soul at all . . . it is the soul alone which deflects or moves itself and it fashions external events to depend upon the judgment which it deems itself worthy to make about them."[36] How can the event depend upon the judgment, how can the event that happens become the event one demands? To do this, Hercules must make representation a type of production, must make representation a kind of creation, must undertake what Deleuze calls a "use of representation," a doubling of physical causality, an ethics of the mime, must re-present the event not as that which occurs but as that which is inside what occurs. Hercules must descend into the depths to return to the surface: "It is always a question of cutting into the thickness, of carving out surfaces, of orienting them, of increasing and multiplying them in order to follow out the tracking of lines and of incisions inscribed on them."[37] Staff-blow philosophy cuts into thickness, brings depths to the surface, multiplies surfaces, tattoos, and inscribes bodies. Representation as Stoic creation, acceptance of one's fate as mastery of one's fate—see here the transcendentalists' old trick: representation without creation as colonization, communication as warfare, strategy without unintended consequences. (See site 18: http://www.ndu.edu/inss/acrpub/act003/a003ch02.html) See here the silence and complicity of the Stoics.

This silence expresses an ethic: "not to be unworthy of what happens to us."[38] It expresses a tranformative salvation: "the point at which death turns against death, where dying is the negation of death, . . . the moment when death loses itself in itself, and also the figure which the most singular life takes on in order to substitute itself for me."[39] Negation? Loss? Substitution? Perhaps we should not be surprised that Deleuze's Hercules is worn out and can labor no more at the surface. The load is heavy, the work is hard, and there are no moral holidays.

Though perhaps unintentional, this silence also expresses the new logic of control and the philosophy of the staff-blow masters without control. In Kafka's penal colony, a machine inscribed crimes on bodies. Though a wondrous assemblage, this machine was not without problems: it was difficult to maintain and not always reliable, could operate continuously for only twelve hours, and required the operations of other bodies to deliver its raw materials, set it in motion, and transport its products. In Deleuze's control society, today's societies, the machines are more sophisticated, more dependable, more efficient, more invisible. They are smooth. They are, in Burroughs's phrase, soft machines. (Deleuze's algebra of production is infinite; Burroughs's algebra of addiction is a zero-sum game.) *We* are these machines, these self-harrowing machines, these self-harrowing addicts. *We* now inscribe our crimes on our own bodies—continuously, efficiently, reliably. *We* are self-inscription industries, masters of inscription and the art of representation, inscribers without control.

Burroughs explained how this is done in terms of audiotape recorders, but today this control operates more frequently and fully by means of video-tape recorders and other newer technologies. This is not your parent's fascism[40] or your parent's panopticon: it is not a matter of being seen, but of seeing yourself being seen, of seeing yourself seeing yourself, a double seeing. Be worthy of how you are seen; be seen as worthy. Be your own panopticon. The smoothest form of control is self-control. See audience members viewing themselves being viewed during the performance of this chapter. See the NYU Ph.D. student viewing herself at her website's real-time broadcast of her writing her dissertation on the topic of auto-performance. See the office workers whose keyboard strokes are counted automatically and displayed on a monitor in a supervisor's office that is displayed on another monitor in front of the worker. See the trucker whose speed, mileage, and fuel use are continuously displayed in the cab next to a monitor that displays a dispatcher recording this data.

See the pedestrians and commuters watching storefront monitors displaying the storefront and street and the pedestrians themselves as filmed by police cameras mounted on building tops and sports stadiums. In Britain, for example, experts estimate that in 2001 an individual on average is filmed daily by as many as 300 different public-funded police surveil-lance cameras. Not counting the vast number of privately controlled cameras, the number of these police cameras is planned to double by 2004 as conventional closed-circuit television is rendered obsolete by new mobile phone technology and open-circuit monitoring systems with encrypted messages.[41] Outside of London, virtually every city center in Britain has its own closed-circuit television surveillance network. According to a 2000–01 estimate, there are more than 2.5 million surveillance cameras in Britain and lots and lots of public warning signs that announce "CCTV in oper-ation" and "CCTV: Watching for You!"[42]

As a result of the September 11, 2001 terrorist attacks in the United States, the Washington, D.C., Joint Operation Command Center of the Synchronized Operations Command Complex houses fifty officials who monitor forty video screens filled with images of travelers, residents, drivers, and pedestrians. With a zoom lens, the officials can focus on the face of anyone walking near the Washington Monument, Lincoln Memorial, or White House. The monitoring system is linked to 200 cameras in public schools, and another 200 cameras are planned for the Metro and public parks. Additional cameras operated by a private firm to catch cars running red lights will soon join the system. There are more cameras in banks and apartment lobbies, hallways, and elevators, and commercial cameras at stores and malls feed digital images of the faces of shoppers into the same system, from which they can be sent around the world at once. This system creates a digital library of hundreds of millions of faces—from terrorists to commuters, criminals to shoppers, sports fans to police, and professionals to children. This system, financed by more than $35 billion during the last two years, is increasingly able to identify, monitor, and track 300 million Americans and visitors.[43] Combined with scannable driver's licenses that provide personal information, generate electronic trails, and can contain digital fingerprints, signatures, and face recognition and other biometrics, Americans increasingly carry their own surveillance in their wallets and purses. Little of this is surprising because the cameras, signs announcing their use, and duplicate public monitors to demonstrate that use are increasingly common. Under this self-surveillance, we watch ourselves being watched.

See the surgeon look up from the operating table, seeing herself as she is recorded by a video camera utilized for possible legal or insurance action. See universities design evaluation processes in which faculty observe themselves being observed throughout an out-in-the-open evaluation process. It is not enough that I am evaluated, inscribed: the evaluators must see that I see them evaluating me, that I inscribe their evaluation process on myself, that I inscribe my evaluation process on myself. Be your own dean. Hammer away with a wrench.

What to do? Become a hammerer? To theorize transgression or change in a society or state that sanctions almost all theorizing is no transgression at all. When corruption takes on new forms and new powers,[44] these theorists are simply court jesters in the corporate take-over of education. Sometimes a wrench cannot do the job of a hammer. Become interdisciplinary? Interdisciplinarity presupposes rather than undercuts disciplines and disciplined self-harrowing. Sometime the novelty of stripping screw heads must wear off. Let us practice counter-disciplinarity. To become a hammerer, a thoroughgoing pan-machinist, even a pragmatist!

But, where then to begin? With ourselves, of course, ourselves already under way (there is no question of beginning), with surface productions and surface machines, military-industrial-information-market assemblages, machinic multiplicities and conspicuous production everywhere. This is no Stoic double or negation of death—Deleuze is dead, finally and fully dead. In response, in pragmatic response, might it be possible to produce a genuinely surface ethic, a genuinely strenuous ethic: To have nothing happen to us that is not worthy of us.

Here it may be tempting to say that we have lost our way. If so, we should resist this temptation, and instead say that we have *made* our way, and now *might* make other ways and other futures, futures not only different but, most of all, worthy of us. Along these ways, in these territories and at these surfaces, the tragic and ironic may give way to humor, the humor of genuine love and sadness, productive humor (see site 19: http://www.vr.net/~herzogbr/kafka/giveitup.htm), Kafka's humor (quoted at this site):

> It was very early in the morning, the streets clean and deserted, I was on my way to the railroad station. As I compared the tower clock with my watch I realized it was already much later than I had thought, I had to hurry, the shock of this discovery made me feel uncertain of the way, I was not very well acquainted with the town yet, fortunately there was a policeman nearby, I ran to him and breathlessly asked him the way. He smiled and said: "from me you want to learn the way?" "Yes," I said, "since I cannot find it myself." "Give it up, give it up," said he, and turned away with a great sweep, like someone who wants to be alone with his laughter.

In these territories, any of us who desires complete directions from someone else—like Kafa characters—can receive none. But we can receive without guilt and share the laughter that these requests must produce. Assemble this new desire: Putting it to the most ordinary uses, let us, Herculean, engage in this new criticism and this now rarely heard ordinary laughter.

Notes

1. Gilles Deleuze, "Control and Becoming," in *Negotiations: 1972–1990*, trans. Martin Joughin (New York: Columbia University Press, 1995 [*Pourparlers*, 1990]), pp. 174–175.
2. These Internet sites, a connected rhizome, move from entries on Deleuze to postmodern mechanospheres to information technologies to information security and control systems to information warfare to, finally, Kafka's policeman. They are referenced here by site address for readers of this essay to access where indicated in the text.
3. Readers should begin this recording at this point. Frank Zappa, "The Chrome Plated Megaphone of Destiny." Words by Frank Zappa, music by Frank Zappa and the Mothers of Invention. © 1968 Frank Zappa Music (BMI). Zappa issued written instructions to his prospective listeners that they must read Franz Kafka's "In the Penal Colony" before listening to this recording. I largely have completed or met these instructions for assembly, in live versions of this chapter at Penn State University, the University of Oregon, and Emory University, all of whose faculty and students have helped me finalize these format requirements.

4. See John Barth, "Author's Note," *Lost in the Funhouse: Fiction for Print, Tape, Live Voice* (New York: Bantam Books, 1968 [1969]), pp. ix–x.

5. Gilles Deleuze, "Intellectuals and Power: A Conversation between Michel Foucault and Gilles Deleuze," in Michel Foucault, *Language, Counter-Memory, Practice*, ed. Donald F. Bouchard (Ithaca, NY: Cornell University Press, 1977 [1972]), p. 208.

6. Gilles Deleuze, *The Logic of Sense*, ed., Constantin V. Boundas, trans. Mark Lester with Charles Stivale (New York: Columbia University Press, 1990 [*Logique du sens*, 1969]), pp. 130, 133.

7. See my "The Humanities, Inc.: Taking Care of Business" in *Genealogical Pragmatism: Philosophy, Experience, and Community* (Albany: State University of New York Press, 1997).

8. In chapters 12 and 13 of *A Thousand Plateaus: Capitalism and Schizophrenia*, trans. Brian Massumi (Minneapolis: University of Minnesota Press, 1987 [*Mille plateaux*, 1980), Gilles Deleuze and Felix Guattari state axioms, propositions, problems. They address three problems: 1) "Is there a way of warding off the formation of a State apparatus (or its equivalents in a group)?" (p. 356); 2) "Is there a way to extricate thought from the State model?" (p. 374); and 3) "How do the nomads invent or find their weapons?" (p. 403). My intention here is to add to their list.

9. Continuing, they state fourteen propositions: 1) "This exteriority [of the war machine to the State] is first attested to in mythology, epic, drama, and games" (p. 351); 2) "The exteriority of the war machine is also attested to by ethnology" (p. 357); 3) "The exteriority of the war machine is also attested to by epistemology, which intimates the existence and perpetuation of a 'nomad' or 'minor science'" (p. 361); 4) "The exteriority of the war machine is attested to, finally, by noology" (p. 374); 5) "Nomad existence necessarily effectuates the conditions of the war machine in space" (p. 380); 6) "Nomad existence necessarily implies the numerical elements of a war machine" (p. 387); 7) "Nomad existence has for 'affects' the weapons of a war machine" (p. 394); 8) "Metallurgy in itself constitutes a flow necessarily confluent with nomadism" (p. 404); 9) "War does not necessarily have the battle as its object, and more important, the war machine does not necessarily have war as its object, although war and the battle may be its necessary result (under certain conditions)" (p. 416); 10) "The State and its poles" (p. 424); 11) "Which comes first?" (p. 427); 12) "Capture" (p. 437); 13) "The State and Its forms" (p. 448); and 14) "Axiomatics and the present-day situation" (p. 460). Deleuze and Guattari, *A Thousand Plateaus*. See also p. 513.

10. Deleuze, "On Philosophy," *Negotiations*, p. 137.

11. Richard Brautigan, *The Abortion: An Historical Romance 1966* (New York: Simon and Schuster, 1970).

12. Deleuze and Guattari, *A Thousand Plateaus*, p. 500.

13. Gilles Deleuze, *Nietzsche and Philosophy* (New York: Columbia University Press, 1983 [*Nietzsche et la philosophie*, 1962]), p. 106.

14. Deleuze and Guattari, *A Thousand Plateaus*, p. 514.

15. Deleuze, *Negotiations*, p. 130.

16. This is a paraphrase of Deleuze's point about Plato, the history of philosophy, and progress in philosophy, *Negotiations*, p. 148.

17. Gilles Deleuze & Felix Guattari, *What is Philosophy?*, trans. Hugh Tomlinson and Graham Burchell (New York: Columbia University Press, 1994 [*Qu'est-ce que la philosophie?*, 1991]), pp. 5–6, 8.

18. See Gilles Deleuze, *The Fold: Leibniz and the Baroque*, trans. Tom Conley (Minneapolis: University of Minnesota Press, 1993 [*Le Pli: Leibniz et la baroque*, 1988]), p. 3.

19. Gilles Deleuze and Felix Guattari, *What Is Philosophy?*, p. 10.

20. Gilles Deleuze & Claire Parnet, *Dialogues*, trans. Hugh Tomlinson and Barbara Habberjam (London: The Athlone Press, 1987 [*Dialogues*, 1977]), pp. 9–10.

21. Gilles Deleuze and Guattari, *What Is Philosophy?*, p. 103.

22. Gilles Deleuze, *Negotiations*, pp. 137–138.

23. Gilles Deleuze and Claire Parnet, *Dialogues*, p. vii.

24. Gilles Deleuze, *Empiricism and Subjectivity: An Essay on Hume's Theory of Human Nature*, trans. Constantin V. Boundas (New York: Columbia University Press, 1991 [*Empirisme et subjectivite: Essai sur las nature humaine selon Hume*, 1953]), p. 106.

25. Deleuze and Guattari, *What Is Philosophy?*, p. 218.

26. *Ibid.*, p. 27.

27. William Burroughs, *The Ticket that Exploded* (New York: Grove Press, 1962), pp. 205–217.

28. Gilles Deleuze & Claire Parnet, *Dialogues*, p. 3.

29. Deleuze and Guattari, *What Is Philosophy?*, p. 98.

30. *Ibid.*, p. 101.

31. *Ibid.*, pp. 108–109.

32. *Ibid.*, p. 110.

33. Gilles Deleuze and Felix Guattari, *Anti-Oedipus: Capitalism and Schizophrenia*, trans. Mark Hurley, Mark Seem, and Helen Lane (Minneapolis: University of Minnesota Press, 1983 [*L'Anti-Oedipe*, 1972]), p. 374.

34. Gilles Deleuze, *The Logic of Sense*, p. 143.

35. Epictetus, *The Enchiridion* (New York: Bobbs-Merrill, 1948 [c. 123]), p. 20.

36. Marcus Aurelius, *The Meditations* (Indianapolis: Hackett Publishing, 1983 [c. 170], p. 44.

37. Gilles Deleuze, *The Logic of Sense*, p. 143.

38. *Ibid.*, p. 149.

39. *Ibid.*, p. 153.

40. Felix Guattari notes, "All over the world the totalitarian machine is experimenting to find the structures best suited to the situation, in other words, best fitted to capture desire and harness it to the profit economy. "The Micro-Politcs of Fascism" in *Molecular Revolution: Psychiatry and Politics* (New York: Penguin Books, 1984 [*Psychanalyse et transversalite*, 1972; *La Revolution moleculaire*, 1977], p. 229. In this light, consider this call from the head of the FBI's anti-cybercrime unit, a call for closer cooperation among federal agencies, corporate America, and the FBI-led multiagency National Infrastructure Protection Center: "Information warfare is obvi-

ously something the United States, the National Security Council, The Department of Defense, the CIA, the FBI and our private-sector partners are very concerned with." *International Herald Tribune*, 21 March 2001, p. 18.

41. *London Times*, 11 March 2001, section 1, p. 10.
42. Jeffrey Rosen, "A Watchful State," *New York Times Magazine*, 6 January 2002, p. 92.
43. William Safire, "The Great Unwatched vs. the Age of Surveillance," *New York Times*, 18 February 2002, p. A19.
44. See Deleuze's "Postscript on Control Societies" in *Negotiations*, pp. 177–182.

CHAPTER 6

From Consciousness of Doom to Criticism: Non-Dialectical Critical Theory

Great Opportunity Awaits[1]

What if female members of a militant German political group had not stormed Theodor Adorno's lecture podium, removed their clothes, embarrassed him by mock-attacking him with flowers, and humiliated him by mock-erotic caresses? What if they had not proclaimed from the podium that Adorno was dead? What if Adorno had not found himself required to respond to his critics that he could not have guessed that people would want to put his theory into practice by means of Molotov cocktails and terrorism? What if Habermas had not called Adorno's philosophy "a strategy of hibernation"? What if critical theory after, or for that matter before, Adorno had never attempted to base itself in universal knowledge constitutive interests or ideal speech conditions or necessary communicative competencies or any other supposed subject whose constitution independent of history is possible only on the basis of a transcendental philosophy of identity that Adorno rejected? What if the philosophical spirit of our age had not been constituted jointly by "the philosophically dubious cult of primordiality practiced by Heidegger," a "reverentially conceptless, passive hearkening to a Being that always speaks Being, without any right to critique anything that can appeal to the shimmering mightiness of Being," and, on the other hand, the positivism that expresses the "reified consciousness of uninspired bright boys" with "a reverence for reified reality" viewed as the criterion of its own truth?[2] And, what if, as the American television program *Saturday Night Live* used to ask, Eleanor Roosevelt had been a B-52 plane, flying over Germany in World War II, her arms outstretched, dropping bombs? Would war have ended sooner? Would we now make theories and bombs from the standpoint of redemption? Would we believe in any standpoint of redemption, safe from "perversion into delusion," happily theorizing with "a spontaneous relation to the object?"[3] Would critical theory have become true?

Hope

Some philosophers believe that they should strive above all else not so much to produce concepts or make life more significant but rather to hold true beliefs, assert true propositions, and write books filled with truth. They think, moreover, that good philosophers not only strive for truth but that they succeed in this task most or much of the time, regularly holding true beliefs and frequently speaking and writing and otherwise asserting propositions that are true. Of course, these philosophers recognize that holding true beliefs or asserting true propositions may have, just incidentally, a critical dimension or serve a critical function sometimes or even all the time. Nonetheless, on this view, the proper, ultimate concern of philosophers is truth, truth *qua truth* rather than truth *qua criticism*.

Claiming that truth is objective rather than warranted assertibility or plausibility,[4] Adorno, of course, may be viewed as one of these philosophers. From this perspective—in which the search for truth is the goal of philosophy, and the attainment of truth is the measure of success in philosophy—it unhappily may seem that today there is vastly more criticism than truth. After all, there is today no shortage of criticism—for instance, "Kill faggots," or "*Being and Time* is a fascist ontology," "Free Tibet," "Popular music is shallow and unintelligent," "Abortion is murder," "the whole is false,"[5] "Adorno's philosophy ends only in pessimistic resignation," "I don't like the way this chapter is beginning so far," and so on. For these truth-seekers and some others, fortunately for other reasons, criticism is not enough. Instead, on this view, if anyone is going to be concerned with criticism, then it will have to be true criticism, criticism that arises from true belief, criticism carried forward by assertion of true propositions, criticism for which there are and continue to be evidence and argument that demonstrate its truth, criticism that is both valued for and justified ultimately by its truth, criticism that can be redeemed, criticism with a little tag in its pocket certifying that it has been passed by truth inspectors certified by the truth industry, the industry that produces, in Horkheimer's distinction, that new-fangled critical theory rather than old-fashioned traditional theory.

Is it time at last to bring these stars down to earth? And, if so, what are the prospects for this task? For example, "3 December (Aquarius): Make more happiness by more interesting gadgets . . ."[6]

Consider, then, this gadget or tool: "If P, then Q." Following the many mystic analysts and religious thinkers who call themselves logicians, whenever "P" is false then "If P, then Q" is true. Regardless of "Q," if "P" is false, then "If P, then Q" is true. (There are truth tables for this, but there are no criticism tables.) This gadget presents a limitless opportunity, at least in theory, for philosophers (and others) to believe and assert the truth. One need only speak in conditionals, being careful to ensure that the antecedent is false. A kind of conceptual assembly line, this can revolutionize the truth industry and its productivity. For example, if Eleanor Roosevelt had been a B-52, the Allies would have won the war sooner. Or if the goal of philosophy is practical and objective, then we require a new dialectic of theory and practice. Or if criticism of immanence objectively can escape being mere further immanence, we require a new dialectic of immanence and transcendence. Or if concepts in principle are not adequate to objects and their objective truth, then we require a new dialectic of subject and object. Or, just possibly, "if you believe there's nothing up their sleeve, then nothing is cool."[7]

Bring My Happy Back Again

Recall Marx's last thesis on Feuerbach: "The philosophers have only *interpreted* the world, in various ways; the point, however, is to *change* it."[8] It is from this standpoint, of course, that Adorno typically has been dismissed. According to so many of his commentators—a group that, on their own terms, appears devoted more to interpretation and theory than to practice—Adorno's critical theory possibly may have changed interpretation of the world, but definitely did not change the world itself and, indeed, is impotent to do so. In short, so the charge goes: too much theory, too little practice. This judgment presupposes views about the nature of theory, the nature of practice, and the relationship between theory and practice. From his early to his last writings, Adorno called such presuppositions into question. In "Why Still Philosophy," Adorno observed that "anyone who still philosophizes can do so only by denying the Marxist thesis that reflection has become obsolete." He continued: "Praxis, whose purpose is to produce a rational and politically mature humanity remains under the spell of disaster unless it has a theory that can think the totality in its untruth" (WSP, p. 14). What is a theory that *can* think the totality in its untruth? What is a theory that *desires* to think the totality in its untruth? What, then, is the meaning of "theory" for critical theory, and, in turn, what makes this theory "critical"—in theory and/or in practice? And, in contrast, what might be a different kind of theory, a new kind of theory, a more Herculean theory that can think the untruth of thinking the totality in its untruth?

Sad Professor

"People even of supposedly 'normal' mind," Adorno observed in "The Stars Down to Earth," his extended analysis of an astrology column in the *Los Angeles Times*, "are prepared to accept systems of delusions for the simple reason that it is too difficult to distinguish such systems from the equally inexorable and equally opaque one under which they actually have to live out their lives" (SDE, p. 115). Is critical theory, in some or all of its many varieties, a system of delusions, an invention of sad professors designed to float their malcontent?[9] If so, by means of what theoretical or practical project could this be demonstrated? And by whom and from what position and by means of what power?

In advance, what would be the forecast for such a project? "31 January, Sagittarius: Early in the A.M. a prophetic hunch requires that you contact a powerful person who is able to make your inspiration a success. Be exact all through the day" (SDE, p. 48).

Furthermore, if critical theory were to be demonstrated a system of delusions, would this demonstration itself constitute the project of a kind of critical theory, perhaps a new kind of critical theory? In any such new critical theory, would the notion of a system of delusions and the notion of a demonstration of a system of delusions be themselves delusions, and so something other than, something more productive than, delusions? If so, would this shatter the hidden happiness of sad professors, the optimism (beneath all expressions of pessimism and gloom) that perhaps history is on one's side, the dream of a theory with a spontaneous relation to the object, the dream of an objective truth, the dream of complete communication, the dream of contemplation from the standpoint of redemption,"[10] and the longing for that future redemption?

What might the future bring? "10 November, Sagittarius: Get away from that concern that seems to have no solution." "14 November, Sagittarius: Old desires, old acquaintances seem for the moment pretty unsatisfactory." "21 November, Sagittarius: Harassed friends try to pull you down to their level; ambitions seem a long way off" (SDE, p. 80).

Can critical theory negate itself, stop taking comfort in the fact that it does not take comfort in its own idea, stop confining itself to self-satisfied contemplation of its own lack of satisfaction? Can it enlist negation in the service of a suspension of objectification and a non-dialectical criticism? If Eleanor Roosevelt had been a B-52, then these would be requirements that a future, genuinely pragmatic critical theory would give itself.

You're in the Air

From the early days of the Frankfurt School, critical theory called into question the nature of theory and practice and, so, the relation of theory to practice. In his effort to address this question, Adorno explored the nature of immanence and transcendence and, so, the relation of immanence to transcendence in criticism. In an effort to address and overcome what he took to be limits of immanent criticism, Adorno examined the nature of subject and object and, so, the relation of subject to object. Asking "What is theory?" Horkheimer in 1937 differentiated traditional theory, theory that first constructs goals that practice then strives to achieve, from critical theory, theory that cannot identify its goals until they actually are achieved.[11] But if critical theory does not identify in advance goals for practice, how is it possible, and, if possible, what would be its relation to, and value for, practice? Horkheimer wrote:

> If we think of the object of the [critical] theory in separation from the theory, we falsify it and fall into quietism or conformism. Every part of the theory presupposes the critique of the existing order and the struggle against it along lines determined by the theory.... The characteristic mark of the [critical] thinker's activity is to determine for itself what it is to accomplish and serve, and this not in fragmentary fashion but totally. (CCS, pp. 229, 242–243)

However, this begs the question: How does critical theory determine its object and the lines of a struggle? How can critical theory determine its own goals—that is, be self-determining—unless one thinks of the particular objects of critical theory in separation from that theorizing: something Horkheimer explicitly said must not be done? If theory is to be critical (rather than traditional), it cannot view the activity of criticism in separation from the object of criticism. This shows that critical theory cannot be transcendent criticism. Yet, if theory is critical (rather than traditional), if the activity of criticism is not wholly separated from its object, theory participates and is complicit in the existing order against which it would and must struggle. This shows that immanent criticism cannot be critical theory.

It will be said, it has been said: Only a dialectic can save us now.

Suspicion

In a brilliant essay, "Cultural Criticism and Society," Adorno recognized and concisely confronted this problem. He sought to address it by distinguishing *cultural* criticism, which shares the blindness of its object and remains subservient to its culture as it confronts it with its own norms, from *dialectical* criticism, which "heightens cultural criticism until the notion of culture is itself negated, fulfilled and surmounted in one" (CCS, pp. 27–28, 29). Is dialectical criticism, then, transcendent theory? It may seem so. For instance, Adorno did write that a position of transcendence, a position that seems more radical than one of immanence, "is in a certain sense presupposed by dialectics as the consciousness which does not succumb in advance to the fetishization of the intellectual sphere." However, if dialectics requires a consciousness that does not succumb to the culture it would criticize, it remains the case that there is no culture-transcendent position for this consciousness to occupy, that there is no possibility for the existence of this sort of consciousness. (This does not mean, of course, that there is no possibility for the desire, indeed strong desire, for the existence of this sort of consciousness.) Accordingly, "The choice of a standpoint outside the sway of existing society is as fictitious as only the construction of abstract utopias can be. Hence the transcendent criticism of culture, much like bourgeois cultural criticism, sees itself obliged to fall back upon the idea of 'naturalness'. . . . " Rejecting this German "nature-boy" view from nowhere," Adorno claimed dialectical criticism is more essentially immanent than transcendent. This criticism analyzes the form and meaning of cultural phenomena in an effort to determine the contradiction between their objective idea and their pretension to correspond to reality. Adorno wrote: "Such criticism does not stop at a general recognition of the servitude of the objective mind, but seeks rather to transform this knowledge into a heightened perception of the thing itself" (CCS, pp. 31–32).

Here it is worth outlining a future research program of immanent criticism of these judgments of so-called dialectical criticism. Why, for example, is a transcendent standpoint supposedly *outside* of, and unpolluted by, the sway of existing society philosophically more problematic than an immanent standpoint committed to a recognition of a supposedly *objective* mind? Why, further, is a presupposition by transcendent criticism of an *idea of nature* philosophically more problematic than a presupposition by immanent criticism of supposed *things-in-themselves*? Did his view of subject and object allow Adorno to avoid having to raise these kinds of difficult challenges to his notion of dialectical criticism? If so, how?

Adorno provided a first glimpse of his responses to these questions in his recognition that "immanent criticism cannot take comfort in its own idea." He wrote that immanent criticism can neither be vain enough to believe that it can liberate the mind directly by immersing itself in it, nor naïve enough to believe that unflinching immersion in the object will inevitably lead to truth by virtue of the logic of things if only the subjective knowledge of the false whole is kept from intruding from the outside, as it were, in the determination of the object. (CCS, p. 33)

Still the problem remains: Transcendent criticism appears impossible, deluded; immanent criticism appears unsuccessful, doomed.

There "must" be a solution, Adorno explained, or at least the possibility of a solution. Because dialectical criticism rejects the identity of subject and object, it must "be mindful of the duality of moments," "must relate the knowledge of society as a totality and of the mind's involvement in it to the claim inherent in the specific content of the object that it be apprehended as such," must reserve the right to go from transcendence to immanence, from one genus of criticism to another, must "subscribe neither to the cult of the mind nor to hatred of it, must both participate in culture and not participate." Only then, Adorno concluded, does the dialectical critic do justice to one's object and one's self (CCS, p. 33). Better guarantee the truth of this critical theory: If Eleanor Roosevelt had been a B-52, only then does the dialectical critic do justice to one's object and one's self. Of course, without an adequate account of subject and object, this claim about doing justice to one's object and one's self simply begs the question again.

And You Want to Bridge the Schism

If critical theory cannot generate goals for practice from a standpoint supposedly outside culture and cannot accept goals generated from a standpoint merely inside culture (that is, some specific culture), can critical theory generate goals for practice through a dialectic standpoint both/neither/other than outside and inside culture? Would it help to write this—outside-and-inside-culture—with hyphens? How can critical theory form itself, how can it analyze its own self-formation as that which cannot determine "for itself what it is to accomplish and serve and this not in fragmentary fashion but totally"? In his dense late essay "Subject and Object," Adorno noted that neither subject nor object can be grasped independently of the other: something is an object only for a subject who considers it from a particular perspective, and something is a subject only in reference to something objective, a general concept, that makes possible the identification or naming of that individual. As a result, any attempt to define subject and object seems already to presuppose an account of subject and object: "Defining means that something objective, no matter what it may be in itself, is subjectively captured by means of a fixed concept. Hence the resistance to defining subject and object."[12] Adorno demanded that the reciprocity or tension between subject and object be retained and retained as irreducible. This demand is not always clearly or consistently set forth in the earlier *Negative Dialectics.* In many passages in this book, Adorno appeared to give priority and preponderance to the object: "To be an object is part of the meaning of subjectivity; but it is not equally part of the meaning of objectivity to be a subject" and "What mediates the facts is not so much the subjective mechanism of their preformation and comprehension as it is the objectivity heteronomous to the subject, the objectivity behind that which the subject can experience."[13] Even so, he added: "That the object takes precedence even though indirect itself does not cut off the subject-object dialectics. Immediacy is no more beyond dialectics than is mediation" (*ND*, p. 186). And in "Subject and Object," he noted: "If the subject does have an objective core, the object's subjective qualities are so much more an element of objectivity."[14] Finally, anticipating the temptation to grasp subject and object non-dialectically, Adorno cautioned that "the polarity of subject and object may well appear to be an undialectical structure in which all dialectics takes place. But the two concepts are resultant categories of reflection, formulas for an irreconcilability; they are not positive, primary states of fact but negative throughout, expressing nothing but nonidentity. Even so, the difference between subject and object cannot be simply negated. They are neither an ultimate duality nor a screen hiding ultimate unity. They constitute one another as much as—by virtue of such constitution—they depart from one another" (*ND*, p. 174). Accordingly, Adorno frequently leveled immanent criticism at subjective philosophies from Kant to Hegel to Kierkegaard to Heidegger, and objective philosophies from positivism to sociology, for preventing their own theories from critically appropriating their own self-formation.

And You Want to Go Forever

This analysis of subject and object reorients critical theory: To maintain dialectical non-identity between subject and object, critical theory must reach objectivity *through* subjectivity; to maintain dialectical non-identity between immanence and transcendence, critical theory must reach transcendence *through* immanence; and to maintain dialectical non-identity between theory and practice, critical theory must reach practice *through* theory. Critical theory must heighten subjectivity, immanence, and theory until they are negated, fulfilled, and surmounted in one.

To maintain a dialectical non-identity of the culture industry and critical theory, must critical theory reach for itself *through* the culture industry? And, if so, would the culture industry, negated, fulfilled, and surmounted, become critical theory or critical practice or just a different culture industry itself—with critical theory as one of its new products?

If we falsify critical theory by thinking of its object in separation from the theory, do we not also falsify critical theory by thinking of the theory in separation from its object? Here, briefly put, is the problem: If the dialectical relation, the relation of non-identity, between subject and object is irreducible and guaranteed, why would there be any reason to worry, as Adorno did, about the possibility of the absolute reification of mind, the removal of the conditions of possibility for critical theory? Dialectics, Adorno wrote, names this irreducibility, this guarantee, this fact: "objects do not go into their concepts without remainder"; dialectics "indicates the untruth of identity, the fact that the concept does not exhaust the thing conceived"; it is "the consistent sense of nonidentity" (*ND*, pp. 5–7). This is the "pragmatic" value of Adorno's account of subject and object: It provides the permanent possibility or freedom for consciousness to transcend the immanence of culture, the freedom for transcendence without which Adorno did not think it possible to conceive criticism (CCS, p. 29).

How, then, can there ever be a final stage of the dialectic of culture and barbarism, a completely administered world? This could happen only if the concept is, or became, adequate to its object. Despite what Adorno claimed, however, the concept *can* be, and frequently is, adequate to its object because its object is the conceptualized object, the object of reflection, the object of theory. A concept's object is produced, not discovered, by conceptualization. The fact that subject and object are not identical does not establish that objects do not go into their concepts without remainder; it establishes only that concept and object are not identical. The absence of identity need not be the absence of adequacy. More important, however, the untruth of identity is not the truth of non-identity. Subject and object are not non-identical. Instead, they are different.

Adorno called dialectics the consistent sense of non-identity, but non-identity is only difference under the form of identity.

Non-dialectical criticism would be the consistent sense of difference under forms of differences, multiplicities, pluralities.

The inadequacies of the concepts of a non-dialectical criticism would not be measured by the inability of this criticism to reach the supposedly non-conceptual, but rather by its inability, if any, to imagine different concepts by means of a wholly immanent imagination. How would such a non-dialectical critical theory, refusing to think of its object in separation from itself, determine for itself what it is to accomplish and serve? Why conceptualize an object one way or another, if the object really is not one way or another separate from, or transcendent of, this conceptualization? A non-dialectical critical theory must answer this question in terms of desire and will rather than truth and intellect. "Whatever wants nothing to do with the trajectory of history belongs all the more truly to it" (WSP, p. 17), Adorno observed. Yes, but whatever wants everything to do with the trajectory of possibility belongs all the less to it. Under the form of dialectics, negative dialectics is non-dialectical thought. Critical philosophy—criticism—now must reject this form.

Imagine something different. If you want, you can capitulate and imagine something true: If Eleanor Roosevelt had been a B-52, an immanent criticism of negative dialectics would lead to the negation of dialectics. Here philosophy's antidote is not any "disenchantment of the concept," but instead disenchantment with any dialectic of concepts.

Negated Dialectics

Critical theory, which once seemed promising, lies dead because the moment to miss it was realized. The summary judgment that it had really grounded criticism of the world, that confidence in reason in the face of relativism and reification had justified itself, becomes a mistaken optimism of reason after the attempt to change criticism of the world miscarried. Critical theory offers no place from which practice as such might be concretely convicted of the trendiness it is suspected of, now as before. Perhaps it was an inadequate interpretation which promised that it would ground practice. Practice can eliminate the moments its critique depends on. A theory continuously deployed is now the forum for appeals by self-satisfied practice; it is a small justification used by savant authorities to nourish, as necessary, whatever philosophy the theoretical changes would require. Having kept its pledge to remain separate from reality or at the point of realization, critical theory is free to ruthlessly transform itself, to become non-dialectical.[15]

Consciousness of Doom

"Even the most extreme consciousness of doom," Adorno observed, "threatens to degenerate into idle chatter" (CCS, p. 34). Can a non-dialectical critical philosophy escape this fate?[16] Taking this worry seriously, Adorno and Horkheimer may have been too optimistic in thinking that consumers see through the products—at least the intellectual products—they nonetheless feel compelled to buy in the culture industries today. In the same way, it is possible to be too optimistic in believing that philosophers see through both the traditional and the critical theories that they seem compelled to manufacture and sell in the culture industry's concept division and in academic marketplaces. Can criticism now, even non-dialectical criticism, be anything other than an exercise in marketing for some new intellectual products, some new line of academic disposables, some new and improved, lots more comfortable, pleasantly ahistorical and soon obsolete, original relation to the universe? Must a critic today be a merchant, a huckster of mass culture, hawking theory, chattering not so idly and hoping to entice the window-shoppers inside to make a purchase, to buy whatever the critic is selling, to take home some new system or anti-system system, to have the latest concept from Paris or Pittsburgh, to be the first one in the neighborhood to own the future of philosophy or this year's model new lands, new men and women, new thoughts?

Pragmatism and Philosophy as Criticism

William James proclaimed that pragmatism is the future of philosophy. But is it? And, if so, what pragmatism, which pragmatism? And what future? Does philosophy in fact have a future—whether as pragmatism, critical theory, Marxism, Hegelianism, or something else? If, with John Dewey and others (in America, Europe, and elsewhere) philosophy is defined as criticism, as criticism of criticism, a particular type of criticism, then this question becomes the question of whether criticism does in fact have a future. In what relation would future criticism stand to practice—to specific historical, local, plural practices? In what relation would this philosophy as criticism stand to other disciplines—to literature, law, history, the human sciences, for example? In what relation does this criticism stand to its most common institutional home or setting—the university? And in what relations does it stand to each of us personally—to the ways in which we lead our lives? Is philosophy as criticism really a way of life, or just, if one is fortunate, a way to make a living or a quaint hobby, a marketing plan for the self, an absorbing diversion from absorption? Taking seriously these worries and putting aside stories of fictional dialectics, is it possible to think and live critically?

To the extent it is possible, thinking and living critically has pragmatic value just because life does not automatically and endlessly satisfy our desires or conform itself to our values. This was Dewey's point, of course, when he defined philosophy as criticism in the final chapter of *Experience and Nature*. Moreover, life also teaches that efforts to reach goals often fail and that goals, once reached, often are not as satisfying as anticipated. If we were better suited to this life, criticism would be unnecessary, critical reflection would be irrelevant, and the very idea of a genuinely pragmatic philosophy would be self-contradictory.

Criticism is the attempt to bring intelligence to bear on just this situation. It is the ongoing effort to realize in our lives (and not just in our philosophies) values that are more illuminating, more inclusive, and more sustaining.

The view that philosophy is criticism is not a new story. It is not new with Adorno and Horkheimer, Dewey, Foucault, Marx, Hegel, or Kant. If philosophy is love of wisdom—surely an old story in Western philosophy—then criticism is simply this love in practice. This is why Dewey, late in his life, linked the future of philosophy as pragmatism to a "back to Socrates" movement.

What Is Criticism?

Dialectics, Adorno wrote, is "self-consciousness of the objective context of delusion; it does not mean to have escaped from that context. Its objective goal is to break out of the context from within" (*ND*, p. 406). In contrast, Dewey viewed criticism very differently, taking neither the context of delusions nor the goals of critical thought as objective. This nondialectical critical theory contains four points that merit special attention and use today.

First, critical intent is not enough. Critical theory may be distinguished from traditional theory, as Horkheimer did, by mere critical intent *only in theory*. Similarly, genuinely pragmatic reflection, reflection that is actually critical, can be distinguished from idle speculation by mere critical intent *only in theory*. Criticism is as criticism does, and so critical theory, if it is to be critical in anything besides name, requires critical function, critical effect. As pragmatism instructs, we should look away from first things and beginnings to last things and consequences. In social and political philosophy, as much as in aesthetic theory, the intentional fallacy really is a fallacy.

Second, as I have argued elsewhere,[17] criticism in part must be genealogical. It must address how we have come to hold our present values, how our present institutions and practices have come to be, whose present interests are addressed, heard, and served, and what subjects—you and me and others—have been constituted. Insufficient attention to these issues, and to their implications for thinking about them and for living after and in light of them, is one of the real weak spots in much pragmatism. It is not enough, for example, to define critical inquiry as the transformation of an indeterminate situation or the resolution of a problem situation. We must ask: Whose indeterminate situation? Whose determinate problem? Whose resolution? How and by whom were they identified as such? What made this possible, and what consequences were produced? Today, a critical pragmatism must turn itself on its own best-known account of inquiry.[18]

Third, criticism in part also must be instrumental, productive, a tool. Genealogy may situate and so destabilize, but this by itself is not enough—and any destabilizing of something is a new stabilizing of something else. This may clear a place for instrumental reflection, by occupying another place, but to be instrumental it is necessary to begin to articulate an alternative and to devise means to achieve this alternative. It must include, in Dewey's language, a valuation: the identification of an end in view and inquiry into the means (and, in turn, the value of the means) existentially necessary for this end. Criticism, that is, requires vision and strategy. Without strategy, criticism is simply either wishful thinking for the double negation that is synthesis in which reality is reduced to logic, or longing for pure negation in which thinking is unaware of what it posits, produces, effects as it hesitates, interrupts, undoes. Without vision, criticism aims at mere change and difference rather than amelioration and betterness. In the millennium after Dewey, the point of new criticism (if not also old theses on philosophers) is neither simply to interpret nor simply to change the world. The point is to improve it.

Fourth, this highlights the central role that imagination should play in criticism. In historicizing the present, genealogical inquiry can free this imagination, can allow it to refocus from the actual to the ideal (that is an ideal always and only from the standpoint of some actual situation), from what is to what should be, and from our selves to their remaking. It is in this context, I believe, that James declared vision the great fact about persons (even philosophers) and that Dewey observed that we live as persons only in the imagination.

Supposed Transcendence and the Basis of Criticism

James thought that in practice even Hegel was a pragmatist who provided us a critical philosophy without transcendence. In *A Pluralistic Universe,* James wrote:

[Hegel] clung fast to the old rationalist contempt for the immediately given world of sense and all its squalid particulars, and never tolerated the notion that the form of philosophy might be empirical only. His own system had to be a product of eternal reason, and so the word "logic," with its suggestions of coercive necessity, was the only word he could find natural. He pretended therefore to be using the a priori method, and to be working by a scanty equipment of ancient logical terms—position, negation, reflection, universal, particular, individual, and the like. But what he really worked by was his own empirical perceptions, which exceeded and overflowed his miserably insufficient categories in every instance of their use.[19]

Imaginative critical activity is, of course, the activity of some actual person or persons. Like persons, it is historically situated. Indeed, because history provides criticism its subject matter, it is only in virtue of the irreducible historicity of experience that criticism is possible. At times, this criticism seeks, or claims to seek, to *transcend* a given time and place, to surpass or excel or go beyond an existing situation. However, there is nothing *transcendental* about this going beyond previous situations.[20] Like explorers who cross over or transcend obstacles, athletes who surmount or transcend former records, scientists who break through or transcend previous belief, or lovers who deepen or transcend earlier relationships, critics engage in, discover, and produce nothing superhuman, supernatural, or superexperiential. There is nothing universal or necessary about criticism or the transcendence, improvement, ameliorative change and difference it seeks. In criticism, as Adorno observed, metaphysics migrates into "micrology," the place where it finds a "haven from totality."

This, of course, is not a widely popular view. Many philosophers have thought that criticism requires something more—perhaps an epistemological foundation, an absolutist metaphysics, a mystical insight or revelation, or ideal speech conditions. How, they wonder, is criticism possible for pragmatists, contextualists, pluralists, historicists, postmodernists— philosophers all too local, all too temporal, all too human? How could there be, they wonder, a critical philosophy without transcendence? Where in these philosophies, they wonder, is the proof—the self-justified proposition, the truth in all possible worlds, the unchanging reality, the absolute, the ever-ready intellectual stone that can be kicked to refute one's opponents or convince skeptics?

What space is there in pragmatism, postmodernism, and this-worldly radical empiricism for transcendence? Is pragmatic criticism really possible? Pragmatists, like postmodernists, often are duped by this question about the possibility of criticism.[21] Their opponents charge that a philosophy without a foundational epistemology and/or a transcendental metaphysics cannot justify its own critical content. These opponents claim that pragmatism, like postmodernism, historicizes all claims, relativizes all values, and legitimizes all sides of all struggles. Eager to respond, the pragmatists reply that pragmatism really may be politically valuable. But there is no general or complete or final way to demonstrate this *in theory*. Instead, pragmatism, on it own terms, can establish its effectiveness only case by case, only piecemeal, and only in practice through its consequences. For pragmatists to attempt to answer their opponents in any other way would be, as John Lachs has noted, merely to seek to unify theory and practice *in theory* alone, thus allowing philosophy to live on and on whether or not the supposed moment to realize it was missed or has passed. Books about pragmatism are not necessarily pragmatic, and so pragmatists, again like postmodernists, need to undercut this concern. The way to do this, I believe, is to take a cue from Aristotle: The best way to show that criticism—understood in light of pragmatism, understood as non-dialectical—is possible is to show that it is actual. If actuality is prior to potentiality, then, as they say, just do it.

In order to actually exist, does pragmatic criticism require the foundational or transcendental? Do we need, more specifically, to take a Hegelian turn, a return to a more robust, full-bodied Hegel? Yes, but only if the name for this more robust Hegel is Dewey; if the name for this more full-bodied version of *The Phenomenology of Spirit* is *Experience and Nature*; if the name for the resulting historicized notion of transcendence is a transformed account of inquiry; and, if the name for the resulting historicized notion of an Absolute is experience—ordinary plural experiences. Yes, if this is Hegelianism without access to truths supposed to have some sort of necessity and universality; if this is Hegelianism without any world-internal rationality unfolding in history; and if this is Hegelianism without its metaphysics. Yes, if this is a Hegelianism that has become a full-fledged experimental, this-worldly pragmatism.

Hegel is important in this context because he must be viewed as one of the all-time great storytellers, fiction writers, narrators, and cultural observers, an insightful "reporter of certain empirical aspects of the actual."[22] Our desire to make possible critique—and genuinely transformative critique—must not lead us to make that longing the basis of a supposedly *necessary* and *universal* critical philosophy. Similarly, our desire for a better world must not lead us to pretend that we can justify particular desires or agendas on the basis of supposedly necessary truths or meanings, supposedly universal notions of rationality, or a supposedly experience-transcendent reality—a reality that transcends all experience as opposed to this or that experience or my or your experience. One of the first tasks of non-dialectical criticism today is to overcome or give up or just never feel that longing for the necessary, the certain, the universal, the trans-experiential and all the question-begging philosophies that result from these wants. Here it does seem that transcendental and foundational philosophers do *not* see through the theories they apparently feel compelled to produce. In response, pragmatists must simply confront these views case by case, demonstrating in each case the historical bases of a particular view of the supposedly transcendental and ahistorical, the local and temporal basis of the supposedly universal and trans-experiential, and the contingency of the supposedly necessary. This, again, is a task for pragmatic cultural criticism, and it is an irreducibly genealogical task.

Narration, Literature, and the Basis of Criticism

Adorno observed that "Hegel's transposition of the particular into particularity follows the practice of a society that tolerates the particular only as a category, a form of the supremacy of the universal" (*ND*, p. 334). Does a critical pragmatic philosophy that tolerates, indeed demands, the particular as particular require a turn away from system and dialectics to narrative and literature? What are or might be the proper genres of non-dialectical criticism? Philosophy? Literature? Art? Law? Leisure studies or hotel management? To engage in non-dialectical and pragmatic criticism is indeed to take a literary or narrative turn, but this is not a turn away from philosophy (though it surely is a turn away from some philosophies). Though separated, philosophy and literature are not separate because philosophy already is and always has been a kind of narrative. When it is a narrative that masks itself as foundational, transcendental, universal, general, and abstract, then it is a narrative ill suited to critical purposes (though it remains a narrative even so). Literature and art better serve these critical purposes—and so offer a lesson that philosophy should learn—when they avoid these masks. They better serve these critical purposes when they give their audiences places (rather than philosophers' space), lives (rather than philosophers' time), historically situated individuals and communities (rather than philosophers' human nature), and concrete satisfactions and frustrations, celebrations and sufferings, and passages and experiences (rather than philosophers' reality). Accordingly, philosophers should refuse to view, for example, the work of Homer, Sophocles, Emerson, Whitman, Jane Addams, Kafka, Holmes, Beckett, Hemingway, Hurston, Christa Wolff, or Malcolm X as work in *other* disciplines.

Philosophy profitably could do something else as well. If it does not, critical pragmatism becomes and remains nothing but the sort of stories and redescriptions offered by Richard Rorty and others. Rorty's "narrative turn," a kind of armchair pragmatism, strips pragmatism of its critical power because it offers stories without inquiry, because it rejects rather than reconstructs inquiry. Narrative illumination of values can have no critical dimension unless those values illuminated in turn are subjected to inquiry (including a genealogical inquiry into inquiry itself)—unless what is found to be *valued* can be and is shown to be *valuable*. In the absence of this inquiry, there can be no criticism, though there can be aesthetic experience. Because it includes inquiry, criticism ultimately is not negation. All criticism posits, all criticism produces. (Adorno appears to recognize this fact without developing its consequences. For example, he notes: "In a sense, dialectical logic is more positivistic than the positivism that outlaws it. . . . The only way out of the dialectical context of immanence is by that context itself. Dialectics is critical reflection upon that context." Yet he immediately adds: "Such dialectics is negative" [*ND*, p. 141].)

To the extent that philosophy turns this critical inquiry on itself, it becomes a kind of criticism of criticism. As such, it is one level more removed from the problems within experience that first generated particular criticism, but it is not, for all that, first philosophy, last philosophy, post-philosophy queen of the critical sciences or the core or foundation of criticism. As a result, criticism of criticism is not *the* form of criticism par excellence. It is not non-local; rather, it is differently local. Metacriticism is not free from any of the contextual demands or the situatedness of other sorts of criticism. All criticism is local.

Criticism and Its Social Conditions

Although James viewed Hegel as a pragmatist in practice, he harbored little hope that Hegelians would come to share this understanding of their own work. Indeed, Adorno's and Horkheimer's highly negative view of pragmatism—an almost comic misunderstanding of pragmatism—is more or less matched by Dewey's negative assessment of German philosophy and culture (notwithstanding the permanent influence that Dewey realized Hegel's philosophy had had on his own thought). In this vein, Dewey generalized in his 1915 *German Philosophy and Politics*:

> Thus it turns out that while the Germans have been, to employ a catchword of recent thought, the most technically pragmatic of all peoples in their actual conduct of affairs, there is no people so hostile to the spirit of a pragmatic philosophy. . . . But that philosophical absolutism may be practically

as dangerous as matter of fact political absolutism history testifies. The situation puts in relief what finally is at issue between a theory which is pinned to a belief in an Absolute beyond history and behind experience, and one which is frankly experimental. For any philosophy which is not consistently experimental will always traffic in absolutes no matter in how disguised a form. In German political philosophy, the traffic is without a mask. (*MW*8:152, 182)

At this point, experimentalists may be tempted to ask for instructions, to look for the policeman in Kafka's story, to ask how one can engage in pragmatic cultural criticism: How can *I* do this? This question appears to presuppose that criticism is not only a task with instructions but also a task for individuals.

Consider instead another question. Upon what social conditions does criticism, or even the capacity for criticism, depend? I ask this question because I believe that the cultural preconditions of criticism increasingly are being extinguished in contemporary societies. This is not a question about supposed logical or metaphysical or epistemological preconditions of criticism. Rather, it is a question about the ways in which social conditions make possible or impossible the genealogies necessary for communities of memory; the imagination necessary for communities of hope; and the instrumentalities or strategies necessary for a community of agents. It is a question about the ways in which social conditions can virtually eliminate the genealogical, the imaginative, and the instrumental. Faced with these conditions, would-be critics are left to take sides—either dreaming of transcendence, synthesis, and rational necessity, or seeking resistance in nostalgic aesthetics or aristocratic desires for dialectic, pure negation, pure resistance, and pure difference.

Perhaps the most important, most demanding task for a criticism of criticism today is criticism of the social conditions and associations that are washing over and eliminating the very possibilities and preconditions needed for criticism itself. If this is, as I have argued,[23] an educational task in its largest terms, it is one at which educators today, large and small, are failing miserably. Like the culture industry's consumers, would-be critical educators are mistaken in believing that they automatically engage in criticism when they write about criticism in journal articles and books and the occasional popular forum, assign some of those articles and books to students, pick up paychecks and wander home through Adorno's "open-air prisons." Educators, if genuinely critical, must deliver critical genealogies and new possibilities to persons who find criticism pointless because they have much or almost everything they want and who feel good about themselves and content with their world and their position in it. And critical educators should deliver critical strategies to an entirely different, increasingly large group of persons around the world who find criticism pointless because they have almost nothing, almost no capacity to change this fact, and almost no realistic hope for anything better in their lives and in this world.

The delivery of these critical messages is an art. To the extent that philosophers fail to take up this art, they—myself included—participate in the further formation of a postcritical society. To practice criticism, one must raise one's imagination and, with others, strenuously exercise one's will. This task is non-dialectical: It is self-remaking, the art of living, understood as ordinary and transient amelioration. Perhaps critical intelligence will not be able to meet this task. Certainly critical intelligence will not succeed if it fails at least to recognize and take up this challenge.

Notes

1. With a nod toward Adorno's *Minima Moralia* and against his view of American popular culture, the first eight paratactic section titles in this chapter are drawn from R.E.M.'s *UP* (Temporary Music, Warner-Tamerlane Publishing Corp., 1998).

2. Theodor Adorno, "Why Still Philosophy," trans. Henry W. Pickford, in *Critical Models: Interventions and Catchwords* (New York: Columbia University Press, 1998 [1963]), pp. 39, 9–10. Hereafter WSP.

3. Theodor Adorno, "Cultural Criticism and Society," *Prisms*, trans. Samuel and Shierry Weber (Cambridge: MIT Press, 1982 [1967]), p. 33. Hereafter CCS.

4. See Gillian Rose, *The Melancholy Science: An Introduction to the Thought of Theodor Adorno* (New York: Columbia University Press, 1978), pp. 11–12.

5. Theodor Adorno, *Minima Moralia: Reflections from Damaged Life*, trans. E. F. N. Jephcott (London: Verso, 1974 [1951]), p. 50.

6. Theodor Adorno, "The Stars Down to Earth," *The Stars Down to Earth and Other Essays on the Irrational in Culture*, ed. Stephen Crook (New York: Routledge: 1994 [1953]), p. 74. Hereafter SDE.

7. R.E.M., "Man on the Moon," *Out of Time* (Warner Brothers, 1991).

8. Karl Marx, "Theses on Feuerbach," *The Marx-Engels Reader*, ed. Robert Tucker (New York: Norton, 1978 [1845]) p. 145.

9. R.E.M., "Sad Professor," *UP*.

10. Adorno *Minima Moralia*, p. 247.

11. Max Horkheimer, "Traditional and Critical Theory," *Critical Theory: Selected Essays*, trans. Matthew J. O'Connell *et. al.* (New York: Continuum, 1972 [1937]), p. 220.

12. Theodor Adorno, "Subject and Object," in *The Essential Frankfurt School Reader*, ed. Andrew Arato and Eike Gebhardt (New York: Continuum, 1982 [1969]), p. 498.

13. Theodor Adorno, *Negative Dialectics*, trans. E. B. Ashton (New York: Continuum, 1973 [1966]), pp. 183, 170. Hereafter *ND*.

14. Adorno, "Subject and Object," p. 502.

15. Compare Adorno's account of the possibility of philosophy in his "Introduction" to *Negative Dialectics*, an account I negate:

> Philosophy, which once seemed obsolete, lives on because the moment to realize it was missed. The summary judgment that it had merely interpreted the world, that resignation in the face of reality had crippled it in itself, becomes a defeatism of reason after the attempt to change the world miscarried. Philosophy offers no place from which theory as such might be concretely convicted of the anachronisms it is suspected of, now as before. Perhaps it was an inadequate interpretation which promised that it would be put into practice. Theory cannot prolong the moment its critique depended on. A practice indefinitely delayed is no longer the forum for appeals against self-satisfied speculation; it is mostly the pretext used by executive authorities to choke, as vain, whatever critical thoughts the practical change would require. Having broken its pledge to be as one with reality or at the point of realization, philosophy is obliged to ruthlessly criticize itself. (p. 3)

16. The following sections of this chapter appeared in slightly modified form as "Consciousness of Doom: Criticism, Art, and Pragmatic Transcendence," *Journal of Speculative Philosophy*, Vol. 12, no. 4 (1998), pp. 32–50.

17. John J. Stuhr, *Genealogical Pragmatism: Philosophy, Experience, and Criticism* (Albany: State University of New York Press, 1997).

18. See chapter 8 for an extended analysis of this issue.

19. William James, *A Pluralistic Universe* (Cambridge, Mass.: Harvard University Press, 1977 [1909]), p. 46.

20. See chapter 10 for an extended analysis of this issue.

21. See chapter 5, pp. 99–100.

22. James, *A Pluralistic Universe*, p. 49.

23. See chapter 1, p. 17–21.

CHAPTER 7

Genealogy, Critique, and Transformation: In Our Time

"I ain't got time for that now"[1]

> Nick stood up on the log, holding his rod, the landing net hanging heavy, then stepped into the water and splashed ashore. He climbed the bank and cut up into the woods, toward the high ground. He was going back to camp. He looked back. The river just showed through the trees. There were plenty of days coming when he could fish the swamp.[2]

Any announcement of the disappearance of the author today appears premature. Contrary to Foucault's statement in "What Is an Author?" this is not because the disappearance of the author in our time "is held in check by the transcendental."[3] There is nothing transcendental that can hold in check the disappearance of the author—or hold in check the disappearance or the appearance of anything at all. While there is no such transcendental at all, there are still plenty of adherents to, and true believers in, the tradition of this transcendental. As a result, today the author has not fully disappeared or been displaced because the "great efforts" of those who are trying to liberate us from "the historical and transcendental tradition of the nineteenth century" (WIA, p. 120), including the tradition of the apparent author, have not produced equally great results or been joined by equally great numbers.

The space produced jointly by these great efforts and their not so great, sadly meager results is occupied by a small assortment of would-be emancipatory authors, including some who publish unmasked books, essays, and interviews advocating masked authorship. These authors are both enduringly anachronistic moderns, and, at the same time, temporarily up-to-date "postmoderns." On the one hand, these authors—Foucault included—are anachronistic throw-backs because, despite their announcements of the disappearance of the author, they themselves are twentieth-century versions of the "singular type of author" whom Foucault asserted was produced first in nineteenth-century Europe. These are authors whom he called "initiators of discursive practices," authors who, as initiators, thus occupy "a trans-discursive position" and engage in a practice "heterogeneous to its ulterior transformations." These authors, Foucault wrote, are authors not simply of books. They are authors of whole new theories, traditions, or disciplines "within which new books and authors can proliferate," creators of "the possibility and the rules of formation of other texts," authors who perform a "return to the origin" in order to transform rather than trivially redouble or ornament their texts (WIA, pp. 131–135).

However, in returning to the origin of what it is to be an author, these authors are, on the other hand, as temporarily contemporary as they are anachronistic. This is so because they initiate their own disappearance or displacement. They effect the disappearance of the author as this absence, or at least the announcement of this absence, as it is found largely in late-twentieth-century (rather than nineteenth-century) discursive practices. In doing so, they transform authorship by locating (as signatories) the origin of the disappearance of the author in the post-author author-function. Through this transformation of authorship, a work that masters its master and "attains the right to kill, a right to become the murderer of its author" (WIA, p. 117), itself becomes an author-function. Such a work becomes a function that is the origin of the disappearance of an author (who thus comes to occupy a displaced position). Through this transformation, for example, "Foucault" names both an author (or author-product) whose disappearance (or now displaced discourse position) is effected by a particular author-function (or historical conditions of discourse), and names also an initiator (occupying a trans-discursive position) of the discursive practice of this particular author-function.

On the surface, it thus might appear that after Foucault there has been a proliferation, even an explosion, of new texts and, yes, new authors within this very discursive practice. Viewing this explosion, it might seem that transformative critique is not only possible but indeed omnipresent. For instance, the twenty-first century began with more than 25,000 Internet sites about Michel Foucault. *Books in Print* listed more than 300 English-language books on Foucault (as well as 35 by him). During the decade of the 1990s alone, *The Philosophers Index* included on average more than 60 entries per year on Foucault. During this same time, there were an average of more than 500 non-overlapping entries per year on Foucault in the leading, largest indexes in the humanities and social sciences—more than one index item on Foucault per day, every day of the year, every year of the last decade of the twentieth century. In 2000–2002, there were more than a thousand new doctoral dissertations in the United States that were wholly or largely concerned with Foucault's work. Amazon Books, the e-retail company, stocked 155 books on Foucault in 2002, more than on any other writer it classified as a philosopher. Six of Foucault's own books were among Amazon's 30 bestsellers of modern philosophy—putting Foucault just ahead of philosophy's odd couple, Ayn Rand and Friedrich Nietzsche, tied for second in what must be a strangely heated *uber*-sales competition. *The Arts and Humanities Citation Index* has chronicled thousands and thousands—in fact, tens of thousands—of references to Foucault. There is an abundance, then, of gray, meticulous, patient documentation of the proliferation of work on Foucault—of work on an author.

Still, what exactly has proliferated? Work about an author's whole new discursive practice, whether Freud's or Marx's or Dewey's or Foucault's, need not be work within that whole new practice—psychoanalysis, dialectical materialism, pragmatism, genealogy—or even be work consistent with that practice. Moreover, work about an author (say, Foucault) need not be work about an author-function (say, the genealogical analysis of discourse) in which this author disappears or is displaced as a variable in, and product of, specific historical discourse.

Recognizing this point, is it possible to study even a very little of the ever-proliferating body of work on Foucault without finding that its central topics usually include concerns with Foucault as an author? Is it possible to study this body of work without encountering scholars who have manufactured a "speaker's benefit" (that they would extend to Foucault), without being tempted to begin writing *The History of Textuality, Vol. I: An Introduction*, without wanting to sigh in resignation or exclaim in exasperation: You "Other Authors"? Is it possible to stop insisting, with so much passion and with so much supposed but unwarranted superiority to the past, that the disappearance of the author is the product of authors?[4] Is it possible not to attempt to make apparent—to make appear—authors of the disappearance of the author? Worse still, is it now possible not to want to be such an author oneself? If so, is it then possible to stop viewing ourselves as authors, authors of texts about authors of other texts about the disappearance of the author? Must one admit: We "Other Authors." The author is dead; long live the author!

Put differently: Is it possible to write as an author and claim to understand Foucault—not Foucault the supposed author, of course, but Foucault the complex and variable function of genealogical discourse? Can we stop asking: Are you for or against him? Are you attacking or defending the major claims in his writings? Will you show that he was an original author or deny him space in the philosophical canon? Is he more or less great than the Stoics or Descartes or James or Wittgenstein? Are his claims true and his arguments valid? What exactly did he mean? Who has most successfully guarded, even disciplined, his writings? Which interpretation is correct? Can we "stop making sense," stop making this sort of supposed sense?

Consider: Does Michel Foucault's work demonstrate the possibility of transformative critique? This sort of question is familiar, an old habit, and it signals rules of the game that must be clear, signals questions that must be asked: "What are the modes of existence of this discourse? Where does it come from; how is it circulated, who controls it? What placements are determined for possible subjects? Who can fulfill these diverse functions of the subject?" (WIA, p. 138). In any genuinely Foucaldian discourse on the possibilities of transformative critique, Foucault the author can have no place. Foucault the author must disappear, must be displaced, must be dead. Can we displace Foucault, returning to Foucault's texts within the discursive practice of genealogy, returning to Foucault to transform rather than simply to proliferate redoublings and inessential authorial ornamentation, returning pragmatically to pick up tools?

But, in any such displacement, who then is speaking? From what place, how, and with what results is there authorization to speak about Foucault and the possibilities of transformative critique? Well, who wants to know, who is asking? Is it would-be revolutionary, quite well-paid, university-employed, institution-tenured professors with intellectual capital judged professionally adequate or even exemplary, professors talking to one another in weighty tomes and at small scholarly conferences in a comfortable micro-corner of a complex government/business/education economy of subjects, knowledges, and power? And all of them authors?

In "What Is an Author?" Foucault concludes (and we know that he is the one who is speaking), via Beckett: "What matter who's speaking?" (WIA, p. 138).

"I got three passports, a couple of visas, you don't even know my real name" (LDW).

"High on a hillside, the trucks are loading"

Under the trees at the top of the hill, Nick blew on the coals of his campfire. It was cold in the early morning shade. He buttoned the collar of his shirt. Crossing the Dolomites near St. Vito during Nick's last sabbatical, the old Italian professor advised him to reserve the mornings for writing.

> Nick looked in the direction of the river. He squinted and reached for paper
> from his Duluth pack. The sun stayed low in the sky behind the aspens and
> cottonwoods. He sat on a small granite ledge and wrote rapidly. Now there
> was never enough time.

What are the possibilities of transformative critique, a criticism that is something more than abstract inference or some unexamined preference? Isn't
this question too abstract? Any possibility of transformative critique would
be a specific possibility. Transformative critique? By whom? For whom?
Against whom? How? What transformation? An original relation to the
universe? An amusement park on every corner? Democracy as a way of life?
Expanded surveillance and smooth information warfare? A multiplicity
of ordinary joys and regrets without the heavens of philosophic assassins? What possibilities? Where? When?

Even setting aside the need for greater specificity—presumably a need
thoroughly recognized by "specific intellectuals"—the question of the
possibilities of transformative critique in our time remains equivocal. This
question might mean: What is the nature of personal and social possibilities
that particular transformative critique has made, is making, or will
make actual? Just what are the possibilities produced by a given transformative critique? In other words: What change does a particular transformative critique create? What transformations does a given transformative
critique effect? What new subjects, associations, practices, and powers does
a specific transformative critique produce? Here the focus is on *possibilities*.

Understood in this first way, this question about the possibilities of transformative critique presupposes that critique really has some transformative effect. This presupposition points directly to a second way of
understanding the question. "What are the possibilities of transformative
critique?" also might mean: Does critique—either a particular critique or
critique in general—have any genuinely transformative function or effect
for, or on, individuals or society? In other words: What evidence, if any, is
there for the belief that critique is ever transformative? What exactly is
the nature of this transformation? What is the role of critique in this transformation? Moreover, even if one grants the occurrence of such transformations, why view critique as a productive agent or cause rather than an
impotent by-product or epiphenomenal effect of this process? Here the
focus is on *transformation*.

Now, understood in this second way, the question about the possibilities of transformative critique presupposes that critique is possible at all.
This presupposition in turn points immediately to a third way of understanding what the question "What are the possibilities of transformative

critique?" might mean: Is it possible to engage in, or produce, any sort of critique, transformative or not? Can critique take place at all? Is it possible in our time? In other words: What are the prerequisite conditions of critique? What skill or sanction or equipment or tool or condition or cultural climate is necessary in order to engage in critique? What are the formation rules of the game, what discipline is required to play by these rules, and what positions of play are made possible? Here the focus is on *critique.*

"Everything's ready to roll" (LDW).

"Why stay in college? Why go to night school?"

> As the plane banked and rose, Nick looked for the river. He liked to see the ground. It was too cloudy. He watched a blonde flight attendant and asked her for a newspaper and two beers. Terrorists in Algeria had killed thirteen elementary teachers in front of their students. He wanted to see the Atlas Mountains someday. He wondered if there were direct flights to Marrakesch from Rome or Madrid or Nice. Like all American professors, he wanted to go back to Italy and Spain and France. The beer was too cold but he was thirsty. On the last page of the third section of the newspaper, he saw a small advertisement for a new book on the history of impotence. He wrote a note on the back of the folder of his conference paper. He wanted to ask Jake if he could review it for the journal. The flight attendant closed the curtain.

Is critique possible in our time? The answer to this question clearly depends upon what is meant by "critique." Is the possibility of critique the possibility of Kant's *Critique of Pure Reason*? The possibility of Marx's "Contribution to the Critique of Hegel's *Philosophy of Right*?" The possibility of Horkheimer's critique of traditional theory (as he distinguished it from critical theory)? The possibility of Adorno's negative dialectics? Or the possibility of Habermas's communicative competence-based criticism of postmodernism? The answer to the question about the possibility of critique today also, though perhaps less clearly, depends upon what kind of possibility is in question. Is the possibility of critique epistemic possibility? Ontological possibility? Political possibility? Or ethical possibility?

The great bulk of philosophers who have been concerned with the possibility of critique have been concerned primarily with the epistemic possibility of the identification and analysis of false consciousness or ideology, false needs or interests, and false or self-reflectively unacceptable reason. In effect, from Kant to Marx to Habermas, these philosophers have asked these kinds of questions. How can critique free consciousness and true human interests and, thus, produce enlightenment and emancipation? How can critique be reflective or self-referential, rather than objectifying, and thus differ in cognitive structure from science? And, if justified at all, how can critique be justified by self-reflection, rather than mere empirical evidence, and thus how can it differ in mode of confirmation from science?[5]

What are these possibilities, epistemic possibilities, of critique—this critique of consciousness, critique of needs, and critique of reason? My answer: None. Not one. Zero. Despite the genuine desires and clever efforts of many, many philosophers, there is no such possibility at all. There is no false consciousness to critique. There are no false needs. There is no self-reflection. In specific times and places, there are specific forms of consciousness, specific needs and wants, and specific modes of belief justification, all resulting from, constituting, serving, and setting into oppositions and resistances specific subjects and their relations. These are historical realities, however they may be judged by philosophers who desire transcendence. They are not signs of some epistemological deficiency—some supposed lack, loss, negation, interruption, inauthenticity, concealment, or falsehood. Nor are they measures of a need for some epistemological magic or sleight of hand—a proposition about our lives that comes brightly packaged with its own justification, some epistemically (rather than psychologically) self-justified bit of knowledge or self-evident starting point, some presuppositionless theory of knowledge, or other latest gizmo from the clever folks in the marketing department of the epistemology industry.

Paralleling and slightly modifying Foucault, we might say that the disappearance in our time of critique (in this sense) is held in check by belief in the transcendental. This belief has been spread by a whole army of philosophers who have preached the salvation of critique, a philosophical salvation army that has promised salvation through transcendental argumentation. Multiplying such belief beyond necessity—and, thus, to necessity—different philosophical saviors have sought to make good on this promise in different ways: here a synthetic a priori judgment, there a historical dialectic of mind or matter, then a vision of wholeness and multidimensional man (and even woman), and now maybe ideal speech conditions and the necessary commitments of communication.

In all such cases, however, three points must be remembered. First, the transcendental is introduced to provide an epistemic grounding for particular normative commitments, values, or views of right thinking and right living. This transcendental is the product of desire, not the product of any supposedly pure reason. Second, the transcendental always begs the question by assuming the values or view of right thinking or right living that are supposedly grounded by the given transcendental itself. The transcendental move can be justified only on the basis of independent premises and other values that, in turn, are not grounded or (self-)justified by that move. They are, instead, the details and accidents and piecemeal fabrications recorded in the official papers of scribes and the special pleadings of lawyers.[6] There is no necessary and universal basis for any such values. Third, it is not possible to provide a general final proof against any and all transcendental-rooted critiques. Such an argument, of course, would be self-refuting, in effect a critique of critique—and thus proof of the possibility of critique. Instead, the critics of critique must be fallibilists, proceeding patiently case by case, exposing in each case the question-begging logic, demonstrating each time that critique which proceeds by transcendental argument is a form of *smuggling*—even if those engaged in this smuggling do not recognize it.

Efforts on behalf of the disappearance of the author are informed by recognition of this smuggling. I think this point has been best recognized by Dewey and Adorno, perhaps another philosophical odd couple. Adorno put it more briefly and polemically, observing that the transcendent critic assumes a consciousness in a supposedly Archimedean position above the totality of culture and its blindnesses: "The choice of a standpoint outside the sway of existing society is as fictitious as only the construction of abstract utopias can be." He continued: "The traditional transcendent critique of ideology is obsolete. In principle, the method succumbs to the very reification which is its critical theme."[7] The disappearance of the author as transcendent critic, were it to happen, would mark the disappearance of critique and the rejection of its supposed privileges. In this displacement, focus must turn from the author of critique to the critic-function—the possibilities, modes, controls, and positions within a given critical discourse. "Gonna be different this time" (LDW).

Or will it? Authorship, long a habit, is only recently a vice. By itself, recognition of a vice is seldom sufficient to break the habit that sustains the vice. To practice criticism, to write critically—but not as an author: is this possible in our time? Should we address persons dismayed that this is possible, attempting consolation? Foucault observed:

> I know ... how intolerable it is to cut up, analyze, combine, recompose all these texts so that now the transfigured face of their author is never discernible. So many words amassed, so many marks on paper offered to numberless eyes, such zeal to preserve them beyond the gesture which articulates them, such a piety devoted to conserving and inscribing them in human memory—after all this, must nothing remain of the poor hand which traced them, ... of that ended life which had nothing but them for its continua-

tion? ... Must I suppose that, in my discourses, it is not my own survival that is at stake? And that, by speaking, I do not exorcise my death, but establish it: or rather, that I suppress all interiority, and yield my utterance to an outside which is so indifferent to my life, so neutral, that it knows no difference between my life and my death.... In each sentence that you pronounce— and very precisely in the one that you are busy writing at this moment, you who have ... felt yourself personally concerned and who are going to sign this text with your name—in every sentence there reigns the nameless law, the blank indifference: "What matter who is speaking; someone has said, what matter who is speaking."[8]

To practice criticism, but not as an author: should we instead address other persons worried that this is not possible, responding to doubts and providing instruction manuals? Assuming that criticism after the author cannot be an act of sovereign will, what are its historical conditions, operations, and positions of existence? Do they exist in our time?

"Can't write a letter, can't send a postcard, I can't write nothing at all" (LDW).

"Trouble in transit, got through the roadblock"

Nick read his paper to sixteen people in the back rows of the small meeting room. The commentator talked mainly about his own work, and said Nick's paper had arrived too late to give it more attention. Two men told Nick they had written books he should read. After his session, he wasn't hungry, so he slipped out to the museum. Late in the afternoon he sat down on a black and pink chair at the exhibit on bullfighting. He wished he had some paper or his laptop. He wanted to write. A voice from the camera's speaker told him to stay off the chairs. He crossed the street and passed some kids who leaned against a graffiti-covered wall and stared at him until he entered the hotel. He looked for Jake and Emily at the book display.

Criticism after the author: The displacement of the author by the author-function would be (were it broadly to occur), the replacement of the "universal intellectual" by the "specific intellectual,"[9] the replacement of critique by criticism. This criticism is genealogical, and Foucault repeatedly identified the aim of genealogy as the displacement of the author and the disappearance of the sovereign self that is the author. This genealogy does not discover the moment of our emergence, "the roots of our identity," our original relations, or the space that is our homeland—a homeland to which metaphysicians and, now, popular culture promise us a return. Instead, it is committed to the displacement, discontinuity, and dissipation of our identity. It is committed to replacement, different placement: "It is no longer a question of judging the past in the name of a truth that only we can possess in the present; but risking the destruction of the subject who seeks knowledge in the endless deployment of the will to knowledge."[10]

Transforming Nietzsche, Foucault identified three modalities of the performance of this commitment to the dissipation of our identities, three modalities of the performance of genealogy: parody (perhaps Hemingway's Nick Adams as university professor); systematic dissociation (perhaps Foucault freed from May 1968, from homosexuality, from Paris, Foucault with David Byrne and Hemingway in America, on safari in oversized white suits); and destruction of those who maintain "knowledge by the injustice proper to the will to knowledge" (perhaps a speedy dismissal of Kant, Hegel, Marx, and Habermas as transcendental dream weavers and smuggling logicians).

Genealogical criticism has its critics, of course, but it generally is not faulted as epistemically impossible. There is for genealogy, after all, no transcendental. Instead, the critics of genealogy argue and complain that it really isn't criticism at all because it is theoretically impossible for genealogy, on its own terms, to have any positive or prescriptive or emancipatory aim or effect—a supposedly necessary characteristic of criticism, or so these critics stipulate. A genealogical criticism, they assert, is no real criticism at all. A transformative genealogy, they proclaim, is theoretically impossible: If genealogical, then not critically transformative; if critically transformative, then not (just) genealogical.

I will not here examine this sort of criticism (although I recognize that it is probably possible to achieve tenure, promotion, and a thick résumé simply by engaging and responding to a minuscule portion of this work). I do not here want to track its varieties or summarize it at length, explicate it in detail, or evaluate its soundness. In forgoing at present these undertakings, I note simply that this sort of criticism issues from a large, seemingly expanding group that includes many social scientists, policy makers, decision analysts, philosophical analysts, critical theorists, Marxists, historians, phenomenologists, and post-Foucault philosophers who proudly proclaim themselves anti-Nietzscheans, neopragmatists, feminists, liberal political theorists, conservative communitarians, lots of absolutist and transcendental thinkers of all kinds, and the many wardens, therapists, and body engineers that are all around us.

At the risk of offending, by sidestepping, all these foes of genealogical criticism, I note briefly the anticipations and advance responses to these critics in Foucault's own texts. In the first place, there is the response to critics that genealogical criticism in theory may be transformative because in fact it has been transformative. (I take this to be the Aristotelian strategy of showing potentiality by demonstrating actuality.) Genealogical criticism, unlike critique, is a regional system of revolutionary, transformative action. For example:

> Revolutionary action [is the] simultaneous agitation of consciousness and institutions; this implies that we attack the relationships of power through the notions and institutions that function as their instruments, armature, and armor.... We have already started interventions in the asylum, using methods similar to those employed in the prisons: a kind of aggressive enquiry formulated, at least in part, by those who are being investigated.[11]

And, a decade later:

> To say that this work produced nothing is quite wrong. Do you think that twenty years ago people were considering the problems of the relationship between mental illness and psychological normality, the problem of the prison, the problem of medical power, the problem of the relationship between the sexes, and so on, as they are doing today?[12]

A second, more frequent response to the critics of genealogical criticism constitutes a rejection of the demand by foes that genealogy must stand in judgment of the present, specify better alternatives, and set forth strategies to reach those alternatives. Dreaming of a new kind of criticism that multiplies signs of existence rather than judgments,[13] the genealogical critic thus rejects the role of cultural prophet, the notion of genealogy as the future of philosophy, and the task of writing books that "tell people what to do."[14] This does not prevent criticism from being transformative; rather it enables criticism to be genuinely transformative:

> An opposition can be made between critique and transformation, "ideal" critique and "real" transformation. A critique is not a matter of saying that things are not right as they are. It is a matter of pointing out on what kinds of assumptions, what kinds of familiar, unchallenged, unconsidered modes of thought the practices that we accept rest.... Criticism is a matter of flushing out that thought and trying to change it: to show that things are not as self-evident as one believed, to see that what is accepted as self-evident

will no longer be accepted as such. Practicing criticism is a matter of making facile gestures difficult.[15]

Because genealogical criticism does not need to be a deduction that concludes "this then is what needs to be done," the foes of genealogy—typically those who imagine themselves to be the "we" who would or should determine whatever "we" think is to be done—wonder how it can be instrumental for those who fight, resist, and refuse. It is odd that this question persists, because it has been directly addressed:

> It's true that certain people, such as those who work in the institutional setting of the prison—which is not quite the same thing as being in prison—are not likely to find advice or instructions in my books that tell them "what is to be done." But my project is precisely to bring it about that they "no longer know what to do," so that the acts, gestures, discourses which up until then had seemed to go without saying become problematic, difficult, dangerous. This effect is intentional. And then I have some news for you: for me the problem of the prisons isn't one for the "social workers" but for the prisoners.[16]

This refusal to provide concrete alternatives and programs of reform marks a repositioning of intellectuals within the practice of criticism. The specific, post-author intellectual no longer formulates goals from above—"the intellectual's role is no longer to place himself 'somewhat ahead and to the side' in order to express the stifled truth of the collectivity."[17] Instead, it is to provide oppositional subjects tools for confronting systems of power (in which intellectuals participate) that prohibit and invalidate their knowledges.

There is a third reply to the foes of genealogy, opponents who hold that genealogy cannot be transformative because although it can render facile gestures difficult, destabilize previously accepted discourse, and call into question situations that had seemed self-evident, this is all it can do. If genealogy is immanent rather than transcendent criticism (boldly directing us to what is positively to be done), then must it not be merely negative rather than positive?

This question highlights again important points of contact between Foucault's genealogy and both Dewey's account of experiential philosophy as criticism and Adorno's analysis of cultural criticism and the role of subject and object within that criticism. All three of these writers rejected the categories presupposed by their critics, rejected the either/or choice between transcendence and immanence, and between positive and negative criticism. In a blistering repudiation of Hegelian dialectics, Adorno concluded that one of the tasks of a non-Hegelian, negative "dialectical logic is to eliminate the last traces of a deductive system, together with the last advocatory gestures of thought."[18] Because Adorno rejected the alternatives of either calling culture as a whole into question from a supposedly transcendent perspective or confronting culture with its own norms from an immanent position, he argued that "dialectics cannot, therefore, permit any insistence on logical neatness to encroach on its right to go from one genus to another" until "the very opposition between knowledge which penetrates from without and that which bores from within becomes suspect."[19]

But can a dialectic that moves back and forth between transcendence and immanence create suspicion about this opposition which its very operation presupposes? Can such a dialectical logic make possible a different kind of criticism, a criticism of difference, a post–twentieth century criticism? When asked to choose between the two alternatives, Adorno picked both. Like Dewey, Foucault steadfastly rejected not only both alternatives but also any dialectical hybrid that fails to liberate difference by permitting difference only as negation, difference only as non-identity. A genuinely negative dialectic must negate exactly this rule of negation. It must be no dialectic at all. Even Marx, at least in this 1844 passage, saw this clearly. Rejecting designs of the future of the world and proclamations of the future of philosophy, Marx advocated worldly inquiry and ruthless criticism:

> Apart from the general anarchy which has erupted among the reformers, each is compelled to confess to himself that he has no clear conception of what the future should be. That, however, is just the advantage of the new trend: that we do not attempt dogmatically to prefigure the future, but want to find the new world only through criticism of the old. Up to now the philosophers had the solution of all riddles lying in their lectern, and the stupid uninitiated world had only to open its jaws to let the roast partridges of absolute science fly into its mouth. Now philosophy has become worldly, and the most incontrovertible evidence of this is that the philosophical consciousness has been drawn, not only externally but also internally, into the stress of battle. But if the designing of the future and the proclamation of ready-made solutions for all time is not our affair, then we realize all the more clearly what we have to accomplish in the present—I am speaking of a ruthless criticism of everything existing, ruthless in two senses: The criticism must

not be afraid of its own conclusions, nor of conflict with the powers that be. I am therefore not in favor of setting up any dogmatic flag.[20]

Accordingly, genealogical criticism is thought without contradiction, without dialectics, without negation; thought that accepts divergence; affirmative thought whose instrument is disjunction; thought of the multiple—of the monadic and dispersed multiplicity that is not limited or confined by the constraints of similarity. The answer to the problem about the possibility of criticism, then, is answered by displacing and replacing the alternatives—positive or negative criticism, transcendent or immanent criticism, the arbitrary or the absolute—presupposed by the problem itself. On this displacement and replacement of dialectics, Foucault wrote:

> The problem cannot be approached through the logic of the excluded third, because it is a dispersed multiplicity; it cannot be resolved by the clear distinctions of a Cartesian idea, because it is obscure-distinct; it does not respond to the seriousness of the Hegelian negative, because it is a multiple affirmation; it is not subjected to the contradiction of being and non-being, since it is being. We must think problematically rather than question and answer dialectically.[21]

To think in this way is to engage in oppositionality to the ways in which we govern ourselves and others by the production of truths. It is contestation and transgression. Again, it is tempting, perhaps, to try to think of transgression either as a simple negative judgment about what is, or a simple positive judgment about what is not. But genealogical criticism is transgression understood differently, understood problematically and pragmatically, understood as non-positive affirmation:

> Transgression contains nothing negative, but affirms limited being—affirms the limitlessness into which it leaps as it opens this zone to existence for the first time. But correspondingly, this affirmation contains nothing positive; no content can bind it, since, by definition, no limit can positively restrict it. Perhaps it is simply an affirmation of division.... This philosophy of nonpositive affirmation is, I believe, what Blanchot was defining through his principle of "contestation." Contestation does not imply a generalized negation, but an affirmation that affirms nothing, a radical break of transitivity.[22]

Non-positive affirmation, philosophy during wartime: "We blended with the crowd" (LDW).

"Try to be careful, don't take no chances"

Nick ordered another beer and a glass of white wine for Emily. They sat at the bar on the thirty-eighth floor of the hotel. It was dark outside. There were lights below. That night she was reading a paper on music, sexuality, and revolution to a radical philosophy association session. Nick didn't want to go, and he knew she didn't care. She did not want to know anyone in the audience. She would be nervous if her department head came. It was the last year of her three-year contract. Nick saved the receipt to give to the secretary in his office. He told Emily he wished he had a sabbatical to go to France this year or even next year. Emily liked Paris. "Take an unpaid leave of absence," she smiled. In his room, he thought about France and his writing and his salary until it was time to go to the reception. He could not find the ballroom. He was going to ask directions but then he saw Jake across the room and they laughed about it for a long time.

Unlike other forms of criticism, genealogical criticism is both possible and transformative. Of course, an acceptance of the theoretical possibility of genealogical criticism is no guarantee of its practical possibility in particular situations. As a result, even if it is noted that theorizing is a practice, still that very thinking, even in noting this fact, remains theoretical. This result has been intended: I have sought to make difficult a variety of facile transcendental and dialectical gestures in philosophy. No sickness unto death, this is difficulty unto death, the death genealogical criticism effects.

It is crucial that there be no resurrection, particularly a resurrection through a dialectical metamorphosis of genealogical criticism into a new transcendental status, into a new author. In order to prevent this, genealogical criticism must insist that it is a critic-function, a discursive practice (and not simply a theory) of genealogy. And so it must be willing to repeat its new questions: Where does this criticism come from? How is it circulated and contained? Who controls it? What displacements are determined for subjects within genealogical criticism? Who can fulfill these diverse subject functions? These questions address the social (rather than the supposedly epistemological) possibilities of criticism. They suggest that the most pressing site for genealogical criticism today is the complex of social conditions and forces, particularly global systems (including education) of production and consumption that have the capacity to disqualify and even extinguish the genealogical critic-function itself. This may be a real possibility. Without a transcendental author, there is no transcendental resistance.

This makes possible a new meliorism, but it will sound too pessimistic to those who enjoy merely quoting Foucault's remark about his optimism and his belief that so many things can be changed. Again, this new meliorism will sound too pessimistic to those who believe things not only can be changed but now are being sufficiently changed, in part by a politics of recognition informed by genealogy—an expanding recognition of difference across gender, sexual preference, race, ethnicity, nationality, ability, age.

However, just as twentieth-century pragmatic theories of inquiry must be transformed by genealogical criticism,[23] so too genealogical criticism must be transformed by attention to the facile gestures it has not rendered problematic or approached pragmatically. For example, study after study concludes that wealthy female Americans vote more like wealthy male Americans than like poor American women; that middle-class gay Americans prefer housing preferred more by middle-class straight men than by lower-class gay men; that ethnic minority American executives hold political values more like ethnic majority American executives than like the ethnic minority unemployed; that upper-middle-class Asian Americans, African Americans, Native Americans, and Hispanic Americans all favor tax policies most like those favored by upper–middle class white Americans. The disappearance of the author and its replacement by author-functions readily re-enforce, rather than disturb, class functions and the surveillance that enables and partially constitutes them.

What matter who's speaking? Well, does it matter who's not speaking, what author-functions do not take place, what silences as well as what discourses are produced? Does a thoroughgoing pluralism matter? What gestures remain facile and what values remain smuggled when it is thought that it does not matter who's speaking or what is functioning?

In the midst of multiple politics of recognition, the gaps between the wealthy and the poor continue to grow. Is this the climate of a culture after the death of the author? Is this condition postsocialism, or only now, finally and more fully completely, capitalism, global capitalism? Recall Marx's 1858 letter to Engels: "Is [a socialist revolution in Europe] not bound to be crushed in this little corner, considering that in a far greater territory the movement of bourgeois society is still in the ascendant?"[24] Would not such an ascendant global capitalism include its own politics of recognition—the recognition of marketplace equality for all, the marketplace equality of all equal producers and the marketplace equality of all equal consumers? Could author functions become postcritical such that facile gestures of production and consumption will become difficult only when there is too little of either or both? In this context, could the author function find increasingly little space in which to be critically transformative?

These questions about the possibility in our time of genealogical criticism, the possibility of a critically genealogical pragmatic inquiry, and the capacity of genealogical criticism to render problematic its own most facile gestures and smooth inscriptions are practical rather than theoretical. As such, they cannot be answered in advance, in a book, in theory, even a favored theory.

And so, at the end of "Life During Wartime," with gunfire off in the distance and assassins nearby: "You better watch what you say." Hemingway, too, issued this reminder through his novel *In Our Time*. On September 30, 1938, having returned from a meeting with Hitler, Daladier, and Mussolini, Neville Chamberlain told the people of Great Britain: "For the second time in our history, a British Prime Minister has returned from Germany bringing peace with honor. I believe it is peace for our time. . . . Go home and get a nice quiet sleep."

In the future, a transformative genealogical criticism will need to follow a more strenuous agenda if peace with honor is to be different from assassins' lives during wartime.

Notes

1. For all section titles, see The Talking Heads, "Life During Wartime," *Fear of Music* (Sire, 1979), intended to be played at the beginning of this chapter. Hereafter LDW.
2. Ernest Hemingway, *In Our Time* (New York: Charles Scribner's Sons, 1958 [1925]), p. 212. (Note that this is the *only* Hemingway passage quoted.)
3. Michel Foucault, "What Is an Author?," *Language, Counter-Memory, Practice: Selected Essays and Interviews*, trans. Donald F. Bouchard and Sherry Simon (Ithaca, N.Y.: Cornell University Press, 1977 [1969]), pp. 113–138. Hereafter WIA.
4. Michel Foucault, *The History of Sexuality*, vol. I, trans. Robert Hurley (New York: Vintage Books, 1980 [1976]), pp. 3–9.
5. For example, see Raymond Geuss, *The Idea of a Critical Theory: Habermas and the Frankfurt School* (New York: Cambridge University Press, 1981), pp. 1–3, 55–56.
6. Michel Foucault, "Nietzsche, Genealogy, History," *Language, Counter-Memory, Practice* [1971], pp. 144–147. Santayana uses strikingly similar language to make a strikingly similar point comparison of most philosophers to attorneys hired on behalf of some cause.
7. Theodor Adorno, "Cultural Criticism and Society," *Prisms* (Cambridge: MIT Press, 1982 [1967]), pp. 31, 33–34.
8. Michel Foucault, "Politics and the Study of Discourse," *The Foucault Effect: Studies in Governmentality*, ed. G. Burchell, C. Gordon, and P. Miller (Chicago: University of Chicago Press, 1991 [1968]), pp. 71, 72.
9. Michel Foucault, "On Power," *Politics, Philosophy, Culture: Interviews and*

Other Writings, 1977–1984 (New York: Routledge, 1980 [1978, 1984]), pp. 107–108.

10. Foucault, "Nietzsche, Genealogy, History," p. 164.

11. Michel Foucault, "Revolutionary Action: 'Until Now,'" *Language, Counter-Memory, Practice*, p. 228.

12. Michel Foucault, "Practicing Criticism," *Politics, Philosophy, Culture: Interviews and Other Writings, 1977–1984* [1981], p. 154.

13. Michel Foucault, "The Masked Philosopher," *Politics, Philosophy, Culture: Interviews and Other Writings, 1977–1984* [1980], p. 326.

14. Michel Foucault, "The Minimalist Self," *Politics, Philosophy, Culture: Interviews and Other Writings, 1977–1984* [1983], pp. 15, 16.

15. Foucault, "Practicing Criticism," pp. 154–155.

16. Michel Foucault, "Questions of Method," *The Foucault Effect*, p. 84.

17. Michel Foucault, "Intellectuals and Power," *Language, Counter-Memory, Practice*, pp. 207–208.

18. Theodor Adorno, *Minima Moralia: Reflections from Damaged Life*, trans. E. F. N. Jephcott (London: Verso, 1984 [1951]), p. 71.

19. Theodor Adorno, "Cultural Criticism and Society," *Prisms*, trans. Samuel and Shierry Weber (Cambridge: The MIT Press, 1982 [1967]), p. 33.

20. Karl Marx, "For a Ruthless Criticism of Everything Existing," *The Marx-Engels Reader*, ed. Robert C. Tucker (New York: Norton, 1978 [1844]), p. 13.

21. Michel Foucault, "Theatrum Philosophicum," *Language, Counter-Memory, Practice*, [1970], pp. 185–186.

22. Michel Foucault, "Preface to Transgression," *Language, Counter-Memory, Practice* [1963], pp. 35–36.

23. See chapter 8.

24. Marx, 1858 letter to Engels, *The Marx-Engels Reader*, p. 676.

Power/Inquiry: Criticism and the Logic of Pragmatism

Since inquiries and methods are better and worse, logic involves a standard for criticizing and evaluating them. How, it will be asked, can inquiry which has to be evaluated by reference to a standard be itself the source of the standard? How can inquiry originate logical forms (as it has been stated that it does) and yet be subject to the requirements of these forms? The question is one that must be met.

—John Dewey

My problem is rather this: what rules of right are implemented by the relations of power in the production of discourses of truth? Or alternately, what type of power is susceptible of producing discourses of truth that in a society such as ours are endowed with such potent effects? . . . There can be no possible exercise of power without a certain economy of discourses of truth which operates through and on the basis of this association. We are subjected to the production of truth through power and we cannot exercise power except through the production of truth.

—Michel Foucault

Of whatever temperament a professional philosopher is, he tries when philosophizing to sink the fact of his temperament. Temperament is no conventionally recognized reason, so he urges impersonal reasons only for his conclusions. Yet his temperament really gives him a stronger bias than any of his more strictly objective premises. . . . Yet in the forum he can make no claim, on the bare ground of his temperament, to superior discernment or authority. There arises thus a certain insincerity in our philosophic discussions: the potentest of all our premises is never mentioned.

—William James

Toward Logic as an Account of Tools

Charles Peirce wrote that few people care to study logic. This still seems true today in the millennium after Peirce. Peirce explained that the reason for this lack of interest is that people already, if mistakenly, consider themselves proficient in logic. This explanation now seems mostly false. People today do not refrain from the study of logic because they believe they already are good at logic. Instead, they don't study logic because they don't care whether or not they are good at logic. Logic appears to have no relevance to them. Understanding logic does not seem necessary or even very helpful for success in real undertakings and inquiries in agriculture, aeronautics, basketball, business, chemistry, communications, economics, engineering, information warfare, painting, psychology, law, literature, music, medicine, or any other field or enterprise. In short, in practice the study of logic does not appear to be pragmatic.

There is no gap between appearance and reality here. Logic not only almost always appears irrelevant; it almost always *is* irrelevant. This judgment may be distressing to logicians (both dialectical and other), but it should not be surprising. As I indicated in chapter 6, in the context of Adorno's critical theory, any field of study that tells us that "if 'P' is false, then 'if P, then Q' is true" is a field of study that has parted company substantially with real investigations that aim at real amelioration of real problems.

As a result, Dewey was right to observe, in the concluding lines of his *Logic: The Theory of Inquiry* that the separation of logic from a general account of the processes for attaining and testing sound beliefs in any field is a recipe for the intellectual crippling and irrelevance of logic; inattention to the cultural consequences of this irrelevance; and incalculable cultural waste, confusion, and distortion that result from beliefs supported by logics that are independent of the most intelligent methods of inquiry available at any given present time (*LW*12:526–527).

Dewey made this same point more than thirty years earlier in his "Introduction" to his *Essays in Experimental Logic*. Logical theory, he wrote then, "is an account of the processes and tools which have actually been found effective in inquiry, comprising in the term 'inquiry' both deliberate discovery and deliberate invention." This view, he added, should eliminate "a lot of epistemological hangers-on to logic."[1]

A Pragmatic Theory of Inquiry

Dewey's account of logic as the theory of inquiry and his account of the nature and pattern of inquiry signaled a far-reaching revolution in logic, even if this signal has been missed by most professional "logicians" and epistemological hangers-on preoccupied with truth tables and formal systems, Polish notation, modalities and possible worlds other than this actual world, and dialectical bases for criticism. While the full benefits of Dewey's revolution may be both incalculable and still in front of us, the strengths of this approach are determinate. These strengths include the following ten points, briefly summarized below.

First, Dewey's account of logic as the theory of inquiry, like his entire philosophy, is *anti-dualistic*. Dewey clearly and steadfastly rejected any split or separation between logic and the actual methods of the currently most intelligent inquiries. He claimed that ongoing inquiry can develop—and that no other activities or processes are available to develop—the logical standards and forms for further inquiry (*LW*12:13).

Second, Dewey's view of logic is *anti-foundational*. The methodology of inquiry, as Dewey conceived it, has no theoretical foundation or justification independent of inquiry itself. Inquiry, in and over time, is its own justification—a justification that is circular (historically but not viciously), autonomous, self-reconstructing. The only justifications for the methods of a given inquiry are the results of other inquiries. As Dewey argued, understood as the theory of controlled inquiry, logic is autonomous, and does not rest on metaphysical and epistemological assumptions or perspectives.

Third, this account of logic is *anti-abstractionist*. Knowledge, Dewey held, is just the general name of, and for, the results of particular inquiries. These inquiries always arise within particular contexts, particular times and places. Moreover, this is true for the knowledges that are the results of these inquiries. Furthermore, there is no other knowledge, no knowledge unmediated by inquiry (*LW*12:14).

Fourth, Dewey's view of logic is *anti-static*. It is, Dewey said, a progressive and dynamic discipline. Logic is not ever fixed or final because inquiry is unfinished, ongoing, progressive, open to modification and abandonment. It is no more closed than the unfinished universe and open experiences that constitute its subject. There is no guarantee, Dewey wrote, that the now settled conclusion on an inquiry will remain always settled: "The attainment of settled beliefs is a progressive matter; there is no belief so settled as not to be exposed to further inquiry" (*LW*12:16).

Fifth, logic is *operational*. The subject matter of logic is determined operationally; facts are not fixed or merely given, but are always in process of being determined and becoming determinate. Fact finding is fact fixing: it takes place or operates from, and with, a goal or purpose. Accordingly, logical forms, Dewey claimed, are postulational. Similarly, essences and accidents have only functional, not ontological, status. To be essential is simply to be indispensable in a particular inquiry, essential in a particular context; to be accidental is to be unimportant relative to that inquiry (*LW*12:141). Inquiry arises from within, and in turn establishes, the continuity of experience and nature: "There is no breach of continuity between operations of inquiry and biological operations and physical operations" and "rational operations grow out of organic activities, without being identical with that from which they emerge" (*LW*12:26).

Sixth, logic is the theory of inquiry understood as *reconstructive*: inquiry is *existentially transformative*. It remakes the material with which it deals. Accordingly, objects of knowledge are results, not antecedents, of inquiries—just as William James recognized truth, verity, to be the result or consequence of a process of verification. Truth, knowledge, and justification thus are mediated rather than immediate, consequences rather than starting points, effects, products. Logical forms thus originate in, and are produced by, inquiry. And, in turn inquiry is a power: "There is no inquiry that does not involve the making of *some* change in environing conditions" (*LW*12:41). This view of inquiry as power to reconstruct or exercise control of transformation lies at the heart of Dewey's famous definition of inquiry. He wrote: "Inquiry is the controlled or directed transformation of an indeterminate situation into one that is so determinate in its constituent distinctions and relations as to convert the elements of the original situation into a unified whole" (*LW*12:108). This focus on control and power parallels Dewey's earlier thesis "that thinking is instrumental to a control of the environment, a control effected through acts which would not be undertaken without the prior resolution of a complex situation into assured elements and an accompanying projection of possibilities—without, that is to say, thinking" (*MW*10:338).

Seventh, as the theory of inquiry, logic, like Dewey's conception of democracy, is *temporal*. As Dewey noted, inquiry and judgment are not only temporal in the external sense of taking time, but also in an internal sense: "Its subject matter undergoes reconstruction in attaining the final state of determinate resolution and unification" (*LW*12:137). This subject matter, like growth and democracy, is thus irreducibly relative to time—and to a span of time rather than a single moment, since inquiry cannot be instantaneous (*LW*12:136).

Eighth, this temporality of inquiry replaces concern for truth with *concern for warrant*, just as, in another context, taking time seriously replaces concern for the good with concern for particular ends in view.[2]

Taken in the abstract, knowledge simply is "warranted assertibility," and "logical forms accrue in, and because of, control that yields conclusions which are warrantably assertible" (*LW*12:16, 29). While this understanding may highlight the contingency of the results of any given inquiry, this contingency is not mere arbitrariness. When this point is missed, "we pragmatists" (in the phrase of Richard Rorty) may turn to dreams of pure self-creation, and wide-open choices of vocabularies and descriptions. In contrast, Dewey noted that real confusions and real conflicts, like the real selves and surfaces involved in them, exist prior to a given inquiry that neither simply creates nor chooses them.

Ninth, this theory of logic is *counter-disciplinary* in its orientation. As such, it stands in sharp contrast to the familiar compartmentalized, departmentalized, supposedly mutually independent disciplines and areas of investigation. Dewey observed that there is "an urgent need for breaking down these conceptual barriers so as to promote cross-fertilization of ideas, and greater scope, variety, and flexibility of hypotheses" (*LW*12: 501–502). This is a point that pragmatist philosophers, Herculean staffs in hand, would do well to acknowledge—and acknowledge in practice as well as theory. There is a real danger here and potential irony here. This point may be lost or further lost, for example, whenever philosophers write *about*—rather than *by means of* or *through*—a philosopher who urged philosophers to turn away from the problems of philosophers and instead turn toward the real problems and real inquiries of persons.

The subject matter of logic is determined operationally. These operations constitute existential reconstructions or transformations. When these transformations produce control, they yield warranted conclusions. And these conclusions are irreducibly temporal. This perspective allows, even leads to, a tenth point about inquiry and its origins, operations, products, and formalizations. Logic, as the theory of inquiry, is *contextual*. This context, Dewey stressed in early chapters of his *Logic*, is biological and cultural (and it is in this cultural context, and in his account of the role of reasoning in his "pattern of inquiry," that Dewey detailed the special significance of language). Inquiry, that is, is not an exercise in pure reason. It is impure, intrinsically and irreducibly situated. It always arises from, empowers, and constitutes selective interests: "Neither inquiry nor the most abstractly formal set of symbols can escape from the cultural matrix in which they live, move, and have their being" (*LW*12:28). "All inquiry," Dewey wrote, "proceeds within a cultural matrix which is ultimately determined by the nature of social relations" (*LW*12:481).

Toward "That Moment a New Era in Philosophy Will Begin"

At the beginning of the twenty-fourth and penultimate chapter of his *Logic*, in a chapter titled "Social Inquiry," Dewey stressed again this contextual character of logic. He put it succinctly, even impatiently: "The impact of cultural conditions upon social inquiry is obvious" (*LW*12:482).

This is both true and false.

It is true in the sense that it is obvious *that* cultural conditions affect all social inquiry. Indeed, Dewey claimed that cultural conditions constitute the existential matrix of all inquiry. However, it is false to view as obvious the role of culture on inquiry in the sense that it is not at all *obvious what or how* particular cultural conditions impact particular social inquiries.

To inquire, for Dewey, is to control and direct. To inquire is to exercise power. So, what then are the impacts of cultural conditions on the exercise of power that is inquiry, on the exercises of power that are particular, real, plural inquiries? And what are the impacts of cultural conditions for an understanding of inquiry itself and an understanding of its function in criticism?

Do cultural conditions distort, stall, or prevent inquiry? At times, Dewey appears to have set forth this view. For example, the last chapter of the *Logic* surveys the ways in which previous philosophies (i.e., philosophies prior to Dewey's own philosophy) distort the nature of inquiry by "one-sided emphasis" and "selective extraction of some conditions and some factors from the pattern of actual inquiry" (*LW*12:507). The history of epistemology, Dewey argued, is a history of this distortion, a history of the fallacy of selective emphasis,[3] a history of theory having parted company with practice. Dewey wrote: "Because they [epistemologies] are not constructed upon the ground of operations and conceived in terms of their actual procedures and consequences, they are necessarily formed in terms of preconceptions derived from various sources, mainly cosmological in ancient and mainly psychological (directly or indirectly) in modern theory" (*LW*12: 526–527).

This criticism of earlier philosophers is troubling—not because of what it says about other philosophers but because of what it does not say about Dewey's own philosophy and his understanding of logic, inquiry, and criticism. Appearing near the close of his *Logic*, Dewey did not advance this observation as a prelude to a critical examination of his own selective emphases, his own special interests, or his own side of the story. Indeed, he did not identify his own selective emphases, admit their existence, recognized or unrecognized, or even write in a way that makes clear he realizes such interests are in play throughout his philosophy. Instead, he suggested that his *Logic* is a theory set forth without selective emphasis, a theory based "inclusively and exclusively upon the operations of inquiry" itself (*LW*12:527).

This philosophically realistic (rather than transactional) view of the operations of inquiry as facts waiting to be found, rather than facts fixed by the operations of still other, earlier inquiries, is at odds with the operational account of inquiry central to the *Logic*. It is also at odds with Dewey's view in *Experience and Nature* that selective emphasis is inevitable whenever reflection takes place, and is an evil only when its presence is concealed or denied.

Dewey expressed at length this same view with specific reference to logic. In *Essays in Experimental Logic*, for example, he wrote: "Now, it is an old story that philosophers, in common with theologians and social theorists, are as sure that personal habits and interests shape their opponents' doctrines as they are that their own beliefs are 'absolutely' universal and objective in quality. Hence arises that dishonesty, that insincerity characteristic of philosophic discussion." He continued:

> Now the moment the complicity of the personal factor in our philosophic valuations is recognized, is recognized fully, frankly, and generally, that moment a new era in philosophy will begin. We shall have to discover the personal factors that now influence us unconsciously, and begin to accept a new and moral responsibility for them, a responsibility for judging and testing them by their consequences. So long as we ignore this factor, its deeds will be largely evil, not because *it* is evil, but because, flourishing in the dark, it is without responsibility and without check. The only way to control it is by recognizing it.[4]

The "personal factor," ignored and unchecked in the *Logic* and still in need of recognition, is the belief that personal factors and relations of power are not at work in the revolutionary theory of inquiry that Dewey set forth. Dewey's inquiry into inquiry is neither impersonal nor disinterested. It is permeated by power.

Dewey's discussion of prejudice is a second example of his viewing cultural conditions as mere distortions or avoidable blocks to inquiry. He noted that "prejudices of race, nationality, class and sect play such an important role [on social inquiry] that their influence is seen by any observer of the field" (*LW*12:482). The impact of these prejudices on inquiry is surely immense. Indeed, we might add additional prejudices to the list, including prejudices defined by gender, sexual orientation, age, ability, preferences, ethnicity, and species. However, all this begs the question: When is a difference in believing or a difference in living a "prejudice," a judgment unwarranted because it is held prior to and independent of inquiry? And when are differences in believing and living warranted because they result from inquiries of individuals, post-judgments? The point is this: The impact of prejudice on inquiry is no doubt massive, but this impact may well not be seen by those observers who share the prejudice in question and who thus may view the prejudice as warranted or fail to attend to their prejudices at all. As Dewey noted, if we don't see the conditioning of prejudice that exists in our own cases, this failure is "due to an illusion of perspective" (*LW*12:482). For example, are scientism or positivism or realism prejudices? Are operationalism or instrumentalism or empiricism or radical empiricism prejudices? Is pragmatism a prejudice? Is social inquiry, inquiry into human relations, as "backward" as Dewey lamented, or is this judgment of backwardness conditioned by prejudices about the nature of advance and success? How have these prejudices been constituted and what are their effects? What work and what selves do they, as tools, produce?

Dewey's on-target recognition of the general impact of prejudice on inquiry was not followed by a needed first step toward a hermeneutic rehabilitation of prejudice and the circularity of inquiry. Rather it is a misstep in the general direction of the illusion of the possibility of inquiry free of all prejudice and the operations of power. And, it is a missed opportunity for reflection on the power of practices of inquiry, prejudice, and warrant to constitute our selves.

These problems may be avoided if one sees the impact of cultural conditions on inquiry in a different way—not as merely distorting or blocking inquiry, but as constituting and determining it in specific and different ways in specific and different contexts. Fortunately, in much of his *Logic* and in other writings, Dewey appeared to champion this view. For example, as noted above, Dewey repeatedly stressed that inquiry is neither abstract nor static; it is operational and contextual. And Dewey set forth this same view in his earlier work on logic: Inquiry always has a particular purpose, and its success always is a function of particular conditions (*MW*10:327).

However, this view is in considerable tension with Dewey's well-known and central account in the *Logic* of the common "pattern of inquiry." Dewey wrote that all "inquiry has a common structure or pattern," despite the diversity of its subject matters and diversity of techniques for dealing with these subjects (*LW*12:105). According to this pattern, an original indeterminate situation is transformed into a problem by means of reasoning that controls the operation of facts and meanings so as to generate and assess a solution to the problem that produces a new, determinate, unified situation.

This general account of inquiry, this account of the general or common pattern or structure of inquiry, readily appears to decontextualize inquiry. As such, it thus appears to run counter to much of the rest of the *Logic*. This was not, I think, Dewey's intent. And it need not necessarily be the result. However, because of what Dewey did not say, and because of the focus of subsequent scholars on the pattern of inquiry, it frequently has turned out that this actually is the result. Dewey characterized the cultural matrix of inquiry in terms of shared meanings, common purposes, and conjoint activities. As a result, differences (sometimes to the point of oppositions and conflict) in problems, goals, strategies, meanings, operations, and resolutions are omitted from the matrix of inquiry. Dewey simply did not pay sufficient or sustained attention to them, though he could have done so. Instead, he characterized inquiry as "objective" only to the extent that subjectivity, difference, and plurality are eliminated. (It is interesting to note that Dewey here, unlike in most of his work, employed a standard, traditional philosophical dualism—subjectivity/objectivity—without undercutting it.)

This apparent decontextualization of logic is everywhere evident in Dewey's account of this general pattern of inquiry. For example, he claimed:

> We know that some methods of inquiry are better than others in just the same way we know that some methods of surgery, farming, road-making, navigating, or what-not are better than others. (*LW*12:108)

> *We* are doubtful because the situation is inherently doubtful. (*LW*12:109)

> To mistake the problem involved is to cause subsequent inquiry to be irrelevant or to go astray.... The way in which the problem is conceived decides what specific suggestions are entertained and which are dismissed. (*LW* 12:112)

> If we assume, prematurely, that the problem involved is definite and clear, subsequent inquiry proceeds on the wrong track. (*LW*12:112)

> In many familiar situations, the meaning that is most relevant has been settled because of the eventuations of experiments in prior cases so that it is applicable almost immediately upon its occurrence. (*LW*12:116)

> In regulated inquiry facts are selected and arranged with the express intent of fulfilling this office [of resolving a difficulty]. (*LW*12:116)

> For things exist *as* objects for us only as they have been previously determined as outcomes of inquiries. (*LW*12:122)

Compare Foucault: "In the end, we are judged, condemned, classified, determined in our undertakings, destined to a certain mode of living or dying, as a function of the true discourses which are the bearers of the specific effects of power."[5] The *Logic* can seem to plaster a big yellow and black happy face on Foucault's genealogies of power. It may appear to do this by means of mere stipulation—anything that does not exhibit the prescribed pattern of inquiry thus is not defined or classified as inquiry. Or it may appear to do this by means of unexamined circularity—it is a summary generalization of features found in particular inquiries that, in turn, are identified as such by presupposing the pattern of inquiry. As a result, this account of inquiry is importantly if not entirely depoliticized and depluralized—and, so, decontextualized.

The pattern of inquiry, abstract and universal, appears to presuppose abstract, universal, timeless subjects ("we," "us") who do not stand to one another in plural relations of difference, opposition, or power, but instead experience (and seek to experience) common indeterminacies, institute shared problems on the basis of shared past inquiries, and approach the present with shared purposes and selectivities. Thus Dewey talked confidently about *the* indeterminate situation that *we* experience, but he never asked directly the relevant political questions: Who are "we"? Whose situation is indeterminate? How was this indeterminate situation produced? By whom? Whose interests are served by an identification of a situation as indeterminate? What are the consequences of this indeterminate situation's arising? For whom are these consequences? What happens when some persons experience a situation as indeterminate and others do not? Through what cultural institutions, practices, and relations is a situation defined as indeterminate for some, and what interests, values, truths are produced by this?

Similar questions and omissions confront the pattern of inquiry account of the institution of a problem, the next stage of the "pattern." A problem may be instituted, but who is empowered to define the nature of the problem, to determine the way a problem is conceived, to decide a problem is posed with sufficient clarity? What happens when different persons or different groups or different cultures define different problems—or are silenced or not allowed to define their problems? What happens when plural, multiple persons or groups set forth not just different but conflicting definitions or accounts of problems? How does the control of the formulation of problems produce, or reproduce, certain subjects, truths, meanings, and values?

These same questions may be posed and should be posed at subsequent stages in Dewey's "pattern of inquiry." For example, who is able to "operationally institute" the consequences of action? On what basis? Who is excluded and how are such persons constituted? What is presupposed, created, and excluded in this process?

These questions and concerns are not just theoretical. Is a military group a bunch of criminals and terrorists or a band of freedom fighters? Is a new world order really an order at all? Is a conversation at work harmless flirting or sexual harassment? Is a fetus a person or not? Was the election or selection of George W. Bush as president of the United States legitimate? Do people belong to different "races"? Does the execution of a murderer or a prisoner in the "war on drugs" establish a newly unified and determinate situation? What methods of farming and raising livestock are better than others?

These kinds of questions point to real flaws in Dewey's *Logic*. As omissions, these flaws need not be fatal. That is, they need not be fatal if it is possible for post-twentieth-century pragmatism to effect a genuine transformation of the *Logic*. This transformation, a step in the direction of Dewey as a Deleuzian minor philosophy, should begin not with the claim that the social inquiries are branches of natural science because their subject matters are existential (*LW*12:481). Instead, it should begin with the recognition that *all* inquiries, including those of natural and social sciences, are branches of criticism because their operations involve value judgments and exercises of power and temperament. In turn, this recognition demands something other than an account of a single, abstract pattern for all inquiry. Instead, it points to the importance of pluralistic genealogies, multiple genealogies of particular inquiries, genealogies that focus on the specific productions of economies of warranted assertions.

Of course, disciples of Dewey's *Logic* will be quick to rise to its defense and defend its every word, claiming either that a logic need not address the issues that I have raised or that Dewey already did address them sufficiently. This is a recipe for a pragmatism that stands still, a merely twentieth-century pragmatism, and it is itself a situation for further inquiry (and here I share Dewey's meliorism). My point here, of course, is not that Dewey's general account of logic cannot address these issues, or that its ten basic strengths are incompatible with its doing so. Instead, my point is that Dewey did not sufficiently acknowledge or address these issues. To do so is to begin to effect a reconstruction, a transformation, of his logic. It is more consistent with the underlying spirit of Dewey's philosophy to undertake this reconstruction than it is to affirm a form of Dewey fundamentalism.

Along the way, new genealogies of particular inquiries would do well to pause at two important points.

First, if the *Logic* is a recipe or set of marching orders for thinking in shared, warranted, approved ways, is it also a recipe for living in increasingly shared, approved, permitted ways? Is the practical (if unintentional) consequence of an effective "pattern of inquiry" the production of shared indeterminate situations, shared instituted problems, and shared operations toward their resolution? If inquiry just simply shows us that some methods of farming are better than others, or that some methods of thinking are better than others, does it show us—or will it be long until it shows us—that some methods of living are better than others? Does it, could it, will it lead to agreement about, or new powers over, what kinds of living count as being "better?" If so, what are the prospects, if any, for pluralism, and what is the role of inquiry in realizing these prospects?

Second, in the millennium after Dewey, is it the case that the most important task for any logic is, as Dewey thought, the production of determinate, unified situations? Or, instead, is the most important task for a new logic the multiplication of indeterminate situations, the proliferation of determinate problems, the multiplication of operations and experiences, the creation of a more fully pluralistic universe, and the admission that one's conclusions are not the only logical ones but rather, as James put it, "accidents more or less of personal vision which had better be avowed as such"?[6]

Both of these pauses are opportunities for epistemological and logical hangers-on finally to let go and, instead, to embrace a more critical, more genealogical, more pluralistic account of pragmatism, inquiry, and life.

Notes

This essay, with only minor changes, appeared in *Dewey's Logical Theory: New Studies and Interpretations,* ed. Thomas Burke, D. Micah Hester, and Robert B. Talisse (Nashville, Tenn.: Vanderbilt University Press, 2002).

1. John Dewey, Introduction to *Essays in Experimental Logic, John Dewey: The Middle Works,* Vol. 10 (Carbondale: Southern Illinois University Press, 1980, [1916]), pp. 332, 334. Many of the essays in this book appeared earlier in *Studies in Logical Theory,* included in *John Dewey: The Middle Works, 1899–1924,* Vol. 2 (Carbondale: Southern Illinois University Press, 1976 [1903]), pp. 293–375.
2. John J. Stuhr, *Genealogical Pragmatism: Philosophy, Experience, and Community* (Albany: State University of New York Press, 1997), pp. 181–204.
3. John Dewey, *Experience and Nature, John Dewey: The Later Works, 1925–1953,* Vol. 1 (Carbondale: Southern Illinois University Press, 1981 [1925]), p. 34.
4. John Dewey, "What Pragmatism Means by Practical," *John Dewey: The Middle Works, 1899–1924* (Carbondale: Southern Illinois University Press,

1977 [1916]), pp. 113–114. Under the title "What Does Pragmatism Mean by Practical?" this essay was first published in *Journal of Philosophy, Psychology, and Scientific Methods* in 1908, and was revised and reprinted in the 1916 *Essays in Experimental Logic.*

5. Michel Foucault, "Two Lectures," trans. Alesandro Fontana and Pasquale Pasquino, *Pouer/Knowledge* (New York: Pantheon, 1980 [1976]), p. 93.

6. William James, *A Pluralistic Universe* (Cambridge, Mass.: Harvard University Press, 1977 [1909]), p. 10.

CHAPTER 9

Pragmatism, Pluralism, and the Future of Philosophy: Farewell to an Idea

Philosophic Assassins and the Future of Philosophy

In his long poem "Extracts from Addresses to the Academy of Fine Ideas," published in his 1942 collection, *Parts of a World*, American poet Wallace Stevens wrote:

> The law of chaos is the law of ideas,
> Of improvisations and seasons of belief.
>
> Ideas are men. The mass of meaning and
> The mass of men are one. Chaos is not
>
> The mass of meaning. It is three or four
> Ideas or, say, five men or, possibly six.
>
> In the end, these philosophic assassins pull
> Revolvers and shoot each other. One remains.
>
> The mass of meaning becomes composed again.
> He that remains plays on an instrument
>
> A good agreement between himself and night,
> A chord between the mass of men and himself,
>
> Far, far beyond the putative canzones
> Of love and summer. The assassin sings

In chaos and his song is a consolation.
It is the music of the mass of meaning.

And yet it is a singular romance,
This warmth in the blood-world for the pure idea,

This inability to find a sound,
That clings to the mind like that right sound, that song

Of the assassin that remains and sings
In the high imagination, triumphantly.[1]

What can be the future of a philosophy—a philosophy like the pragmatism on which Stevens's poetry draws deeply and self-consciously—that refuses to sing in the high imagination? What can be the future of a cold philosophy that does not romance the pure idea and makes no good agreement with the night?

These questions may seem too optimistic, too hopeful, too question-begging. They may appear to be just more sounds played on just another instrument that once more would recompose in just another way the mass of meanings. *What* can be the future of a philosophy that offers no consolation? No. Ask instead: *Can there be* any future for such a philosophy, for example, a genealogical and pluralistic pragmatism that offers no consolation? *Is* there a future—*is* it possible to make a future—for a philosophy that recognizes itself as three or four ideas, an unarmed philosophy, a philosophy intent on shooting no one, a philosophy that does not strive to be the last philosophy or to triumphantly compose, recompose, or even decompose the mass of meaning? *Can* philosophers be anything other than assassins, and *is* there a future for philosophers who are not assassins?

Throughout the twentieth century, pragmatists frequently characterized pragmatism *as* the future of philosophy, and they proclaimed that the philosophers of the future will be, and/or should be, pragmatists. This self-assurance will startle no one familiar with the history of philosophy. It is anything but exceptional: like true believers everywhere, most Western philosophers have viewed their own philosophies as philosophy's future, or as the means of transportation to any future philosophical destination worth the trip, or, at least, as a map to the future philosophy that now awaits anyone sufficiently fit and able to make that trip.

There is nothing remarkable, then, about pragmatists' having believed, or still believing, that pragmatism *is* the future of philosophy. What *is* remarkable, however, is the steady decline throughout much of the twentieth century in the self-confidence of pragmatists in pragmatism as the future of philosophy. It is important to be clear here. It is not that pragmatists lost confidence *in pragmatism*—in the truth or meaning or value of their pragmatism or in the need for pragmatism. They did not. Instead, pragmatists bit by bit lost confidence *in philosophy*—in the capacity of philosophy to become genuinely pragmatic.

This erosion of confidence in philosophy and the possibility of its future pragmatic transformation has operated at two related but distinct levels. Addressed most fully by William James, this loss of confidence has taken place at a personal level—philosophy as a personal way of life marked by love of wisdom. Examined most directly by John Dewey, this loss of confidence also has operated at a more political, institutional level—philosophy as a professional activity within universities and larger social systems of education and knowledge production.

In light of this two-part declining confidence by pragmatists in pragmatism as the future of philosophy, the commonplace descriptions of pragmatism as a peculiarly optimistic, unsuspicious, naive, downright cheery philosophy of enterprise, expansion, and progress are not only deeply uninformed and mistaken but also deeply ironic. They are the tracks of assassins in unfamiliar country.

I propose to take this pragmatist loss of confidence all the way, to take it without consolation, to take pragmatism as an improvisation and season of belief. I believe that today pragmatists can successfully *stop* seeing pragmatism as the future of personal philosophy, and can successfully *stop* seeing pragmatism as the future of institutional, professionalized philosophy (or even see the future of pragmatism in this context at all). This critical disillusionment and rejection of pragmatism's previous belief in its philosophic Manifest Destiny has important consequences for the future of pragmatism, the future of philosophy more generally, and the future of intelligence and criticism more broadly still. I approach these futures by means of two brief histories of pragmatism's understanding of itself as the future of philosophy. These accounts are genealogies in the sense in which Dewey identified critical philosophy as "intellectual disrobing" by means of a "genetic" approach. They are genealogies also in the sense in which Foucault characterized philosophy as history of the present in the service of becoming different. I follow these brief genealogies with a focus, in this chapter and the next, on issues of personal transcendence and social hope as case studies for indicating a future direction for pragmatism, a direction beyond the future of philosophy.

In raising these questions about pragmatism, pluralism, and the future of philosophy, I want at the outset to stress four points in order to try to avoid misunderstanding. First, in discussing the future of philosophy, I am not peering into a crystal ball or reporting the results of calls to psychic hotlines, claiming to possess objective evidence about the future, grappling with problems of supposed foreknowledge, or suggesting the possibility of a supposedly spectatorial stance on the future. There is no such evidence, foreknowledge, or stance. Instead, my concerns are with hope, possibility, hard work, and transformative engagement. Second, I am not attempting merely to celebrate or praise pragmatism. I take such projects to be themselves at odds with the reconstructive, self-critical productive character of pragmatism at its best. Instead, my concern is with reshaping philosophy and reshaping pragmatism. Third, I am not simply urging that philosophy in the future should become more pragmatic. If ever this was sufficient, surely it is not so any longer because what counts as "pragmatic" or "experimental" or "intelligent" or "critical" or just plain "better" is contested, and contested from multiple traditions and perspectives and interests. Accordingly, pragmatism, as it strives to produce a pragmatic future for philosophy and culture, would do well to take seriously, indeed to extend, this pluralism. Fourth, in pursuing this project, I am not opting for pluralism over pragmatism. I reject this either/or option and the philosophical strategies that it informs. Instead, I seek to reconstruct a more pluralistic pragmatism, a more pragmatic pluralism, and in so doing to change both pragmatism and pluralism. Pragmatists who say with James that they will not allow the logic of non-pragmatist philosophies to trump their experiences and their lives should strive, in turn, to ensure that this logic does not trump the experiences and lives of others. Pragmatists who fail in theory to do this in effect pretend to inhabit some spectatorial stance, some meta-philosophical view from nowhere. To them, I offer a strong plea for a more pluralistic philosophy. And pragmatists who fail in practice to do this ignore the meaning of democracy as a way of life and the need for work on its behalf. To them, I offer a strong call, even a staff blow, to action—but not the songs of assassins.

James and Pragmatism: From Conquering Destiny to a Future of Maybes

James published *Pragmatism* in 1907. Rather than explicate or critically assess the themes, claims, or arguments of this book,[2] I want to call attention to three features of James's own understanding of this book. First, James often asserted that his pragmatism was *not* particularly novel or unique philosophically. In this spirit, he subtitled the book "A New Name for Some Old Ways of Thinking," and dedicated *Pragmatism* to the memory of John Stuart Mill "from whom I first learned the pragmatic openness of mind and whom my fancy likes to picture as our leader were he alive to-day."[3] In this spirit, he wrote that the philosophical tendencies of pragmatism are "tendencies that have always existed in philosophy" (*P*, p. 5). Finally, in this spirit, he declared that pragmatism "represents a perfectly familiar attitude in philosophy" and asserted that there "is absolutely nothing new in the pragmatic method," here citing Socrates, Aristotle, Locke, Berkeley, Hume, and Hodgson as some of its skilled practitioners (*P*, pp. 31, 30).

Second, although James believed that the pragmatic attitude and method had long been present in philosophy, still he believed that his *Pragmatism* constituted a revolution and radically different future for philosophy. In this spirit, he identified the revolutionary impact of his work in its self-conscious unification of prior pragmatic tendencies in philosophy, and in its bringing these tendencies to consciousness of "themselves collectively" and to consciousness of "their combined mission" (*P*, p. 5). In this spirit, James described the pragmatic method as a revolutionary way of really "settling metaphysical disputes that otherwise might be interminable," and characterized the pragmatic attitude as the first philosophy with both irreducibly tough-minded and tender-minded elements (*P*, pp. 28, 13). In this spirit, he admitted believing "that a kind of new dawn is breaking upon us philosophers" and reported feeling "impelled to try to impart to you some news of the situation" (*P*, p. 10). Finally, in this same spirit, he wrote that forerunners of pragmatism used it only in fragments: "Not until in our time has it generalized itself, become conscious of a universal mission, pretended to a conquering destiny. I believe in that destiny, and I hope I may end by inspiring you with my belief" (*P*, p. 30)

This immediately suggests the third important aspect of James's own understanding of his *Pragmatism*: his initial overflowing confidence in pragmatism as the future of philosophy. In this self-assured spirit, he wrote to his brother Henry, "I shouldn't be surprised if ten years hence it should be rated as 'epoch-making,' for of the definitive triumph of that general way of thinking I can entertain no doubt whatever—I believe it to be something quite like the protestant reformation."[4] (After reading *Pragmatism*, Henry James replied to his brother: "You are immensely and universally right.")[5] In the same spirit, John Dewey later argued in *The Quest for Certainty* that the intellectual consequences of Kant's philosophy were merely Ptolemaic and that pragmatism—and pragmatism alone—constituted a Copernican Revolution in philosophy (*LW*4:229). Calling Kant a "mere curio," James added that the path of philosophic progress lies "not so much *through* Kant as *round* him."[6] James's own experience provided evidence for his confidence: he turned down hundreds of lecture invitations, delivered addresses to overflowing audiences, and saw his *Pragmatism* book go into five printings in its first year. Of course, not all the response was positive, but James anticipated criticism in a spirit of supreme confidence about pragmatism as the future of philosophy: "I fully expect to see the pragmatist view of truth run through the classic stages of a theory's career. First, you know, a new theory is attacked as absurd; then it is admitted to be true, but obvious and insignificant; finally it is seen to be so important that its adversaries claim that they themselves discovered it" (*P*, p. 95).

Three years after the publication of *Pragmatism*, William James died. In the course of these three years, James's confidence that his pragmatism was "*immensely* right" never waned, but his confidence in his brother's judgment that his pragmatism was "*universally* right" and his confidence in pragmatism as *the* future of philosophy dropped substantially. This slipping self-confidence is evident in his most important later writings. Seeing more fully and consistently that pragmatism was not simply a philosophic method (and that pragmatism could maintain no sharp separation between issues of method and issues of content or substance), James developed radical empiricism as the metaphysics of pragmatism, set forth both pragmatism and radical empiricism as pluralism, and developed the moral content and consequences of this pluralism. Throughout this work, James increasingly and insightfully recognized that pragmatism, immensely right in theory, was unlikely to be a "definitive triumph" in life because it constituted in practice a philosophy that is insufficiently a live option or is a far too demanding and strenuous an option for many persons.

Once again, I focus on three features of James's own understanding of his radical empiricism, pluralism, and late pragmatism. First, following publication of *Pragmatism*, James more and more claimed real novelty for his views. Pragmatism, James increasingly recognized, was not so much a new name for an old way of thinking as it was a quickly familiar name for a very new and radical way of thinking. In this spirit, James wrote that

> the fantastic character of the current misconceptions [about his pragmatism] show how unfamiliar is the concrete point of view which pragmatism assumes. . . . It also shows, I think, that the second stage of opposition, which has already begun to express itself in the stock phrase that "what is new is not true, and what is true not new," in pragmatism, is insincere. If we said nothing in any degree new, why was our meaning so desperately hard to catch?[7]

Second, as James became more and more convinced that his philosophy was genuinely novel and original, he became less and less convinced that it would constitute the sole future of philosophy. Instead, in the spirit of pluralism, he became increasingly convinced that pragmatism could be simply *a* future of philosophy, one of many futures for philosophy, one of many future philosophies. James saw pragmatism as a future philosophy for those few persons with pluralistic attitudes and hardy temperaments (*P*, p. 124). In this spirit, he questioned his own belief in the existence of widespread and deep philosophic unrest. He doubted his earlier belief in the real possibility of general upheaval in the existing philosophic atmosphere, and he recognized the power of shopworn traditions of abstraction and absolutism. He began to view his earlier hopes and beliefs as largely functions of his own biases, personal feelings, desires, will to believe, and his own discontent with the status quo and its "extant solutions."[8] In this spirit, he concluded "A Dialogue" between pragmatist and anti-pragmatist with the observation that at present many persons simply cannot or will not bring themselves to become in practice pragmatists, and that in the future this may—but also may not—change. James concluded with a wave toward a possible future and resignation toward a real present: "Well, my dear antagonist, I hardly hoped to convert an eminent intellectualist and logician like you, so enjoy, as long as you live, your own ineffable conception. Perhaps the rising generation will grow up more accustomed than you are to that concrete and empirical interpretation of terms in which the pragmatic method consists." He concluded: "Perhaps they may then wonder how so harmless and natural an account of truth as mine could have found such difficulty in entering the minds of men far more intelligent than I can ever hope to become, but wedded by education and tradition to the abstractionist manner of thought" (*MT*, p. 159). Pragmatism as the future of philosophy? "Perhaps," James concluded.

Here is the third important aspect of James's understanding of his pluralistic and radically empiricist pragmatism. As a pluralistic philosophy, pragmatism, James increasingly realized, will have the same difficulty in the future that it has in the present in entering the minds of abstractionists and absolutists. Why is this so? James's answer, in short, was that pragmatism—actually living as a pragmatist, and not just nodding at pragmatism in a lecture hall or in the pages of a book like this one—is too demanding and too hard for many persons. Characterizing pluralism as a "willingness to live without assurance or guarantees," James concluded in "The Absolute and the Strenuous Life" that this pluralism "is bound to disappoint many sick souls whom absolutism can console" (*MT*, p. 124). In "Pragmatism and Humanism," he thus observed that the pluralistic, pragmatic "idea of this loose universe affects your typical rationalists in much the same way as 'freedom of the press' might affect a veteran official in the russian bureau of censorship. . . . It is a set of stars hurled into heaven without even a centre of gravity to pull against. . . . Such a world would not be respectable, *philosophically*" (*P*, p. 123).

These "sick souls" who long for certainty and permanence and a rote relation to the universe, who seek self-transcendence and origins, and who hope for redemption and some kind of other world here or elsewhere, demand guarantees that pluralism and its "world working out an uncertain destiny" cannot provide. For pragmatism, James concluded unflinchingly, "Shipwreck in detail, or even on the whole, is among the open possibilities."[9] Pluralism, James observed succinctly, is a "philosophy of maybes." A philosophy that offers us destinies of maybes—indeed, maybes followed by death—is a philosophy, James came to recognize, that demands too much and promises too little to many persons.[10] They want the future of philosophy to be more comfortable and warm, to offer a better agreement between themselves and night, to include a revolver big enough to keep composed the mass of meaning and to assassinate the chaos.

Dewey and Pragmatism: From the Recovery of Philosophy to Ideas as Seasons

If there is no reason for confidence in pragmatism as the future of personal philosophy—the embodied philosophy that will be commonly practiced and widely lived by individuals in the future—there is even less reason for confidence in pragmatism as the future of philosophy that pervades institutions, social relations, and cultural practices. John Dewey recognized this long ago. In his well-known essay "The Need for a Recovery of Philosophy," Dewey foresaw and warned about several gray, tedious, and unimportant futures for philosophy, futures that are anything but recipes for original relations to the universe: philosophy as now irrelevant chronicle of its own past; philosophy as now ineffective apology for its diminished position relative to the natural sciences that have emerged from it; and philosophy as now antiseptic formalism in retreat from the real world and its real problems. In the face of these possible futures, Dewey argued that philosophers creatively must bring to consciousness the needs and principles of success of their own times and places.[11] Today, many years later, however, Dewey's worries about the profession of philosophy seem right on target—as evidenced by cloistered philosophy departments and philosophy associations full of historians, apologists, and formalists, the major contemporary varieties of philosophic assassins. And, I hasten to add, this prediction encompasses most of what has come to pass for pragmatism and scholarship on Dewey. This is evidenced by university pragmatists busily chewing the historic cud of pragmatism, reducing it to more woody fibre for like-occupied and like-consoled professionals who today ironically are pragmatism's own historians, apologists, and formalists.

It is crucial to grasp once more not only the substance but also the spirit of this pragmatic demand for a recovery of philosophy. First, Dewey believed that philosophy needs to change, that the need for this change is large, and, most important, that the source of this need for large change lies outside—not inside—philosophy. Second, closely related, Dewey believed that the justification for sweeping change in philosophy also lies outside—not only inside—philosophy. He viewed the future of philosophy as something dependent on changes in cultures, on the actual future. Dewey thus saw pragmatism as a possibility that emerges as older philosophies are overturned in practice—overturned by the good and bad changes of politics, economics, technology, and scientific inquiry across virtually all aspects of everyday life. By contrast, he did not view the future of philosophy as something to be determined by the arguments or commentary of philosophers—by, say, Emerson, James, Adorno, Deleuze, or even Stuhr here and now saying this. Moreover, he did not view pragmatism as some sort of superior theoretical proof of the inadequacies of previous thought. Accordingly, he did not view pragmatism as an attempt at theoretical disproof of other philosophies, a kind of extended heated journal article, the effort of a would-be last assassin. Instead, he rejected this model of philosophy, observed that the entire history of Western philosophy is but a brief and provincial episode, and called for critical change consonant with the real and rapid changes in human life. Philosophy, he bemoaned, "is likely to be a dressing out of antithetical traditions, where criticism of one view is thought to afford proof of the truth of its opposite (as if formulation of views guaranteed logical exclusiveness). Direct preoccupation with contemporary difficulties is left to literature and politics. If changing conduct and expanding knowledge ever required a willingness to surrender not merely old solutions but old problems it is now" (*MW*10:4).

Third, Dewey's focus on the extraphilosophical sources of the need to reconstruct philosophy for the future, and his focus on the extraphilosophical justification of any such philosophy demonstrate his belief in the possibility of something better. More specifically, they signal a call to action in order to realize that possibility. Dewey's work manifested a spirit of hope and display tough-minded faith in the future. It exuded meliorism. Perhaps it is almost the embodiment of the Platonic Form of meliorism: "Faith in the power of intelligence to imagine a future which is the projection of the desirable in the present, and to invent the instrumentalities of its realization, is our salvation. And it is a faith which must be nurtured and made articulate, surely a sufficiently large task for our philosophy" (*MW*10:48).

Is this task, however, too large for our philosophy? By 1949, at the age of ninety, more and more doubtful about the capacity of institutional, professional philosophy even to take up, much less accomplish, this task, Dewey asked bluntly in the title of an essay, "Has Philosophy a Future?" Responding to his own question in this essay (and in several other related pieces written about the same time), he made three major points. First, asserting that philosophical problems and issues are related intrinsically and irreducibly to time and place, he argued that because of rapid and wide-spread cultural change, philosophy's past cannot and will not be, or control, its future. Indeed, its old problems must be abandoned, its old habits must be broken, and its conservative reluctance to do just this must be overcome. The very features of past philosophies that rendered them useful and illuminating, Dewey wrote, now equally render them "unfit for service in a radically changed human situation" (*LW*16:361). Accordingly, if philosophy is to have a genuine future, it cannot be merely as an extension of the already remote concentration on the study of past systems. Because such scholarship, Dewey wrote, is "not conducted in order to discover the light these past systems shed upon what philosophy should now engage in, its outcome is a matter of history rather than of philosophy" (*LW*16:361). Similarly, if philosophy is to have a future, it cannot be merely an extension of the current focus on supposed forms and relations. Because such technical skill, Dewey wrote, is comprehensive only by virtue of its abstraction, it results "in forms that are useful only in producing more forms of the same empty type" (*LW*16:362). Philosophy, pragmatism included, has no living future, Dewey concluded, as mere history or mere formalism. Such philosophy may remain one of the so-called liberal arts, but it has long since ceased to be in practice a "liberating art" (*LW*15:261–285). Instead of the "recovery of philosophy" and "faith in the power of intelligence" he called for more than thirty years earlier, Dewey more frequently saw philosophy in "retreat from the present scene" and permeated by "a defeatism that has not the courage to search out a philosophy that shall be relevant" (*LW*16:362). The need for a new, future philosophy is undeniable. However, the capacity of institutional and professional philosophy both to specify and to meet this need is highly questionable.[12] In "Philosophy's Future in Our Scientific Age," Dewey wrote impatiently that philosophy's future won't be "post-philosophical" but may just be extraphilosophical: as long as work gets done, "to mankind in general it makes little difference what group does the needed work; and, in any case, the work itself is much too large to be restricted to the members of any one calling" (*LW*16:380)—including philosophy.

Second, philosophy's lack of courage, Dewey found, often had led it beyond defeatism and passive retreat from intelligent inquiry to absolutism and active subordination of intelligence to the supposed authority of particular institutions, practices, and traditions. Dewey wrote:

> The old form appeals to a supernatural spiritual authority; the new one bases itself upon economic affairs as strictly materialistic. . . . Each one claims an authority which is so final and absolute as to confer upon the institution it represents not merely the right but the duty of enforcing by means of oppression and suppression, a special way of life for all mankind. . . . The assumption that history is marked by movement toward a final goal is equally that of the Church on the one hand and of Totalitarian Bolshevism on the other. The difference between them concerns only that which is assumed to be the final goal. (*LW*16:362–363)

Among these monoliths, Dewey recognized, there is precious little room for pragmatism and its pluralism and its maybes, or for intelligence, inquiry, and fallibilism.

Moreover, there is only a little—very little—that institutional, professional philosophy and that individual professional philosophers can do about this. This is Dewey's third main point: The future is not wide open for pragmatism, and pragmatic philosophy, by itself, can do only a little to open it any further. Any future pragmatic reconstruction of philosophy, Dewey recognized, can be only a small part of a larger and broader, more far-reaching and "indefinitely long" reconstruction of cultural institutions— the cultural institutions that are the source of the need for reconstruction and the locus of its justification, if any. In any such future reconstruction, philosophy can have only a small share of the work that instead must draw on the cooperative practical efforts of persons in all occupations (philosophy surely included). Pragmatist philosophers, that is, cannot alone or fully secure for pragmatism the future of philosophy (*LW*16:366–368). Rather, Dewey noted that any pragmatic reconstruction of philosophy, like any broader pragmatic reconstruction of culture, requires a cultural climate unfavorable to old traditions, values, and attitudes, and instead favorable to new experiment and experience and many maybes. Pragmatism might be made the future of philosophy, Dewey realized, only as it is sustained by, and in turn contributes to, a pragmatic "climate of belief"—a pragmatic culture extending far beyond book knowledge, pragmatic lives reaching far beneath conscious thought and will. Like Stevens, Dewey articulated this law of seasons of belief: "Without such a cultural climate even the most important undertakings are born out of due season; they fade and die" (*LW*16:380).

The Pragmatic Temperament and a Future Farewell

Dewey died three years later in 1952 at age ninety-two. Since his death, the once-future philosophy on the whole has moved around pragmatism at least as much as through it. Was pragmatism born out of due season, born without a sufficiently sustaining "climate of belief" or prevailing cultural climate, born to fade and, unlike Dewey himself, die early? Or, alternatively, was pragmatism born in a micro-climate of belief, at least so far nurtured but also confined? Was pragmatism born in an intellectual niche environment, a wholly local destiny of three or four ideas or, say, five men, or possibly six?

What would it mean for pragmatism to be—for pragmatism to have become, to have been made—the future of philosophy? As James suggested, would the arrival of pragmatism as the future of philosophy be at hand when its assassin adversaries tire of calling it absurd and, later, tire of viewing it as insignificant, and instead begin to claim that they themselves discovered pragmatism and that they themselves are pragmatists?

Or, to abandon this problem for another: Would the arrival of a future pragmatism be at hand when pragmatists stop pulling revolvers and stop viewing pragmatism as the future of philosophy? Isn't it possible in the future to think and live a pragmatic philosophy that begins to recognize itself as just one season of belief in just some persons and places, just one original relation to the universe? Couldn't this kind of future pragmatism begin to improvise a new song that does not seek to cling to the mind as the one right song? With hard work, might not a future pragmatism begin to affirm its future, to say yes, by surrendering the idea of itself as the future, by saying no? Isn't it time for a future pragmatism, in the words of Wallace Stevens in his "The Auroras of Autumn," to say farewell?

> Farewell to an idea ... The cancellings,
> The negations are never final. The father sits
> In space, wherever he sits, of bleak regard,
> As one that is strong in the bushes of his eyes.
> He says no to no and yes to yes. He says yes
> To no; and in saying yes he says farewell.[13]

In order for pragmatism to say yes to no, to affirm that it is not the future of philosophy, it must become—must make itself—more thoroughly pluralistic, more consistently pluralistic than even William James. James set the stage for, but did not really undertake, much less complete, this task by connecting brilliantly philosophy with individual temperament and vision. However, he most often did not recognize sufficiently the ways in which this connection resulted from and reflected his own peculiar pragmatic, pluralistic temperament—a temperament, acknowledging selective emphasis, I find extremely close to my own. As a result, James did not adequately grasp the fact that pragmatism is a presupposition as much as a solution to what he called "the present dilemma in philosophy." Nor did he grasp adequately the ways in which a pragmatic classification of "the types of philosophic thinking" *presupposes* rather than justifies pragmatism itself. A parallel, structurally similar problem occurs in Dewey's philosophy, as argued in chapter 8, where the commitment to the use of methods of social intelligence and inquiry *presuppose* as much as warrant or justify particular pragmatic values and particular arrangements of power.

To pragmatism as the future of philosophy, as conquering destiny, as method of intelligence: I say farewell to this idea, an idea more at home among assassins than pragmatists. To pragmatism as a season of belief, an improvisation within the mass of meaning: I offer a disillusioned greeting and passionate embrace.

In "The Present Dilemma of Philosophy," the first chapter of *Pragmatism*, James described the history of philosophy as largely a history of different, often clashing temperaments covered by supposedly impersonal reasons for one's conclusions.[14] Temperament, James wrote, loads the evidence one way or the other, makes evidence one way or the other, and gives even professional philosophers a stronger bias than any supposedly more objective premise: "He *trusts* his temperament. Wanting a universe that suits it, he believes in any representation of the universe that does suit it. He feels men of opposite temper to be out of key with the world's character, and in his heart considers them incompetent and 'not in it,' in the philosophic business." James concluded with a look ahead: "The one thing that has counted so far in philosophy is that a man should see things, see them straight in his own peculiar way, and be dissatisfied with any opposite way of seeing them. There is no reason to suppose that this strong temperamental vision is from now onward to count no longer in the history of man's beliefs" (*P*, pp. 11–12).

James made a similar, parallel point a few years later in "The Types of Philosophic Thinking," the first chapter of *A Pluralistic Universe*. Despite the fact that philosophers claim that their own conclusions are the only universally valid and sound ones, in reality all their different conclusions, like their "professional shop-habits," are "accidents more or less of personal vision." Philosophy, James wrote, is the irreducible personal expression of intimate character. Different philosophic systems are "personal flavors," "just so many visions, modes of feeling the whole push, and seeing the whole drift of life, forced on one by one's total character and experience, and on the whole *preferred*—there is no other truthful word—as one's best working attitude."[15]

Having affirmed a pluralism of temperament and vision, the existence of many different peculiar ways and total characters, James made three points. First, despite proclaiming that "individuality outruns all classification" (*APU*, p. 7), James set forth a classification of temperaments and visions, a typology of philosophies. In both *Pragmatism* and *A Pluralistic Universe*, he identified and characterized two main, subdividable types of philosophy: tender-minded, monistic rationalism and tough-minded, pluralistic empiricism. James recognized, I'm confident, that philosophies could be grouped or divided or typed in lots of different ways for lots of different purposes. He did not believe tender-minded philosophies and tough-minded philosophies constituted natural kinds. Instead, he found this classification to be a useful way to illustrate the inadequacies of these philosophies.

This was his second main point. Both types of philosophy, he argued, are inadequate and unsatisfying. It is a dilemma to have to choose between just them in an effort to hold an adequate philosophy. But, how are these two types of philosophy inadequate—and inadequate not just intellectually but inadequate and without "some positive connexion with this actual world of finite human lives" (*P*, p. 17)? They are inadequate, James argued, because both are one-sided failures to embody a trusted temperament and peculiar way of really seeing things and actually living life. Both are one-sided failures to reflect one's vision, the whole drift of life, the total character and preferred working attitude. In *Pragmatism*, James addressed directly his reader, writing that "you" do not want an empiricism without humanism and religion, or a rationalism without concrete facts and multiplicity. Instead: "You want a system that will combine both things, the scientific loyalty to facts and willingness to take account of them, the spirit of adaptation and accommodation, in short, but also the old confidence in human values and the resultant spontaneity, whether of the religious or the romantic type" (*P*, p. 17). And in *A Pluralistic Universe*, he similarly rejected philosophies that fail to provide a "background of intimacy": "The majority of men are sympathetic. . . . It is normal, I say, to be sympathetic in the sense in which I use the term. Not to demand intimate relations with the universe, and not to wish them satisfactory, should be accounted signs of something wrong.... We are invincibly parts, let us talk as we will, and must always apprehend the absolute as if it were a foreign being" (*APU*, pp. 19–20, 23).

It is not difficult to see James's third major point in these passages: Pragmatism constitutes a third way—neither tender-minded, monistic rationalism nor tough-minded, pluralistic empiricism. It is a way to hold on to facts *and* values, religion *and* science, nature *and* spirit, concrete temporality *and* intimacy, causation *and* hope. In short, pragmatism is a way to have it all. What could be more American? How could any theory have a larger "cash value"? James believed pragmatism would be a conquering destiny because he believed it to be a theory that satisfies the demands of practice, experience, life, a theory that satisfies your "own peculiar sense of a certain total character in the universe." It is a new type of philosophy, one that will provide escape in the future from the present dilemma in philosophy.

Is pragmatism really this successful?

No.

Is it at all likely that it will be this successful, the least bit reasonably likely then or now, with hard work, to become the future of philosophy?

No.

Why not? Like any other philosophy, pragmatism at most satisfies its own criteria for the success of a philosophic theory; it does not satisfy the criteria of other theories (and indeed transforms and does violence to these criteria when it claims to have satisfied them). Pragmatism resolves the problems of other philosophies, but only if they adopt a pragmatic account of what counts as problems and their resolutions. And so:

1. Unless one already presupposes pragmatism, then tender-minded, monistic rationalism and tough-minded, pluralistic empiricism are not the only or even main types of philosophies. From other angles of vision and ways of feeling the whole pull of the world, one just as well could say the main types of philosophies, for example, are: personalism and impersonalism; premodernism, modernism, and postmodernism; dialectical and non-dialectical; traditional and critical; bourgeois and revolutionary; feminist and non-feminist; and so on.

2. Unless one presupposes that one lives already as a pragmatist, both rationalism or empiricism might be highly adequate and thoroughly satisfying philosophies. Certainly many persons at least seem to have experienced these philosophies in this way, seem to have found these

philosophies make "some positive connection" with their actual world and finite lives, and reflect their own preferred working attitude. Indeed, as James has noted, throughout history religion has driven irreligion to the wall. As James would counsel them, these persons reject any philosophy, pragmatism included, that would oppose or suppress their strong personal vision. *To* whom is James speaking, after all, when he writes that "you" want empiricism with religion and want rationalism with concrete? To whom is he speaking when he writes that "you" want a system that combines both of these? To whom is he speaking when he writes about longing for a background of intimacy and about the abnormality and wrongness of anyone who desires and lives in a way that is not sympathetic—indeed "sympathetic in the sense in which I [James] use the term?" To whom is he speaking when he claims that the Absolute must always be apprehended as if it were a foreign being? To whom, what particular persons in particular times and places, is he speaking?

Perhaps in the end he really is speaking to and for himself. Perhaps he is speaking for himself and for persons (whether technical philosophers or not) who live as pragmatists. Perhaps he is speaking for five people, or possibly six, or maybe some number more. Surely James recognized that he did not and could not speak for everyone, that there are too many irreducibly other visions, modes of feeling, ways of seeing the whole drift of life, preferences, and total characters and experience. If he did not recognize this, or did not consistently recognize it, then he allowed his pragmatism to override his pluralism and recognition of the varieties of experience, allowed his pragmatism to pull a revolver. Once again, *for* whom is James speaking? For who else could a thoroughly pluralist James speak: "In the end it is our faith and not our logic that decides such questions" (*P*, p. 142), and I deny the right of any pretended logic to veto my own faith.

3. Finally, unless one lives as a pragmatist and presupposes pragmatism, pragmatism is not a way to have it all. Unless one is a pragmatist, the philosophy of pragmatism does not synthesize or aggregate or reconstruct; rather, it eliminates. In the executive lounges of the epistemology industry, CEOs as different from one another as Bertrand Russell and Josiah Royce have found that James's pragmatic account of truth is *not* an account of *their* truth. Perhaps this pragmatism is too relative, too changing, too psychological and personal, or just too fuzzy, but it is not the truth that functions in *their* visions, experiences, and working attitudes. Similarly, in the gathering places and holy sites of the world's great religions, Dewey's "common faith" is *not* an account of their faith,

his naturalization of religious experience is *not* an account of their life of spirit and transcendence, and his humanization of the concept of God leaves *no* room for their God or their worship or their lives as believers or their felt yearning for transcendence—for their very real experience of themselves as something other than absolutist "sick souls." And, as one final example, in the headquarters of groups of fundamentalists and dogmatists, in the secret meetings of hate groups, and in the boardrooms of propagandists and so-called public opinion brokers, Dewey's commitment to inquiry and democracy, and his faith in intelligence would *negate* and wipe out these ways of life and their conceptions of progress and their bases for hope—if, contrary to fact, Dewey's pragmatism here found any significant resonance, connection, or home in character and vision.

Pragmatism has not been the future of philosophy, is not now the future of philosophy, and has no future lock or inside track on being made the future of philosophy. When pragmatists proclaim pragmatism as the future of philosophy, the one future philosophy for all persons, they offer themselves consolation and they become just more philosophic assassins. In saying farewell to this idea, in taking a hard and disillusioning genealogical look at themselves, future pragmatists may become more thoroughly pluralistic—and, just perhaps, more thoroughly pragmatic.

Of course, old habits are not easily transformed, and so it may be tempting to ask: Would a more fully pluralistic, self-consciously genealogical pragmatism be a more true pragmatism or a more justified pragmatism or a pragmatism that leads more directly and fully to reality? Yes—for persons who have come to hold pluralistic, pragmatic views of truth, justification, and reality. Yes—for persons who think and live, who have been educated to think and live, both pragmatically and thoroughly pluralistically. Yes—for persons who trust this temperament, and believe that what counts is seeing things straight in one's own way, a way that is this way. Yes—for persons whose whole character and experience force on oneself this way of seeing, feeling, attending, and working. Yes—for persons for whom ideas are men and women—this idea too.

Finally, it is crucial to understand that in becoming more fully pluralistic in thought, a person would *not* become thereby or automatically more fully pragmatic. To become more fully pragmatic, a pragmatist would have to become more fully melioristic. This is a matter of how one acts and works and lives. It is a matter of effort and striving and producing, perhaps Herculean producing, a matter of character and will. To be more pragmatic, a pluralistic pragmatist would have to *act* in ways that create, sustain, and enlarge a "cultural climate" that is broadly experiential and broadly strenuous, a "climate of belief" that is unfavorable to absolutism, fundamentalism, monism, scientism and the warm songs of high imaginations. This action is irreducibly intellectual, but it is not detached, remote, or merely professional.

Reflecting on the creation of new climates of belief, Dewey observed that "campaigns of persuasion and education carried on by those of ardent faith are intrinsic parts of the effective initiation of any new movement" (*LW*16:380). Yes. Whatever the future may be, pragmatists need to engage in the inquiry and hard work needed to produce as much as possible a more fully pragmatic cultural climate. A commitment to pluralism neither abandons nor even weakens the effectiveness of this work. Pragmatism's universe is pluralistic. This universe, however, is not complete and ready-made; instead, it is something always to be produced and retooled, always under way and in process. Indeed, future pragmatists may escape being pragmatists merely in theory only if and when they undertake this action. Moreover, pragmatists who do undertake this action may escape being assassins only when they refuse to veto different temperaments or indeterminate situations or problems or visions or faiths in a pluralistic cultural climate.

This thoroughly pluralistic pragmatism, only one possible future of philosophy and only one possible future of pragmatism, includes the recognition that its own season of belief is local and transient. In the face of this recognition, it generates no need for consolation. And, at least to philosophic assassins, it offers no consolation.

Pluralism and Exclusion

A philosophy that offers no consolation, a philosophy intent on shooting no one, is not, for all that, a philosophy addressed to everyone. It is an invitation—an address to some but not all—and as such constitutes an exclusion. So if not every temperament or vision or faith is welcome at the table of this pluralistic pragmatism, then how pluralistic is it? At what point does it run out of generosity? And then what is to be done?

I've suggested pragmatism needs to be fully pluralistic in order to address a tension between its meliorism and its pluralism. This pluralism is crucial for how pragmatism responds to other, different points of view. What does this mean, theoretically and practically? Theoretically, it means first that pragmatism must be a philosophy of *openness and real possibility*. It must recognize that it is not the future of philosophy for every "you" and cannot promise to provide every "you" with what "you" want. Pragmatism should not view itself as a triumphant assassin. Moreover, of course, it should not be an assassin while viewing itself as something else.

Second, it means that pragmatism must be fully a *philosophy of experi-ence*—that is, *plural experiences of plural persons*. It must recognize that persons whose lives, upon clear and honest reflection, do not give rise to pragmatism's problems and pragmatism's responses will not and should not freely affirm pragmatism as the philosophy of their futures. Imagine someone trying to argue: Cezanne offers lovers of Rembrandt all they want and more; or, Duke Ellington resolves the predicament created by those who most prefer the music of Beethoven and those others who most prefer the music of R.E.M.; or, Charles Simic is the future of all poetry, or Ernest Hemingway is the future still of all novels. Pragmatism should not proclaim any less pluralism and difference in philosophy than it finds in life, in plural lives, temperaments, and the mass of meaning.

Third, it means that pragmatism must be *a genealogical philosophy*. It must recognize that it is addressed only to some of these lives and that it is compelling and "living" only for, and in, some of these lives. On prag-matist grounds, there is no argument in *A Pluralistic Universe* that compels absolutists or monists to become pragmatists or pluralists. There is no argument in *A Common Faith* that compels fundamentalists to become naturalists or humanists. And, there is no argument in *Freedom and Culture* that compels theocrats to become democrats. As a result, James is wrong to call absolutists "sick souls"—without, at least, making clear the relativity of this judgment through a genealogy of his own preferences, his temperament, his vision. He is not wrong, however, to say that abso-lutist, monist, rationalistic philosophies are "out of plumb and out of key and out of 'whack,' and have no business to speak up in the universe's name," or in his name, or for his name. Pragmatism, accordingly, should grasp itself as a season of belief.

Practically, this more thoroughly pluralistic pragmatism points to a large cultural agenda, a whole cluster of social tasks. Pragmatists should work on many fronts, including many that may not seem immediate or directly relevant, and should work in many ways to produce cultural condi-tions that give rise to experiences, meanings, and values that, upon careful and honest reflection, lead persons to be pragmatists and thoroughgoing pluralists. To take up this immense task is to recognize that pragmatism will not be the future of philosophy unless future experience, future life (and not just future reflection), is pragmatic.[16] Of course, this won't moti-vate persons uninterested in pragmatism in practice, and I don't pretend here to address any such "yous." I offer these persons no consolation—not even the consolation of a pretend invitation that does not acknowledge the meta-philosophical costs to those who would accept it. Supposedly open invitations are fine things—at least to those who are empowered to decide what counts as openness, dialogue, and polemics. It is enough for a philosophy to draw deeply on, illuminate, and render more meaningful and so transform the thinking and living of those who hold it and those who may come to hold it in the future. It need not (and cannot) do so for everyone.

Pluralism, if it is to be pragmatic, must be practiced. And pragmatism, if it is to be pluralistic, must say farewell to assassin visions of the future of philosophy and assassin cultural climates, and it must begin working on behalf of different ones, ones that really do offer no consolation.

Notes

1. Wallace Stevens, *The Collected Poems of Wallace Stevens* (New York: Alfred A. Knopf, 1993 [1942]), pp. 255–256.
2. See "Pragmatism versus Fundamentalism" and "The Idols of the Twilight: Pragmatism and Postmodernism" in my *Genealogical Pragmatism: Philosophy, Experience, and Community* (Albany: State University of New York Press, 1997), pp. 63–114.
3. William James, *Pragmatism* (Cambridge, Mass.: Harvard University Press, 1975 [1907]), p. 3. Hereafter *P*.
4. *The Letters of William James*, Vol. II (Boston: Atlantic Monthly Press, 1920), p. 279. Cited in *Pragmatism*, p. xix.
5. F. O. Matthiessen, *The James Family* (New York: Knopf, 1947), p. 343. Cited by H. S. Thayer in his introduction to James's *Pragmatism*, p. xix.
6. William James, "The Pragmatic Method," *Essays in Philosophy* (Cambridge, Mass.: Harvard University Press, 1978 [1898]), p. 139.
7. William James, *The Meaning of Truth* (Cambridge, Mass.: Harvard University Press, 1975 [1909]), pp. 99–100. Hereafter, *MT*.
8. William James, *Essays in Radical Empiricism* (Cambridge, Mass.: Harvard University Press, 1976 [1912]), p. 21.
9. William James, *Some Problems of Philosophy* (Cambridge, Mass.: Harvard University Press, 1979 [1911]), p. 73.
10. James himself wavered and changed his mind on this issue. In "The Moral Philosopher and the Moral Life," he argued that only a world with a God—and no mere religion of humanity—can effectively call forth the strenuous mood that slumbers in all persons. History has shown, he concluded, that religion drives irreligion to the wall. *The Will to Believe and Other Essays in Popular Philosophy* (Cambridge, Mass.: Harvard University Press, 1979 [1897]), pp. 157–159. Ten years later in "The Absolute and the Strenuous Life," much less confident in pragmatism as the future of philosophy, James viewed this desire for guarantees and absolutes as a mark of "sick souls." I critically analyze James's "Moral Philosopher and the Moral Life" and present an alternative account of the moral life in "Persons, Pluralism, and Death" in *Genealogical Pragmatism*, pp. 277–295. Ralph Barton Perry claimed that the tough view set forth in

writings like "The Absolute and the Strenuous Life" reflects James's own orientation, while the views set forth in essays like "The Moral Philosopher and the Moral Life" represent his openness and tenderness of mind toward the views of others. See Perry's *Present Philosophical Tendencies* (Westport, Conn.: Greenwood Press, 1972 [1912]), p. 374.

11. In a passage referred to in chapter 1, Dewey wrote: "I believe that philosophy in America will be lost between chewing a historic cud long since reduced to woody fibre, or an apologetics for lost causes (lost to natural science), or a scholastic, schematic formalism, unless it can somehow bring to consciousness America's own needs and its own implicit principle of successful action." John Dewey, "The Need for a Recovery of Philosophy," *John Dewey: The Middle Works, 1899–1924*, Vol. 10 (Carbondale: Southern Illinois University Press, 1980 [1917]), p. 47. See pp. 12 and 128 below.

12. Dewey wrote: "Even were there space for a consideration of what philosophy will specifically consist in the future, it would contradict what has been said to attempt even to list its articles of doctrine" (*LW*16:381).

13. Wallace Stevens, "The Auroras of Autumn," *The Collected Poems of Wallace Stevens*, p. 414. Aiming to develop a genealogical and disillusioned pragmatism, I quoted this passage in "The Idols of the Twilight: Pragmatism and Postmodernism" in *Genealogical Pragmatism*, p. 102. I did so to signal some ways in which pragmatism and postmodernism provide challenges to, and resources for, each other—some of the ways in which each leads the other to say farewell to some of its ideas. I want to recall that project here. Far more important, I quote again from this poem in order to signal ways in which pragmatism, at its pluralistic core, contains challenges to, and overcomings of, itself—ways in which pragmatism, despite its historians and formalists and apologists, says farewell to some of its own ideas and self-identity.

14. James's language here followed the conventions of his day: his subjects, philosophers, are always male, never female. It is obvious that this language is not at all gender-inclusive. It is less obvious that James's thought is not at all gender-inclusive, but it is difficult for me to believe that there is no connection at all between James's speech and his thought. Perhaps more important, it is less obvious still that James's pragmatism is not, consistent with, or could not easily be rendered consistent with, feminist concerns—and even strongly supportive of them. I raise this issue here not to attempt to settle it but rather to stress that James's account of the history of philosophy as the clash of temperaments is a view that, on its own terms, is saturated by James's own temperament, bias, vision, and very person, and is not an impersonal, objective account, an assassination of anyone with a different feel for what is "out of whack."

15. William James, *A Pluralistic Universe* (Cambridge, Mass.: Harvard University Press, 1979 [1909]), pp. 14, 15. Hereafter, *APU*.

16. This call to action is not a recipe for quietism, a loss of nerve, or a backing away from pragmatism's traditional commitment to amelioration. The practical issue, of course, involves power: Who gets to decide what count as

problems or their amelioration? A pragmatism that is not sensitively pluralistic will not be maximally transformative because it will not be successful in dealing with non-pragmatists and non-pragmatic cultural climates. Just calling a philosophy or practice ameliorative doesn't make it so, except perhaps to those doing the calling. At the same time, the transformation of cultural climate need not involve any rush to relevance. A genealogical and pluralistic pragmatism would do well to avoid employing the very values and meanings and conceptions of relevance that it seeks to transform.

CHAPTER 10

No Consolation: Life without Spirituality, Philosophy without Transcendence

Choosing What to Sacrifice

In *The Last Puritan*, George Santayana's popular 1936 novel published a century after Emerson's call in *Nature* for an original relation to the universe, one of the main characters, speaking about another, observes:

> I tell him he has no soul, because he feels no need of spiritual things, and seems not to suffer for missing them. . . . His virtue is bodily, his charm is bodily, his happiness is, and always will be, bodily. And in singly exercising his natural gifts—and what more can we ask of a free soul justly?—he must offend the world, and he must neglect the spirit. Nobody can unite all the virtues. Our Lord himself could not be a soldier, nor an athlete, nor a lover of women, nor a husband, nor a father: and those are the principal virtues of the natural man. We must choose what we will sacrifice. The point is to choose with true self-knowledge.[1]

After the last puritan, might there be time and place, a season and cultural climate, for a happiness that is always bodily and a pragmatism that feels no need of spiritual things, for a life without spirituality and a philosophy without transcendence?

At the risk of offending the world, or at least some of its inhabitants, I singly exercise my natural gifts, trust my temperament, sing the body, plural bodies, electric, and strive to embody—not to know but to be—an original relation to the universe. In doing so, I live without *any* experience of spirituality, live without living without anything. Reflecting on my life (and taking philosophy as memoir or testimony, but not as confession), I think without *any* clear or distinct or vivid understanding of spirituality, and conclude that it does not exist, that it is out of whack in my universe, a depth or height without meaning at the surface. *Desiring* no spirituality (because I experience no need of it) and *sacrificing* nothing spiritual (because I cannot give up what does not in the first place exist to be gained), I pursue the only real virtues, the virtues of human beings, inescapably embodied beings, irreducibly temporal beings.

Choosing *what* to sacrifice when I am far-sighted or lucky, I know as time passes and death is nearer—it is always near—that I cannot choose *whether* to sacrifice. Choosing with the self-knowledge that it is always myself that I sacrifice in choosing, I live and grow as much as possible as a natural, embodied man: athlete *and* lover *and* husband *and* father. This much is honest memoir in the form of philosophy, not a novel but rather a short, all too short, story.

Every existence is an event. Yes. Consciousness does not exist, except as a function. Yes. The self does not have a history; it is a history. Yes. Don't ask me to stay the same, don't check my papers. Yes. Create new concepts. Yes. I seem to be a verb. Yes.

Experiencing the fallibility of natural men and women, I realize, of course, that I may be mistaken, that it is possible that all this is wrong, that my memoir may be more fiction than fact. First, it is possible that spirituality exists even though I have no experience of it, or do not know I experience it, or do not believe it exists. Second, it is notoriously difficult to prove conclusively through any inquiry that anything—for example, the Loch Ness monster, Elvis, an alien abduction, reincarnation, eternal recurrence, virgin birth, or spirituality—does not exist. And third, of course, I realize that it is especially difficult to prove conclusively that something does not exist when large numbers of persons previously have claimed, and today still do claim, direct experience of it (and even greater direct desire for it). How can one prove, for example, that the Loch Ness monster or prior lifetimes do not exist to persons who honestly report seeing Nessie or remembering earlier lives as their own? Would there be any point to this endeavor?

Similarly, many persons claim direct experience of spirituality, maybe not while reading this chapter, but sometime and someplace. Perhaps they claim experience of spirituality while at worship or on a pilgrimage, on a whitewater river or wilderness hike in the mountains, in battlefield trenches or a hospital room, while reading particular poems or listening to certain pieces of music, or while lost in a narcotic haze or found in the clear eyes of a loved one.

The lives of natural persons, on the one hand, and spiritualists, on the other, aside, does spirituality exist? Well, does *what* exist? What does this question mean? Like Elvis, there are reports and sightings of spirituality everywhere, yet it remains elusive. Like conceptual scuba divers in a metaphysical Loch Ness, we need to know what we are looking for so that we might know it if we come face to face with it or even just cross its trail. Picture FBI photos in post offices and philosophy departments, CIA mug shots on the Internet and milk cartons, and a special episode of *America's Most Wanted*: spirituality, master of disguise, have you seen it?

What, then, is *spirituality*? Once defined as the members of the clergy and as the property or revenue received for spiritual services, spirituality now is defined and typically understood as the quality or condition of being or having regard for spiritual things as opposed to material things. Of course, to define spirituality in terms of relations to spiritual things is not much of an advance.

What things, then, are spiritual? The *spiritual* is typically defined as that which pertains to the spirit or soul, to religious and sacred things, to immaterial and supernatural beings, and to the church, clergy, or the highly refined. Again, to define the spiritual as whatever has the character of spirit is not to make our ideas very clear.

So what, finally, is *spirit*? There are many definitions or senses of spirit, including the following: the animating or life-giving principle in living things; the immaterial part of a corporeal being, typically the seat of thought or action or feeling; a supernatural, immaterial, or wholly intelligent being, regarded as usually imperceptible to humans but capable of becoming visible at will; the divine nature or essential power of God; a particular or essential character or liveliness or assertiveness of a person or thing; a wind or breath; and, a refined substance, vapor, or fluid such as distilled alcoholic liquor for drinking.[2]

To live without spirituality, of course, is not to live without breath. It need not be to live without distinctive character or liveliness, although, as William James pointed out (in different words), spirituality junkies may feel the need for something more. And, to live without spirituality need not be to live without vapor or liquor or other refined substances. However, to live without spirituality is to live without the immaterial, without the non-corporeal, without the supernatural, without the omniscient or omnipotent or eternal, without the divine. (Put positively, it is to live *with* all these withouts.) Life without spirituality is life that is material, corporeal, natural, fallible, limited, temporal, and human.

In definition, the essence of spirituality is negation, absence, lack: Spirituality is defined traditionally as non-natural or supernatural, non-material or immaterial, non-corporeal or soul rather than body, non-human or divine. A life of spirituality, accordingly, is a life that goes beyond matter, body, nature, ignorance, weakness, time, and ordinary human life. It is a life of transcendence. This is a life defined as one that goes beyond, climbs over, surmounts, becomes above, exceeds limits, becomes independent, excels, unifies, and ascends beyond the otherwise limits of human reason, experience, and values.

The pragmatic meaning of spirituality is transcendence.

Philosophical issues about spirituality, when genuine, are living, practical issues about prospects for transcendence of or in our reason, language, experience, meanings, and values. Accordingly, a life without spirituality, if it is possible, requires a philosophy without transcendence.

Is a philosophy without transcendence possible? This question may be asked in several contexts—for example, contexts of epistemology, metaphysics, and ethics. Consider: 1) What notions of transcendence and self-transcendence, if any, are required by the notion of philosophy itself, by the notion of reason scrutinizing itself, by the notion of a critical philosophy or philosophy as criticism, by the demand to know thyself? 2) What notions of transcendence and self-transcendence, if any, are required by the very notion of being, by being itself, by the notion of what really is rather than what merely is perceived, apparent, or experienced? and 3) What notions of transcendence and self-transcendence, if any, are required by notions of individual fulfillment and the self-realization (of a self presumably not always, if ever, fully realized), by notions of community and social well-being, and by the practice of any hope and hard work on behalf of this fuller self and community?

Although epistemological and metaphysical and metaphilosophical issues of transcendence arguably have most occupied philosophers, in the end all issues of transcendence are ethical issues, issues about values. Transcendence is an irreducibly normative notion. Going beyond, climbing over, surmounting, becoming above or independent, exceeding, excelling, and ascending are not merely ways of becoming different; they all are, supposedly, ways of becoming better. Transcendent knowledge, transcendent existence, and transcendent values are not just different from their non-transcendent counterparts; instead, they are better, better because more— more secure, more complete, more moving, and more lasting. In short, transcendence, traditionally, is good. This is why no one prays to go to a heaven that offers an eternal life that is like living in Pittsburgh in 1950. Heaven, it is thought, if it is to be heaven, must be considerably more transcendent.

Most philosophies promise their adherents and would-be adherents some sort of heaven, some kind of transcendence: an epistemological heaven—universal and necessary truth, or at least certain knowledge, that transcends everyday belief; an ontological heaven—reality, real Being, that transcends appearance and how things merely seem; and, an ethical heaven—heaven proper, the valuable, what is worthy of being valued, that transcends what is merely valued at various times and places. These heavenly philosophies that promise the true, the real, and the good, do *not* require us, contrary to the beliefs of the last puritan, to choose what we will sacrifice, much less to choose with true self-knowledge what we will sacrifice. Without the true, the real, and the good, these philosophies teach us, we have nothing. Having nothing, we have nothing to sacrifice: "when you ain't got nothing, you got nothing to lose."

In these philosophies of robust transcendence, there is no call simply to sacrifice; there is only a call to surmount. Thus, these philosophies, although some claim otherwise, do not demand of us sacrifice; instead, they stand by like financial planners with investment opportunities guaranteed to yield a high rate of return, conceptual smugglers and alchemists ready to help us convert belief into truth, experience into reality, and preference into the good. See Plato, Aquinas, Descartes, Leibniz, Hegel all running cult sweepstakes for their readers: not the Reader's Digest kind of sweepstakes—no purchase necessary but you may already be a winner; instead, a different sort of sweepstakes—purchase absolutely required (buy this philosophy), but everyone who makes a purchase will be a winner.

Santayana's philosophy sees through and renders naked these philosophies of transcendence. His views constitute an alternative to this tradition, and something of a spiritual halfway house between it and pragmatism. Seeing through these traditional notions of transcendence and spirituality, Santayana, as the last puritan, nonetheless clings to a notion of spirit as that which recognizes these illusions of transcendence. And the last puritan nonetheless embraces a notion of transcendence as a surmounting of illusion, a disillusionment about revelation. In this context, Santayana wrote: "The spiritual man lives tragically, because his flesh and his pride and his hopes have withered early under the hot rays of revelation. Even the Church is no home for the spirit. . . . Religion ceases to be a radical conversion, a thorough cleansing of the heart. It becomes a local heritage, a public passion, a last human illusion for the spirit to shed."[3]

Here transcendence takes the form of disillusionment, and spirituality is the permanent immaterial, non-corporeal ontological possibility of illusion and disillusion. Spirit, as Santayana said it, has "transcendental rights." In this philosophy of disillusioned transcendence, like more traditional and commonplace philosophies of robust transcendence, there is no sacrifice because the attentive, sympathetic sacrifice of illusion is liberation. And this liberation is salvation, an eternal possibility because of the fact, for Santayana, that all intelligent beings "have one foot in eternity."[4] One foot in eternity, in the immaterial, the non-corporeal, the non-natural: the last puritan is still a puritan, rowing for heaven, both oars in the water as Cotton Mather instructed, as calculating as the Odysseus of the *Dialectic of Enlightenment.*

Still Feeling the Need: Pragmatism as Forced Relocation

Has pragmatism been, then, a philosophy without transcendence, a philosophy that neither claims nor understands "transcendental rights"? No, in its first millennium, it was not this. Instead, it has constituted, a forced relocation, a long march, of traditional notions of transcendence and spirituality. It has relocated transcendence *within* immanence, relocated spirit *within* nature, relocated affirmation *within* negation, relocated salvation *within* a great community.

Pragmatism's forced relocation of transcendence and spirituality—if one wanted to take a linguistic turn, which one should not, this could be called a forced translation—has created several major industries within pragmatic philosophy: the naturalization of epistemology via broadly biological and experimental accounts of intelligence and inquiry; the naturalization of metaphysics via radically empirical and transactional accounts of existence; and the naturalization of ethics via humanistic and relativistic accounts of valuation and self-realization. These industries continue to produce and produce; like theologians with their proofs of God, pragmatists apparently can never have too many naturalized accounts of the true, the real, and the good. I will not here detail any of these accounts, relying instead on your familiarity with them; if this assumption is mistaken, then I take consolation in the fact that there are available many naturalization industry tours (watch out for forklifts). These products of pragmatism's naturalization industries, appropriately, have had a high exchange value. They include, for instance, truth without the problems of certainty; justification without the problems of foundations; nature and access to it without the problems of supernaturalism or solipsism; values without the problems of absolutism or emotivism; and distinctively religious or spiritual experience without idealism, dualism, or institutional religion.

In short, via forced relocation, pragmatism has claimed to offer everyone—to offer "you"—spirituality without spirit and transcendence without transcendentalism. This is not surprising. From the beginning through its first century, pragmatism has offered its customers a two-for-one sale, a sale that is no doubt particularly appealing (but not exclusively appealing) to its American customers who want it all: radical empiricism *and* the will to believe, scientific fixation of belief *and* God, experience and nature *and* the religious, philosophy as criticism *and* democratic faith, self-creation or, at least, private fulfillment *and* solidarity. Like idealistic philosophies of robust transcendence and materialistic philosophies of disillusioned transcendence, these naturalistic and immanent pragmatic philosophies of relocated spirituality and transcendence require no sacrifice because supposedly the existence, or the possibility of existence, of spirituality and transcendence is not rejected, lost, or sacrificed. After the last puritan, after Santayana's epiphenomenal materialism, and after Emerson's call for a perpetually ongoing original relation to the universe, twentieth-century pragmatism still offered its audience transcendence and spirituality, only now—supposedly—better theorized.

In the end, however, pragmatism's forced relocation of spirituality and transcendence is not very successful. I think it is time that pragmatists recognize this. This pragmatist project has not been successful on two fronts. First, pragmatism has lost, still loses, and cannot prevent losing over and over a rearguard fight about spirituality and transcendence. Pragmatism's naturalization of spirituality *transforms* spirituality even as (and because) pragmatism claims to preserve and sustain spirituality within a philosophy that does not transcend a natural, material, corporeal, temporal, fallible, changing, and thoroughly human reality. Similarly, pragmatism's naturalization of transcendence *transforms* transcendence as—and again, because—pragmatism claims to preserve and sustain transcendence within a philosophy that understands itself as immanent cultural criticism and understands reality as a this-worldly world of experience. Accordingly, proponents of a more robust spirituality and transcendence always can and usually do claim that pragmatism's relocation or recontextualization or reconstruction of spirituality and transcendence constitutes a denial or destruction or downright loss of *their* spirituality and *their* transcendence. As a philosophy that takes context seriously, pragmatism now needs to compel itself to recognize the difficulty that this claim presents on its own pragmatic grounds. If pragmatism requires itself to establish some counterpart to the old mind/brain identity thesis, it is bound to fail. There simply is nothing in pragmatism's account of spirituality and transcendence that it can *identify* with the spirituality and transcendence theorized by those who claim to participate in and experience non-naturalistic, non-pragmatic, more robust spirituality and transcendence.

Pragmatism cannot win this rearguard battle—a battle against, or on behalf of, persons for whom pragmatism is not a live option from the start. Accordingly, it is time to stop fighting this battle. The naturalization of spirit and transcendence is a transformation of spirit and transcendence. This transformation is not simply reconstruction but also loss. It is a loss: it is recognized rightly by pragmatism's critics as the elimination of spirit and the elimination of transcendence in more robust and also in more disillusioned senses. Pragmatism needs to make explicit this loss, this violence, this difference, this elimination. Pragmatism is not simply a philosophy that satisfies in part both the "tender-minded" and the "tough-minded"; it is a philosophy that fails to satisfy in full everyone who is other-minded.

Just as James concluded that consciousness does not exist, except as a function, post–twentieth century pragmatists must be ready to conclude that spirit and transcendence do not exist, except as a function. What is that function? It is evaluative difference. Transcendence is difference, differencing, that is preferred. To call a belief, experience, or value transcendent is only, but importantly, to say that it is preferred from a particular point of view.

There is nothing transcendent about this, of course, except from another particular point of view. And, there is nothing immediately "natural" about these different preferences. They are socially produced, socially mediated, and socially productive. We must resist the temptation to embrace what Adorno called the religion of "nature boy." The practical task facing pragmatism, or any other philosophy, is not to pretend that these preferences have some spiritual or transcendent or immediate status or unity that recommends them. Pragmatism's task is to deliberate about particular preferences on the way to different preferences and action on their behalf. Community designates no non-natural fact or unity; it designates a practical agenda. As practical agenda, this deliberation does not have "one foot in eternity." Instead, it has both feet, temporarily, in embodiment and enactment; or, rather, it is those two feet.

This pragmatism, moreover, is not a celebration of the ordinary—which, if celebrated, is no longer ordinary. It is the honest admission of the ordinariness of the ordinary, a preference for this ordinariness, and a sacrifice of self-righteous philosophical notions of sacrifice. The sacrifice of sacrifice, extraordinarily ordinary: In the end, is a philosophy without transcendence possible? No argument or thin string of concepts can prove or disprove this. Instead, if a life without spirituality—plural lives without spirituality—can be actual, then a philosophy without transcendence, a pragmatism that bodily answers anew its own call, is not only possible but also demanded.

Pluralism, Hope, and Hard Work

How is it possible to make good on this demand? In working toward a new cultural climate, a new season of belief, pragmatism offers important resources that reach far beyond its forced relocation of spirituality and transcendence. What can pragmatism offer a way of thinking and living without transcendence and spirituality, a pragmatism of temporal difference embodiment, and multiplicity in action?

Posed this way, the question is too *abstract* and *general*. First, there is *no one pragmatism, no one American philosophy*, and no one way in which any philosophy alone might contribute to a new cultural climate and season of belief.[5] Second, when pragmatism is viewed, as is often the case, within an American context, it is important to make clear that there is *no one America*. Instead, there are many Americas—North, South, and Central, of course; within North America, philosophies in the United States, Mexico, and Canada; and, within the United States alone, a vast number of overlapping, intersecting, sometimes opposed and sometimes parallel, always different philosophies rooted in particular histories, places, cultures, and experiences. Third, and perhaps most important, there is *not just one* kind of contribution that pragmatism may make, not just one kind of relevance it may have in different times and places. It is important to reject abstract and overly general understandings of pragmatism, postmodernism, American philosophy, education, and humankind. The point is not simply to speak in a more qualified, concrete, and particularistic manner—for example, to ask, What can some specific pragmatism contribute to some specific education and cultural change of some specific people at some specific times and places? It is not simply, in James's phrase, to "thicken up" philosophy. Rather, the point is that life and education are irreducibly local affairs, and so any philosophy content (or arrogant enough) to offer only thin logical considerations, abstract pronouncements, and general truisms will make no contribution at all to the concrete lives and thoughts of real persons.

Rendered sufficiently specific and concrete, however, this is an *important* question—important because *practical*. It directs groups of philosophers to look up from the different answers that divide them on the shared questions that unite them. It directs them to look out from theoretical concerns encrusted with both ancient commentary and contemporary jargon. It directs them to all kinds of practical problems and issues that confront human beings (most of whom are not philosophical theorists), living issues that supply both the origin and the measure of adequacy of any philosophy that also is alive. This is a question about the pragmatic value of pragmatism.

This question can be answered in many different ways. Upon hearing it, friends of pragmatism may feel that they are children who have been invited into a candy store. It will seem that there are so many goodies, so much from which to choose. These choices, of course, reveal as much about the child's tastes that guide given choices as they do about the actual quality of what is chosen.

Friends of Charles Peirce, for example, may construe the possible contributions of pragmatism toward new cultural climates as preeminently Peircean: the rejection of Cartesianism, the insistence that philosophical problems originate in genuine doubt, the demand for inquiry unblocked by methods of fixing belief that do not work in practice, and the commitment to fallibilism. This is compelling stuff: in a world scarred by dogmatists, fundamentalists, and absolutists, a lesson in fallibilism indeed would be a major contribution to new educations and assassin-free cultural climates.

Similarly, friends of Josiah Royce, for example, may conceive of the resources of pragmatism and American philosophy as characteristically Roycean: the distinction between a society and a community, the linkage of community not with uniformity or conformity but with a wise provincialism, and the articulation of an ethics of loyalty and respect for persons and their ideals. In a world of selfish, narrow individuals striving for lives in gated neighborhoods, a lesson in the great community would be an invaluable contribution to a newly pluralistic and tolerant season of belief that might escape the defects of liberalism.

Once more, friends of George Santayana, for example, may view the possibilities of philosophy as Santayanaesque: the substitution of animal faith for empty skepticism, a tired smile for all philosophical systems, a pluralism about values and lives and human natures, and the conception of spirit irreducibly tied to matter. In a world in which many persons are willing to live marking time for an afterlife, and many others are willing to die for an afterlife, a this-worldly, no-afterlife toughness about the finitude of human life constitutes a crucial lesson, though one not fully beyond spirit, still unlearned by humankind.

Surveying pragmatism, other persons will pick out other favorites and highlight other potential contributions: James's radical empiricism; Dewey's experimentalism and commitment to democratic community; Mead's notion of the irreducibly social self; Emerson's self-reliance; Thoreau's civil disobedience; Bowne's personalism; Goldman's anarchism and egalitarianism; DuBois's account of "the veil" and "the problem of the color-line" and his insistence on the centrality of race in American lives and thoughts; Charlotte Perkins Gilman's analysis of the domestic economy, women, and the need for feminism; Alain Locke's account of the "New Negro" and his critical pragmatism; and so on. Here, in the work of these and other pragmatist and pragmatist-influenced American philosophers, there are more insights than I can put to use, more than I can even merely list, more in fact than I recognize. Fortunately, friends of these and other American philosophers make their cases in detail.

When all these cases are made, the legacy of pragmatism will not be found in any doctrine, thesis, or proposition. It will not be found by asking familiar questions. Is Emerson, for example, the greatest American thinker? Is Peirce's doctrine of pragmaticism correct? Is James's thesis of the will to believe justified? Is Dewey's postulate of immediate empiricism true? Is Santayana's epiphenomenalism superior to idealism? What parallels are there between James and Deleuze, or Dewey and Foucault? These issues matter, but from the standpoint of cultural climate and season of belief, the standpoint of the broad education of humankind—the standpoints of the educations of many different human beings—they do not matter very much.

The most important resources that twentieth century pragmatism can make to the education of humankind are not championed figures, a correct doctrine or two, some justified theses, or pages of true propositions. It is not a matter of belief at all. Instead, it is a matter of temperament. It is a matter, as William James said, of vision. At its best, American philosophy has a temperament and a vision that are pluralistic and melioristic. Pragmatism does not always live up to this vision, and American society lives up to it even less often and less completely, but I am convinced that it is the most important contribution that pragmatism can make to new ways of thinking and new ways of living.

In a world where people kill, injure, abuse, degrade, exclude, impoverish, disenfranchise, hate, or just hope to assimilate those who are different, the pluralism of pragmatism—and the capacity of pragmatism to become even more thoroughly pluralistic—has never been a more scarce or more needed resource. In a world where different experiences, different ways of knowing, and different values and ways of living are a fact, the recognition of this fact of plurality in the ontologies, epistemologies, and moral theories of pragmatism forms a mother lode of theoretical honesty. In a world in which the question of whether we will choose to live with others has been replaced by the question of how we will choose to live with others, the pluralism of pragmatism, of a thoroughly pluralistic pragmatism, points us toward a sane way to begin to answer that question.

But pluralism remains pluralism in theory alone unless it is enacted. Meliorism supplies the motivation for this action. Against the pessimistic true disbelievers who are sure that things cannot be more as they want, and so see no need to try to make them so, the meliorism of pragmatism provides hope and preaches hard work. Against the optimistic true believers who are sure that things will be more as they want and foresee, and so see no need to try to make them so, the meliorism of pragmatism guarantees nothing and preaches hard work. And against the shallowness and smugness of pessimists and optimists alike who refuse to inspect critically the origins and consequences of what they want and the terms in which they think and live this want, pragmatism provides a genealogy and preaches hard work. In a world in which many persons live without hope, and many others live on false promises, the meliorism of pragmatism constitutes a tough-minded faith without spirituality and transcendence, and a call to action on behalf of a future that is not fixed. In the sense in which Dewey identified immaturity as a precondition for growth, the meliorism of pragmatism is a fountain of youth in a world that often feels itself old. In a world of despair and apathy and inaction, this meliorism is an announcement that our moral holidays are over. Meliorism—hope and hard work— in the service of genuine pluralism and ordinary life: I can think of no more valuable contribution that any philosophy might make to the ongoing renewal of thought and life.

In the spirit of this meliorism, however, it is crucial to grasp that questions about pragmatism's theoretical resources have only limited importance. Can pragmatism contribute? Is it able? Does it have the resources? This kind of question concerns ability and capacity. I am sure pragmatism can contribute, sure that its successes and even its failures can contribute something to the education of humankind and the ongoing creation of different cultural climates. The most important question, however, is not a question about ability but, rather, a question about will and imagination. This is a personal question, a question about each person, a question about you and me. Will you and I contribute to the education of humankind, to a new climate of belief, to a new season of belief by helping to invent and employ the means to do so? If so, how and when? To consider drawing upon and moving beyond pragmatism is to confront a world that educates persons that philosophy is unimportant and presents professional philosophers who mostly act as if to prove that this is true. What pragmatism can contribute to the development of original, insightful relations to the universe is a moot question if individuals do virtually nothing.

Drawing upon pragmatism requires not only determination but also imagination and self-reflection. The obstacles and difficulties are many. For example, although philosophy may be the corruption of youth, as it has been since Socrates, in much of the contemporary world there is a youth culture that sees no need to be corrupted. Similarly, philosophy may be love of wisdom, but in the millennium after Emerson and James and Dewey, the objects of desire are data and information. And philosophy may advocate an examined life, but many persons do not want to think too hard, and the life of a reasonably paid happy pig may seem preferable to that of an unsatisfied Socrates with no steady source of fixed income.

In these and so many ways, efforts to think beyond, but not without, twentieth-century pragmatism (or twentieth-century postmodernism or twentieth-century philosophy more broadly) seem out of touch. These efforts, after all, take the form of print in a visual culture; hard work in a culture of entertainment and lotteries; reflection in a talk-show, sound-bite, and money culture; difference and displacement in a culture of thinking and living in line; critical distance in a culture of persuasion, manipulation, and information warfare; and endless disagreement in a culture that wants its experts to agree.

Pragmatism can contribute much needed pluralism and meliorism (and much more) to ways of thinking and living that can move beyond this. It needs to steel its will to make this contribution. And it needs to apply its imagination to the ways in which it does this. There is no reason for optimism, but there is every need for pluralism, hope, and hard work.

Antagonizing without Spirituality

Santayana closed *The Last Puritan* with a dialogue with himself:

> The trouble with you philosophers is that you misunderstand your vocation. You ought to be poets, but you insist on laying down the law for the universe, physical and moral, and are vexed with one another because your inspirations are not identical.
>
> Are you accusing me of dogmatism? Do I demand that everybody should agree with me?
>
> Less loudly, I admit, than most philosophers. Yet when you profess to be describing a fact, you can't help antagonizing those who take a different view of it, or are blind altogether to that sort of object. In this novel, on the contrary, the argument is dramatised, the views become human persuasions, and the presentation is all the truer for not professing to be true. You have said it somewhere yourself, though I may misquote the words: After life is over and the world has gone up in smoke, what realities might the spirit in us still call its own without illusion save the form of those very illusions which have made up our story?[6]

This is an eloquent illusion, characteristically eloquent but still an illusion. After life is over, notwithstanding the appeal of this illusion during life, there is no longer an us, there is no spirit in us, and there are no longer realities for us to call our own and strive to change, with or without illusion. "Our story"—really it is our plural stories—is not a story that must give rise to the mystery of being or the wonder of being or the problem of being or quests for spirituality or transcendence. There is nothing mysterious or extraordinary about this life. Indeed, who would have thought it otherwise? Here Deleuze's Hercules readies his staff.

Lots of people quite obviously have and still do think otherwise. Changing this cultural climate constitutes a broadly educational task, an exercise of invitation, evocation, suggestion, imagination. In pointing to this task, do I demand that all others should agree with me? No. No, although philosophy has pushed and taught, pushes and teaches me, to make this demand, to eliminate pluralism, to make identical our inspirations, to demand converts to one's own truths, thoughts, and experiences. Still, after the twentieth century, it is possible to think and live without this dogmatism and without this self-understanding.

This philosophy is, as Santayana recommends, a thoroughly human persuasion, the drama of a thoroughly human self, dramas of some plural human selves in some seasons of belief, dramas of embodied enactments (neither spiritual nor material)—fulfillment and frustration, love and sadness, appreciation and criticism, creation and difference.

Here is an ordinary drama of thoroughly human selves. A few years ago, when my father-in-law died suddenly, my mother-in-law sought to comfort my son, then eight years old, at a memorial service on a cold winter afternoon in a small town south of Pittsburgh. Quietly and surely, she whispered to him: "Gramps has gone to a better place." My son replied through his tears with a different sureness, "Granny, there is no better place for us than being here with you and me."

Another drama, thoroughly ordinary with thoroughly human selves: When my cousin and I were young we telephoned strangers and recorded the funny conversations on our reel-to-reel tape recorder. Once we called a bar in Des Moines and told the guy who picked up the phone that he had won a prize from a new radio station's public relations promotion. We offered him either a new wool suit or new wool pants. He growled, "I'll take the pants." Surprised and trying unsuccessfully not to laugh, we asked if he understood that the suit was a pair of pants *and* a jacket, that the suit included the pair of pants *and more*. He replied, "A suit ain't no more than a pair of pants if you ain't got no need for a jacket." Without need for jackets, spirit, or transcendence, and with the hopes and hard work of many, we lived as natural boys, as natural gods neither spiritual nor non-spiritual. We lived as Hercules in time and body and in action, lived without lack, lived without living with or without spirituality and transcendence. I still have that tape.

This is not the sacrifice claimed by, and in the name of, spirituality or transcendence—in the end no sacrifice at all.[7] It is the sacrifice of ordinary selves, collective self-sacrifice, a principal virtue of a life that feels no need of spirituality and a philosophy that reflects no need of transcendence.

Amour et Regrets

Near St. Paul de Vence in southern France, the bright yellow mimosa blooms and the citrus trees are heavy with fruit even in February. From the paradise of La Colombe d'Or just outside the walled medieval city, green fields and palm trees, stone walls, pastel shutters, and red tile roofs stretch from the Alps to Nice and the Mediterranean. The light and air that attracted Picasso, Miro, Leger, Chagall, Cocteau, and others cannot be said or thought.

Cimetière St. Michel lies on the other side of the village just beyond the city walls with their arrow slits and cannons on three terraces that descend gently to the abrupt edges of St. Paul's hill. Most of the tourists who come in buses to walk the steep, narrow stone streets and look at the art galleries windows with Visa and Mastercard stickers do not go to the cemetery. Still, the sign on the entrance gate advises "pique-niques inter-dits" and asks visitors to be quiet and respectful.

The cemetery's small, simple Chappelle Saint-Michel was mentioned in written accounts as early as 1356. Walking from the chapel along the paths among the tombs, it thus seems surprising that almost everyone now legibly recorded in the stones as buried there, Chagall included, died in the twentieth century. Most of the gray tombs appear older by many genera-tions, family tombs bearing French and Italian names. Most of the tombs are simple massive concrete rectangles with thick tops and thicker walls that rise three or four feet from the ground. There are fresh flowers and watered plants; the tombs are mostly well tended. Looking toward the mountains or the sea, the evidence of impermanence beside every step, still the cemetery seems almost permanent and beyond.

On many of the tombs and on the few more recent graves, there are pictures of the deceased, photographs that are somehow effectively glazed or sealed or imprinted on stone and glass mounted on little stands and tripods, photographs barely touched by weather even many, many decades later. A man in his fifties who died shortly after World War II. A baby girl who died days after birth in the 1960s. A long-haired, smiling young man who died in his twenties in the 1970s. A woman in her nineties who died a month ago; the photograph of her is surrounded by small vases of cut lilacs.

From family and friends and neighbors, there are also notes, poems, tributes, declarations fused on more stones the size of paperback book pages on small stands on the tombs. The stones speak of love that never dies, memory that never fades, life that never ends. "Ce n'est qu'un revoir." "L'amour ne meurt jamais." "Le temps passe, le souvenir reste." "Ton souvenir restera toujours gravé dans mon coeur." "Notre pensée est toujours pour toi." "La vie éternel." Looking toward the cemetery from my study in La Colombe d'Or, returning in the light of days, looking through the locked gate in starry darkness, standing in silence on the gravel paths, helping an old woman carry a heavy metal pail of water to flower urns, looking down the terraces to the seamless meeting of brilliant blue sea and sky: tradition, continuity, presence, and again, almost but only almost, permanence.

On one side of the highest, oldest terrace, directly across from the chapel, winter rains have washed out completely the soil from under one tomb. It has slid down the hill, split open, and lies broken, apparently empty except for a thin layer of wet dirt and some broken pieces from the top concrete slab. It is surrounded by newly placed orange plastic warning cones and yellow and black caution tape. A photograph and stones with two messages from the top of this tomb have been retrieved and set on the remaining thin strip of ground that used to ring the tomb. Free of suggestion that death is only "revoir," or that love and memories and thoughts do not pass or die with those who love and remember and think, these two messages of love and sadness are simple and straightforward. From a wife and children, one reads: "Ta femme et tes enfants qui t'aiment plus que tout." The other, unattributed, says only in large print: "Regrets."

Without spirituality and transcendence: with the most love, embodied and enacted love, and the most sadness, embodied and enacted sadness.

The edges of the tombs on both sides of this landslide hang precariously over the edge, and the path in front of all three is closed, blocked by temporary blue-and-white "Déviation" signs. Like Emerson, here the children of the fathers and mothers might demand and receive their own works, hard thought and hard work to do, many kinds of work for many different persons. And in this thoroughly ordinary work, without spirituality and transcendence, without any desire to leave, there is sadness, embodied and enacted sadnesses, and there is the most love, embodied and enacted loves. Here the sun shines today also. And tomorrow.

Notes

An earlier version of sections 1, 2, and 4 of this chapter appeared as "Life Without Spirituality, Philosophy without Transcendence" in *The Hedgehog Review: Critical Reflections on Contemporary Culure*, Vol. 3, no. 3 (fall 2001), pp. 57–72.

1. George Santayana, *The Last Puritan: A Memoir in the Form of a Novel* (New York: Charles Scribner's Sons, 1936), p. 254.

2. I draw these definitions from the *Oxford English Dictionary* (Oxford: Clarendon Press, 1993). Other major dictionaries offer nearly identical definitions.

3. Santayana, *The Last Puritan*, p. 255.

4. George Santayana, "Liberation," *The Realm of Spirit in Realms of Being* (New York: Charles Scribner's Sons, 1937), pp. 736–767.

5. I want to stress here a point that, paradoxically, appears to be increasingly misunderstood. Pragmatists, American pragmatists, and classical American philosophers (some of whom are pragmatists), have been just some of the many groups of philosophers and philosophical thinkers in America. They can be identified in terms of definite personal, historical, and philosophical connections, connections that are themselves linked to multiple aspects of American culture. To identify some American pragmatists as "classical" (just as, for example, certain dramatists or physicists are "classical") is to note that their work constitutes an early and influential development in philosophy in America. To note this fact about this philosophy is not, in itself, to claim that this philosophy is "classic," outstanding, or best. This is why it is important to distinguish classical American philosophy from classic American philosophy. Similarly, to note this fact about this philosophy is not, in itself, to claim that it is prior, unrelated, or superior to any number of other philosophies inside or outside America. For a more extended discussion of these issues, see my "Sidetracking American Philosophy," *Transactions of the Charles S. Peirce Society: A Quarterly Journal of American Philosophy*, Vol. 34, no. 4 (fall 1998), pp. 841–860.

6. Santayana, *The Last Puritan*, p. 602.

7. Recalling Santayana's observation that we must choose what we will sacrifice, I most definitely am not denying that persons whose lives and philosophies are marked by commitments to notions of spirituality and transcendence strive to surmount and leave behind the ordinary and strive to realize other values and meanings. They do so strive, often with great effort, and they experience themselves so striving. However, I resist calling this activity "sacrifice" because I believe it is marked, and marks itself, more by a sense of investment and improvement and surmounting than by a sense of loss ("shipwreck") and difference and differencing.

Index